JAVANESE SHADOW PLAYS,
JAVANESE SELVES

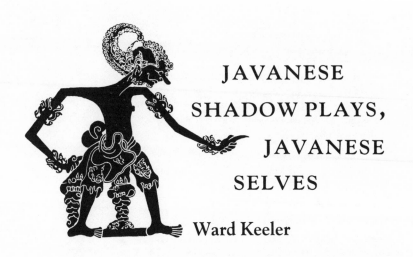

JAVANESE
SHADOW PLAYS,
JAVANESE
SELVES

Ward Keeler

PRINCETON UNIVERSITY PRESS, PRINCETON, NEW JERSEY

For James T. Siegel

Guruku

CONTENTS

Acknowledgments   ix

Introduction: On Interpreting a Javanese Art Form   3

1. Language, Power, and Asceticism   25

2. Family Relations   51

3. Village Politics   85

4. Potency, Possession, and Speech   109

5. Ritual Celebrations   141

6. The Status of Dhalang and Ritual Sponsors   165

7. The Dhalang, the Troupe, and the Tradition   180

8. The Pleasures of the Performance   202

9. On Javanese Interpretation   243

10. Conclusion   261

Glossary   269

Bibliography   273

Index   279

ACKNOWLEDGMENTS

As a general rule, Javanese say "thank you" (*matur nuwun*) only in impersonal situations: in very formal encounters, or in addressing groups. True gratitude and indebtedness cannot be reduced to stock phrases, no matter how refined. In fact, to say "thank you" in Java can arouse disappointment, since it implies that such words can cancel the bonds between people that exchange relations set up. A student offers his teachers deference, and whatever material gifts he can muster. To his friends, he offers good company and the unspoken promise of support through thick and thin. But he never presumes that the debt he owes them could be paid, whether materially or by the expression of thanks.

I have been fortunate to find friends among my teachers, and teachers among my friends. I wish to acknowledge the debts I owe all of them, without presuming that such debts could ever be cancelled.

Benedict Anderson and James Siegel introduced me to the study of Indonesia, and since my first days as an undergraduate at Cornell I have benefited immeasurably from their insightful writings, from their classes, and from their advice and encouragement of my own work. Terence Turner and Victor Turner, in addition to James Siegel, were my first teachers in anthropology, and they imbued the field with the sense of excitement that it still holds for me—an inestimable gift.

I have turned to those same teachers many times since leaving Cornell, but I have also benefited greatly from the advice and encouragement of other scholars I have met more recently. Alton Becker, Judith Becker, Donald Emmerson, Clifford Geertz, Hildred Geertz, Wendy O'Flaherty, Valerio Valeri, and Paul Wheatley all helped me formulate my ideas about Javanese culture, and to them I am deeply grateful.

If my teachers in the United States have provided me with questions and skills, countless teachers in Java have provided me with the information, advice, and friendship that made living in Java such an enriching experience. Lest I appear unduly nostalgic, I should say that to be a Westerner in Java occasionally has its trials. Then again, being a Westerner strikes me as a fairly arduous business anywhere, in as well as outside the West. Teachers and friends in Java received me with unfailing graciousness, and I must attribute what sense I have made of Javanese culture to their wonderful patience and generosity.

To single out any among the many people who showed me such kindness seems tendentious. Yet I would feel remiss were I not to mention Bapak Sastrapustaka of Jogjakarta, and Ki Dhalang Sarwadisana and Ki Dhalang Gandawijaya, both of Klaten, for their invaluable teaching and kindness. I treasure the memory of the times I spent with each of them, times in which I felt, as the phrase in *wayang* puts it, cool as though bathed in a thousand waters.

The ethnographic literature tells us that a special bond often unites ritual initiands. I feel just such bonds with friends whose researches in Indonesia overlapped, at one point or another, with my own. Anthony Day, Joseph Errington, Barbara Hatley, Ron Hatley, Terrence Hull, Valerie Hull, Jenny Lindsay, Anton Lucas, Ann McCauley, Gerry Meister, Hisako Nakamura, and Mizuko Nakamura provided intellectual stimulus and good fellowship during the two stays in Java on which this study is based. Shelly Errington conducted research in Sulawesi, not Java, but conversation with her has proved particularly important for all my thinking about Java.

In writing and rewriting this study of *wayang*, I have obtained invaluable advice from many quarters, including many of the scholars I have already mentioned. I am particularly grateful to Alton Becker, Thomas Beidelman, and David Sapir for excellent suggestions about the entire text, and to Peter Metcalf for an extraordinarily close and helpful reading. I appreciate as well the comments made on portions of the text by Judith Ferster, Susan McKinnon, Leslie Morris, and Nancy Munn.

The Indonesian Institute of Sciences granted me research permits during both of my stays in Java, and I am indebted to Ms. Syamsiah Ahmad and Mr. Napitupulu and other members of that institute for their assistance in making my research possible. Mr. Humardani and Ki Dhalang Sutrisno of the Akademi Seni Karawitan Indonesia in Solo kindly sponsored my research in 1978-1979. My research in 1978 was supported by a Fulbright-Hays predoctoral grant, and in 1978-1979 by a grant from the National Institute of Mental Health. The latter grant also provided support during the writing of my dissertation. I revised and expanded the text as a Fellow at the Institute for Advanced Study in Princeton in 1983-1984, supported by a grant from the National Endowment for the Humanities, and as a Mellon Fellow in the Department of Anthropology at New York University in 1984-1985.

Finally, I am grateful to Gail Ullman and Sherry Wert, both of Princeton University Press, for their excellent guidance in preparing the manuscript for publication.

Wayang viewed from the shadow side. Men watch while sitting on mats, as is the traditional style. The *dhalang* can be glimpsed on the other side of the screen; the puppet box sits to his immediate left, with bronze sheets (*keprak*) hung on the side of the box, by the puppeteer's right foot. Drawing by Suharso.

Wayang viewed from the *dhalang's* side. Invited guests, visible on the other side of the screen, are seated on chairs, as is now the standard practice in most city performances. Some members of the audience are nodding off— not surprising, since the puppets on the screen indicate that the time is well past midnight. A refined knight, on the right of the screen, faces three *punakawan*, or servant-clowns, on the left; they are playing the scene in which the *punakawan* first appear. Drawing by Suharso.

JAVANESE SHADOW PLAYS,
JAVANESE SELVES

INTRODUCTION: ON INTERPRETING A JAVANESE ART FORM

N*dhrog-dhog-dhog*. The puppeteer rapped a heavy wooden mallet against the side of the puppet box to his left, starting a performance of the Javanese shadow play (*wayang kulit*). The great gong sounded and the Javanese orchestra arranged behind him began to play. A man in his early sixties, with the wide-set eyes and wide jaw characteristic of lowland Javanese, the puppeteer (*dhalang*) sat cross-legged in front of a long white screen with a red border, a bright light suspended above his head. Banana-tree trunks, held by supports about a foot off the ground, ran along the base of the screen. The portion of the screen directly in front of the dhalang was filled by a single puppet, called the *kayon*, an all-purpose prop shaped something like an inverted cone. On it were depicted in brilliant colors an enormous tree, with monkeys and birds in its branches, monstrous heads on either side, and a gateway and pool below. A few inches to either side of the *kayon* began a long row of puppets extending to the ends of the screen and beyond. Each of the dozens of flat leather puppets, intricately cut and elaborately painted, was secured to the banana trunks below the screen by means of a pointed grip made out of horn, which was jabbed into the trunks' spongy flesh. The puppets were arranged in ascending size. Nearest the dhalang were small, delicate puppets depicting babies, women with demurely lowered faces, and some gods. Refined knights with half-closed eyes, bare chests, and narrow waists; more gods dressed in long gowns and turbans; larger, bolder males; then giants and monsters with huge round eyes, bared teeth, and paw-like hands completed the series on either side.

As the orchestra, called the *gamelan*, began to play, Ki Cerma, the dhalang, pulled the stem of the *kayon* out of the banana trunk with his right hand and, gripping its tip with the fingers of his left, held it over his head while he murmured ritual spells to stave off danger. Then he twirled the two-foot-high *kayon*, secured it in the banana trunk to one side of the open area of the screen, and began to bring out the puppets that would appear in the first scene. A prince, maidservants to attend him, and knights figured among these. Ki Cerma held the stem of each puppet in one hand as he moved it across the screen, and with the other hand he grasped the two lighter grips, also made out of horn, connected to the puppets' palms. The arms of shadow puppets are very long and jointed at the shoulders and elbows, but these are their only movable parts. The dhalang moved each puppet and manipulated its hands in a manner appropriate to its particular character and station, the maidservants moving with elegant grace, the knights with dignified resolve.

A number of microphones, some of them flat ones that looked like old parts from a car, one flashy new one recently made in Japan, were fastened to the banana trunk in front of the dhalang. They were linked to loudspeakers inside and outside the house in which the performance was taking place, and as Ki Cerma began to speak, his voice flooded the scene. He spoke in a long, rapid, and heavily stylized stream of words, describing in an idealizing and conventionalized but rather obscure vocabulary the kingdom and court of Pringgadani, in which the story opened. Throughout his narration, the gamelan played softly in the background. The dhalang timed his delivery to mesh with a series of strokes on the various gongs in the ensemble, and he occasionally interrupted his description with a few sung lines of Old Javanese poetry (suluk). The account ended as the dhalang identified the characters now assembled in formal audience with the prince.

With great deliberateness, the prince of Pringgadani, Gathutkaca, exchanged greetings with each person present in turn. The order in which he did so, and the titles and degree of linguistic formality he used in each of these exchanges, were determined by the status of each of his interlocutors. An elder visiting from another kingdom received long, elaborate thanks and offers of refreshment. These greetings were graciously acknowledged by the guest, the refreshments modestly declined. Knights who were members of the prince's own retinue received less elaborate greetings, but they themselves expressed gratitude at their prince's concern for their well-being, and they greeted the guest present at the royal audience.

The exchange of greetings took several minutes to complete. Following it, Prince Gathutkaca summoned his prime minister, Bajradenta, to come forward, in order to discuss a matter that was causing him great disarray. The dhalang now sang another suluk, after this half-hour or so of preliminaries, and the focal point of the story was about to be revealed. Only at this stage did many members of the audience leave off chatting and start paying much attention.

Preparations for the performance had begun months prior to this long and stately opening. Most performances of wayang sponsored by private families (as opposed to those put on by organizations, government offices, an entire village, etc.) are held in conjunction with some rite of passage. Weddings and circumcisions are celebrated with a performance especially often, but other events, such as the birth of a child, a roof-raising, or the final ritual in a long series of funerary observances, can be appropriate times at which to sponsor a shadow play. The sponsors must first select an auspicious date on which to hold a ritual, in accordance with rather complicated numerological calculations. Then they must choose which dhalang they wish to approach, and inquire, often through intermediaries, whether he can perform on that date and what his fee might be. A dhalang's calendar and his fee both depend on the fame he enjoys, though the criteria by which he is judged are diverse. Dhalang with strong voices and quick wits are often very popular, very busy, and quite expensive to engage. Older dhalang whose voices have lost their flexibility and power may nevertheless be valued due to their greater experience and wisdom. Ki Cerma's age and the travails of his life had taken the sweetness from his singing voice, and he had also lost some of the energy that had made him, twenty years earlier, a renowned performer very much in demand. Nevertheless, he was still a respected dhalang, and he performed at least a few times each month during the dry season, when most performances are held.

If a dhalang is free to perform on the evening the sponsors wish, negotiation of a fee then ensues. The fee depends on several factors: whether the sponsors wish to engage only the dhalang plus one or two musicians, assembling the rest of the singers and musicians on their own, or wish to let the dhalang bring musicians with him; whether the sponsors will rent puppets and screen from someone else, or will ask the dhalang to bring his own; whether the sponsors wish the dhalang to perform only at night, or wish to have him or a person delegated by him perform during the day preceding the more important nighttime performance as well; and whether the sponsors can by virtue of some kinship, friendship, or other relationship with the dhalang expect special consideration when the dhalang names a fee. The dickering is occasionally protracted, but it must be done with discretion, since the relations between dhalang and their sponsors must never be thought to resemble those between buyers and sellers at the market. When an agreement has been reached, the dhalang is given some portion of the fee as a retainer. In this case, Ki Cerma was performing in the home of people living in a village near his own. He had agreed to a fee somewhat lower than his usual one because neighbors are expected to put good relations above financial interests.

Several days before the performance itself, in anticipation of the many guests who would come both before and during the performance, relatives and neighbors had gathered to help the sponsors in their preparations. Men first took the front off the house. The front of older-style Javanese houses consists of a long row of wooden doors. These are removed and the floor and roof extended to accommodate the gamelan and musicians when a performance is to be held, or simply to accommodate guests when a ritual celebration is held without any type of entertainment. Plaited coconut palm leaves were put up to decorate the open sides of the performance area that extended into the yard, and mats were unrolled to cover the floor. (In newer, Western-style houses, the front wall is made of cement, and only the windows and door can be removed to permit casual spectators a view of the performance.) Inside, the screen was set against two of the wooden posts that support the roof of a traditional style house; beneath the screen were the banana trunk runners in which the puppets were secured. Chairs were set up in the area behind the screen, closer to the inner section of the house, so that invited guests who came to see the performance would be able to watch it on this, the more prestigious side, where shadows rather than the puppets were visible. Traditionally, and still in some villages near Jogja, there were not chairs but mats spread on the floor behind the screen, where invited guests sat.

Behind the house, in the kitchen area, women had cooked enormous quantities of food to serve the many guests. People who came before or during the day of the ritual celebration to contribute money toward the costs of the event, as well as those who came to see the performance itself, were served snacks with tea, then rice with side-dishes, and again snacks and tea. A small army of women prepared these refreshments, cooking day and night from long before as well as during the event, and even afterwards, to feed the people who helped to clean up.

Early in the morning of the day the performance took place, the gamelan arrived, carried on an ox-cart, with copious amounts of straw protecting the bronze gongs, pots, and keys from scraping. Until the performance started, children and youths tried their hands at various instruments, occasionally attempting to play together, often simply banging out notes on their own. Since a rented tape recorder and loudspeaker blared cassettes of pop music and gamelan at deafening volume throughout the day of the event, these additions to the general noise level went largely unnoticed.

The sponsors had chosen to hold a performance of wayang during the day, in addition to the nighttime performance, so by about nine or ten in the morning a troupe of performers had arrived. They were greeted and served a meal by the sponsors. Although the same musicians played for both the daytime and nighttime performances, the dhalang in this case was a "representative" of Ki Cerma, who was to perform in the evening: his next to oldest son, Sigit. In other families, it is often a brother or other relative to whom the principal dhalang passes on the task, and whom he pays, usually rather little, out of the total sum received from the sponsors. Few dhalang perform both all day and all night, though in the past apparently this was not uncommon. Ki Cerma had done so in his youth and early adulthood, on the insistence of his father, himself a dhalang. Many dhalang develop their skills by performing during the day. But if they begin to receive frequent invitations to perform at night, they can cease to take on the unprestigious and onerous job of daytime performing. Ki Cerma's oldest son had practiced his skills by performing during the day for his father, but now received a fair number of invitations to perform at night, and so happily let his younger brothers take his father's place during the day instead.

One reason that daytime performances are so lacking in prestige is that the audience consists primarily of children. They cluster around the gamelan, hanging onto the posts supporting the extended roof or struggling to get a spot where they can stand near the platform on which the musicians are seated. On the shadow side of the screen sit men who have escorted their wives or other female relatives on a preliminary visit to the ritual celebration. These women bring contributions to give the sponsors, something they do with a circumspect gesture when greeted by the female sponsor further inside the house. The men watch the performance briefly while eating a meal that they are served. The shadows barely show in the daylight, however, and the men take little interest in this entertainment. Within a half-hour or so they leave again, along with the women they have escorted. They are soon replaced by other guests, who make equally brief visits.

The evening performance matters much more than any daytime one, although the stories are drawn from the same repertoire. (Occasionally sponsors request that the daytime and nighttime performances treat related stories, but more often the stories are not directly linked.) In this case, since there had been a daytime performance, the musicians rested and ate another meal during the hour or two after it ended and before the evening performance began. Ki Cerma arrived during this period. In the past, a dhalang usually arrived on foot, on a bicycle, or occasionally in a horse-drawn carriage. Now Ki Cerma rode up on an old German motorbike, bought long before in the flush of his great early successes. (Very wealthy dhalang arrive in a car or minibus with several attendants.) The sponsor couple greeted him and served him and the musicians a meal. At seven-thirty he joined the gamelan, and a concert began. Often the dhalang himself plays the drums during this concert, but Ki Cerma's son Sigit, who had performed the daytime wayang, was a particularly skillful drummer, trained at the national music academy (Akademi Seni Karawitan Indonesia) in Solo, so he drummed for the concert. He later went on to accompany his father's performance and was relieved at last only at about three-thirty in the morning, when another younger brother took a turn at drumming.

If the dhalang is very popular, people of all ages, though almost exclusively males, start gathering outside the house where the wayang will be held during the course of the concert, or even earlier. In the case of Java's four or five most popular dhalang, hundreds of people, sometimes well over a thousand, assemble, crowding together in whatever space the arrangement of houses nearby affords. Boys often climb trees to get a better view of the screen—sometimes in such numbers that the trees collapse. Although Ki Cerma's popularity was not so great, nevertheless on the paths and roads near the performance itinerant sellers set up stalls and laid out mats where people could buy refreshments or toys, or could gamble. In the yard, immediately behind the gamelan, people sat or squatted while watching the performance, though spectators on the sidelines stood. These people's attempts to get a better view, plus the constant coming and going of spectators, often made it impossible for others to see the screen without standing up.

At about nine, Ki Cerma rose, advanced toward the screen, and sat down cross-legged in front of it. He took puppets that he would use in the first scene out of the puppet box, and checked to see that another son, Harsa, who was sitting behind him ready to assist him, had taken out others that he would need later. He then took up the wooden mallet and started the performance by rapping the side of the puppet box to his left.

Many of the invited guests arrived after the performance had begun. They came on bicycles or motorbikes if they lived outside the hamlet where the sponsors' home was located. They had to make their way among the vendors and spectators to where vehicles were parked, overseen by the neighborhood youths, who handed out numbered parking checks. Then they passed along a receiving line as they entered the sponsors' house. Although some women accompany their husbands to evening ritual celebrations, most of the guests who came at this time were males. They were escorted to the area behind the screen by a relative or friend of the sponsors and shown a place to sit, its proximity to the screen depending on their social status. Women spectators—there are rarely very many—sat further inside the house, behind the men. Invited guests struck up conversation among themselves, whether they had been previously acquainted or not. Few of them paid much attention to the performance until the dhalang sang the lines of the suluk indicating that the exposition of the plot was about to begin.

The pace of the long opening scene quickened once Prince Gathutkaca and his courtiers and guests broached the issue at hand. Gathutkaca revealed to his prime minister that his disarray was due to the disappearance of his father, Werkudara, one of the five virtuous Pandhawa brothers. Gathutkaca and his minister, Bajradenta, were still discussing this grave turn of events when the arrival of a priest (*pandhita*) caused a great stir at the court. The priest, named Begawan Durawicara ("Priest False Speech"), aroused great suspicion among some of the courtiers, but his assurances that he could find Gathutkaca's father impressed the prince, who entrusted all responsibility for the kingdom to him. Durawicara informed Gathutkaca that all he needed to do to meet up with his father was to enter the magical pocket in his, the priest's own, robes, while the sage did meditation. Gathutkaca and the priest then left the audience hall together, to the general dismay of the court.

Once the long formal opening was past, most spectators listened to the dhalang as he took on each puppet's voice, and they watched more attentively as he moved each puppet's hands as it spoke. The dispute between Durawicara and one of the courtiers doubtful of the veracity of his claims was typical of such opening scenes. Although the characters had to observe the constraints upon their acts and gestures that the prince's presence imposed, these figures argued quite heatedly, and the barely suppressed tension riveted the spectators' attention. To be able to make characters enter into arguments, counterposing their different points of view convincingly, is considered a very valuable skill in a dhalang.

The shrewd and powerful Kresna, who is an incarnation of the god Wisnu, and his brother Baladewa arrived in Pringgadani to find the courtiers greatly distressed at their prince's departure with Durawicara. Kresna entered the palace to learn more about the mysterious sage. Inside the prince's chambers, Gathutkaca entered Durawicara's magic pocket only to find himself growing strangely and suddenly weaker, while the priest crowed that he would now kill the prince. Durawicara invited his son, Lesmanagandrakumara, to come forth out of his other pocket. When he did so, it was apparent that this son had taken on the exact same form as Gathutkaca himself. His father told him that now the young man would be able to fool Gathutkaca's wife, Pregiwa, into thinking that he was her husband, and he would be able at last to fulfill his long frustrated amorous desires for her.

By now it was past eleven o'clock at night. In a scene included in virtually all performances of wayang, the prime minister, Bajradenta, reviewed the royal troops in preparation for the battle that was sure to follow upon the recent, unsettling events. In this "departure of the troops" scene (budhalan), the dhalang displayed his singing voice in the lines of the suluk he sang, and he displayed his ability at manipulating the puppets as he represented the characteristic gestures and styles of movement of the different puppets. Among the guests and musicians there was also considerable movement, since by this time young people had begun distributing snacks and glasses of tea on either side of the screen. Invited guests were served individual portions. Had the sponsors been wealthy, each guest would have received a little paper plate or even a cardboard box of snacks, but these sponsors had only modest means and served only the usual cylinders of sticky rice with a bit of spiced meat inside (lemper) and a little piece of cake. For the musicians, peanuts fried with garlic, flat cakes of coconut and rice, brilliant pink cupcakes, lemper, and several other kinds of goodies were piled high on plates and laid on the mats among the instruments for the musicians to snack on throughout the night. The dhalang ate nothing, drinking only occasional sips of tea from a glass to his right. He did smoke strongly flavored clove or incense cigarettes all night long, however, as did many of the men present, endowing the scene with a heavy, musky scent.

After the departure of the troops, in most performances the scene shifts to another kingdom, often to one "across the sea" where particularly rapacious or crude characters have their kingdoms. By means of a subtle cue to the gamelan players, the dhalang signals them to begin playing a specific musical composition, and after a few minutes of music, he begins another narrative description, far less lengthy than in the opening scene but like it formal and highly stylized. The guests, and particularly the uninvited spectators, let their attention wander during such introductions, a few of them dozing off. When the action resumes, they focus once again on the puppets and on the question or problem that will lead these new characters into conflict with those in the first scene. In this particular performance, the story was relatively less complex—atypically so. Rather than open another story line at this point by shifting to another kingdom, the dhalang continued to follow Kresna in his pursuit of the evil priest. But as often happens in the course of whatever scene follows the departure of the troops, the performance was interrupted. When all the guests had been served a plate of rice with side dishes, a representative of the sponsors took a microphone and addressed the assembled company, announcing to them the nature of the ritual event while expressing to them the sponsors' thanks for their attendance and apologies for any shortcomings. Finally, he invited the guests to eat the food they had been given and urged them to stay until the performance's end. If the moderator at a ritual celebration is particularly prolix, or if distinguished guests are asked to make speeches, such interruptions can last half an hour or more, often to the irritation of the dhalang; but in this case it only lasted twenty minutes. The guests then took up their plates and ate the little bits of curried meat, stewed soybeans, and sweet pickled cucumber that are the usual Javanese ceremonial fare, all of them placed atop a mound of rice.

Invited guests can leave when a decent interval has elapsed after they eat. Some may choose to stay until after a battle has taken place between characters introduced in the earlier scenes, a battle that usually begins by about midnight and invariably ends in a draw. In this performance, the battles pitted Kresna and Baladewa plus the royal troops of Pringgadani against Begawan Durawicara, but the latter was able to make himself invisible and elude them all, escaping into a great forest.

In a third major scene—which took place, as is conventional, in a sage's hermitage—the servant-clowns first appeared, and they sang popular, catchy tunes with the assistance of the female singers sitting with the musicians. This singing plus the servant-clowns' joking lasted about an hour. Following it, Gathutkaca's cousin, Abimanyu, a delicate figure possessing the slight frame of very refined knights, paid homage to the venerable Abiyasa. This revered sage urged the downcast knight to persevere in his search for Werkudara by seeking out yet another sage, named Senawangi. The scene concluded as the gamelan played another, more classical gamelan composition and the servant-clowns set off to accompany their master, Abimanyu, on his journey. At this point most of the invited guests left, filing out of the house in a steady stream. Only an exceptionally famous and popular dhalang can keep many invited guests watching the performance later than this time, about one in the morning.

Once the invited guests had left, boys and a few older youths entered the area behind the screen, where they watched, joked around, and/or slept through the rest of the performance. They took great pleasure in the battle between the refined Abimanyu and a series of monsters that followed in the course of his journey, and in the clowns' comic battles with those monsters. At about three in the morning, the gamelan played another longer composition, and the dhalang made another formal introduction of characters and scene, this time of the priest Senawangi and the ancient and wise white monkey Anuman. By now most of the boys behind the screen had dozed off, and the area in front of the house was close to deserted. The musicians, too, were given to falling asleep once this composition was over and dialogue resumed. (Some sponsors serve them coffee and another meal at this time to help keep them moderately alert.) Much of the story line was developed and resolved in the time between this last long musical composition and the series of battles that took up the final hour or so of the performance. Senawangi was revealed to be the missing Werkudara, Anuman and the god Sang Hyang Tunggal persuaded him to return to his responsibilities in his own kingdom, and Abimanyu and his attendants arrived in time to escort him there. In Pringgadani, Pregiwa was not quite deceived by the false "Gathutkaca," whose aims were therefore thwarted. She fled into the forest, the same forest in which Durawicara had earlier sought refuge. Durawicara's efforts to kill Gathutkaca failed, and all the characters joined battle. These battles were enacted to a heavily accented, repetitive musical accompaniment, waking the sleeping boys and attracting some early risers among the neighbors to watch, including some women carrying their babies. At about five in the morning, as the sun began to make the horizon glow in the east, the battle music suddenly resolved into a closing musical piece. There was a very brief gathering of characters at the court of Pringgadani. Ki Cerma then took out a wooden hand puppet (a *wayang golèk*) and made it dance in front of the screen for a few minutes as an entertainment that the victors held to celebrate their triumph over adversity. The performance that had begun at nine o'clock the night before finally ended with the conclusion of this dance, as the dhalang replaced the *kayon* in the center of the screen. The sun was just about to rise.

The dhalang stood for the first time since the performance began, and he and the musicians and singers gathered inside the house, where they were served more snacks and another meal. The sponsors discreetly slipped the dhalang his fee, and the dhalang's wife paid each musician once they went outside about an hour later, when they were all about to leave.

Some of the musicians, many of whom were relatives of the Cerma family, accompanied the Cermas home, where they continued to talk and joke for an hour or two. They were exhausted, but also excited, and this time seemed necessary for them to work off their excitement. Eventually they dispersed, and Ki Cerma then went to bed, though if he had had business to attend to or work to do in the fields, he would have put off sleeping for several hours. He was unlikely in any case to sleep for very long at one stretch until that evening. But if he had been a very popular performer, or if it had been a month in which many people hold ritual celebrations, he might have had to make do with whatever sleep he could catch during the day, since by evening he would have set off once again to perform. Javanese often cite this grueling schedule as one reason why dhalang are said to die young.

At the sponsors' home, meanwhile, the morning was spent returning the house to its usual condition, cleaning up the yard, taking down the loudspeaker, returning rented plates and chairs, and finally serving up yet another meal to the kin and neighbors who had helped out. Everyone was weary.

SHADOW PLAYS AND SOCIAL SCIENCE

Javanese wayang is an eight-hour performance that draws on the energies of a great many people and fits into a larger event that can mobilize dozens or even hundreds more. It is by no means the only major art form in Java. On the contrary, Java offers a remarkable number and range of performing arts. These include village performances in which men go into trance, commercial folk drama, several courtly dance traditions, stand-up comics, singers of Indonesian, Javanese, and Islamic pop music, and many more. It is true that some traditional performances are now nearly forgotten. Few are the performances of *topèng* (dance with masks) or *langen mandra wanaran* (a performance in which players sing, but gesture only from a kneeling position) that take place in contemporary Java. But new forms crop up, and the Javanese taste for all forms of theatre shows no sign of diminishing. In fact, theatre seems to pervade Javanese life. Whenever Westerners speak of polite Javanese encounter, with its elaborately orchestrated conversations and choreographed gestures, they fall almost instantly into theatrical metaphors. But in all the dramaturgy, the shadow play stands out as the preeminent art form in Java. It is the tradition that Javanese themselves consider the most important, the most prestigious to sponsor or perform, and the most distinctly Javanese. Even Javanese who don't much care for wayang, and there are many such people, nevertheless speak of it as uniquely meaningful, or as they put it, "full." Its influence on other traditional art forms is great. Much of the court dance tradition consists not only of stories adapted from the shadow play tradition, but also of movements modeled after those of its flat leather puppets. In fact, such dance is called *wayang wong*: a human shadow play. When in conversation Javanese speak of someone showing up or leaving a place, they often illustrate the point with a particular gesture. They hold one hand in front of their chests, fingers pointing upward and the back of the hand facing outward. They then move their arm to the side, raising and lowering it slightly, in imitation of the way a puppet moves across the screen.

Wayang's influence goes beyond the arts and beyond conventional gestures. Imagery taken from wayang crops up frequently in Javanese speech, and the art form provides many a metaphor to Javanese comments on all sorts of events. Children are nicknamed after the servant-clowns, and the labels for kinds of characters are used to characterize kinds of humans as well. In a religious mode, people often remark that we are all really just puppets, moved by the ultimate dhalang, God. In political discourse, any important political official is liable to be labeled a puppet manipulated by an unseen dhalang. Much discussion about the current regime has centered on who at any given movement the real dhalang is.

As these last two examples suggest, the dhalang himself holds particular fascination for Javanese, as well he might. The extent of his learning and his ability to create narrative and dialogue on the spot are usually remarkable, and he is often an extremely clever comic. His authority over the performance is total. He crafts the story, manipulates all the puppets, takes all their voices, and directs the gamelan, all at the same time. In the course of a performance, as dhalang are fond of putting it, the dhalang is king.

Yet as I have tried to suggest in the foregoing description, there is something puzzling about wayang in performance. The tradition fascinates people, but most individual performances do not. Relatively few people watch an entire performance. Granted, Java's four or five most popular dhalang will keep a large crowd present all night. But even they cannot keep spectators attentive through the narrative introductions to many scenes, nor awake through the entire eight-hour performance. The vast majority of dhalang keep very few people watching beyond halfway through the performance. And in the half of the performance that many people do see, the first half, the story is only barely set in motion. Most of the story, as I have mentioned, develops much later, after about three in the morning. The rest of the performance is filled with set pieces, music, and comic exchanges. The stories themselves, for that matter, particularly those stories popular at present, of which *Senawangi* is a somewhat simplified but still fairly typical example, are highly conventionalized, and their outcomes are easily predicted. So there is little reason to follow them very closely. Wayang seems in many ways to preoccupy the Javanese, yet they pay it only intermittent attention. I wish to analyze the reasons both for its allure and for what sometimes looks, to an outsider, like its willful neglect.

The central difficulty that confronts researchers of a non-Western art form is that they must avoid using it as a screen on which to project their own preconceptions, yet they cannot restrict themselves wholly to native exegesis. Indigenous commentary is essential, of course. Yet an art form can express more than any one spectator, or any one performer, recognizes consciously. Claude Lévi-Strauss's demonstrations of recurring patterns in different registers within a culture should permit us to presume that an art form can be motivated at least in part by constraints as deeply felt but also as effectively hidden from consciousness as any kinship structure or pattern of exchange (Lévi-Strauss 1964). And Victor Turner's observation that a ritual's symbolism can express conflicting values, even if native exegesis does not acknowledge such contradictions, applies to performances as well (Turner 1967). The problem then is how to surpass description without imposing alien judgments, how to remain sensitive to cultural context without limiting oneself to indigenous exegetical "traditions."[1]

---

[1] In studying non-Western arts, Westerners have tended to follow one of two approaches. Either they have provided more or less appreciative descriptions, or they have devised more or less arbitrary interpretations. The descriptions are sometimes dazzling in their detail and presentation. Yet they often leave the reader still curious as to why an art form has developed in a particular place and in a particular way.

In Java, one need only turn to Pigeaud's voluminous *Javaansche Volksvertoningen* (Pigeaud 1938) and J. Kats's beautiful *Het Javaansche Tooneel* (Kats 1923) to see what standards the Western scholarship on performing arts can attain. These and other studies of *wayang kulit* have focused primarily on three major concerns: 1) the description of the puppets themselves, and of the setting and manner of performance; 2) synopses of representative plots; and 3) discussion of the probable origin and purpose of wayang in the remote past. (See for the last point Rassers 1959.) Some more recent studies, such as those of Seno-Sastroamidjojo and Ulbricht, have tended toward a mystical interpretation (Seno-Sastroamidjojo 1964; Ulbricht 1970). In *The Religion of Java*, Clifford Geertz provides a psychological reading of wayang, linking it in partic-

The resolution of this problem lies in considering an art form in light of the relationships its performance occasions. Those relationships are many: they include those among performers, between performers and their sponsors, between sponsors and their guests, etc. Most important of all, however, are the relations between the artistic illusion itself and its audience, and implicit in these links, the relations between artist and spectator. These relations immediately suggest certain questions: what effect upon the audience is sought; what the nature of the spectators' satisfaction is thought to be; and what reactions the performance elicits. Much of this material can be obtained from indigenous commentary, though perhaps as much in casual remarks about particular performances as in more formal, generalized pronouncements. But commentary must be judged in view of what actually happens at performances, as well: how performers use the conventions of the art form, and what arouses the spectators' interest, approval, and/or censure. Commentary and practice do not necessarily coincide on any of these points, and any disparities demand particularly careful consideration.

To understand a performance as a relationship does not simply permit investigators to challenge commentary with observed reactions, however. It permits them, much more significantly, to integrate the art form with other kinds of relationships that obtain among the members of that culture. It is here that aesthetics, sociology, and ideology meet: in recurrent patterns in the mediation of self and other. My analysis of wayang develops out of this premise, that an art form constitutes a relationship, or really, a series of relationships, that can be compared with other (i.e., social and political) relations.

By taking this approach, I hope to avoid a conundrum that bedevils analysis of performing arts, namely, whether the arts are simply "reflections" of other, more important aspects of social life, or are themselves effective agents in the world. (Peacock 1968 struggles with this issue in his account of another Javanese performing art, the transvestite melodrama called *ludrug*.) My contention is that both so-

___

ular to the viewpoint of the aristocratic component in Javanese society (C. Geertz 1960). Benedict Anderson sees in wayang diverse models of behavior, models that underlie Javanese tolerance of a range of personal styles (Anderson 1965). A Dutch scholar has recently presented a wealth of sociological data about dhalang, their backgrounds, and training (Clara van Groenendaal 1982).

cial life and aesthetics develop out of deeply held assumptions about the world, and that neither one need be seen as cause or effect of the other. The responsibility of the analyst is to discern what those un-derlying assumptions might be, and how they shape both social life and aesthetic activity.

Paul Ricoeur states, "One of the aims of all hermeneutics is to struggle against cultural distance" (Ricoeur 1981:159), and clearly the cultural distance between Java and the West—the gap between their assumptions and ours—is great. A. L. Becker addresses just this point when he prefaces his very subtle and valuable discussion of Jav-anese wayang with some general remarks about how to "recreate a conceptually distant context." He distinguishes four types of rela-tions that must be examined when dealing with any text: those within parts of the text; those with other, prior texts; those among author, text, and hearers and readers; and those between the text and non-literary events (Becker 1979). In this list Becker has set much of the program I have tried to follow.

My approach begins with analysis of the more palpable relation-ships in Javanese life, and proceeds to the more elusive domains of aesthetics and epistemology. After discussing Javanese understand-ings of the self (Chapter 1), I consider relationships as they can be observed in daily life: interaction within the family (Chapter 2), in villages (Chapter 3), and among those people deemed spiritually powerful and their suppliants (Chapter 4). I then examine relation-ships as they are occasioned by a performance: the interaction that takes place among sponsors, performers, guests, and other spectators (Chapters 5, 6, and 7). Finally, I discuss relationships as they are de-fined more abstractly: the interaction, taken now in a broad sense, among individuals, aesthetic illusions, and knowledge (Chapters 8 and 9).

The figure at the center of all these stages in the analysis is the dhalang. He is foreshadowed in the fathers, village headmen, potent and/or prescient figures, and ritual sponsors that are the foci of Chap-ters 2 through 5. He takes his place at the center of a performance of wayang, and of my discussion, in Chapters 6 and 7. His power and effectiveness, thought at once enticing and suspect, and the varying responses they elicit, point to the ambiguous status of art and knowl-edge, as discussed in the concluding Chapters 8 and 9.

If interaction is the connecting thread in my analysis and the dhalang the central figure, three topics that recur frequently are self, power, and language. To speak of interaction is to speak of selves. But mention of self immediately poses an essential problem in any anthropological inquiry: How is the self understood in a particular culture? Since cultural assumptions about the self impinge fundamentally on all interpersonal relations, one must ask what the critical attributes of an individual's identity are thought to be. In Java, the self is defined most crucially in two ways: as placed in the social hierarchy, and as in possession of a particular concentration of power. Hierarchy is constantly at issue in Javanese interaction; social status shapes interaction everywhere, but in Java its effects are quite precisely registered. The concept of concentrations of power, meanwhile, provides Javanese a way of conceiving, justifying, and at times even trying to alter, much about one's social status.

In referring to a person's "concentration of power," I am alluding to Javanese ideas about a kind of spiritual energy that individuals possess in varying degrees, understandings that Moertono and Anderson have brilliantly analyzed (Moertono 1968; Anderson 1972b). People's actions, their speech, and their fortunes are all thought to be affected by the spiritual potency they wield, and by the potency others wield. Among those "others" are their parents and ancestors, political leaders, specialists in ritual and curing, and dhalang. Interaction with any of these figures always implies a concern with potency: its concentration or dispersion, its attainment or loss, and its implementation or avoidance. In wayang, not only are many of the incidents portrayed on the screen informed by an abiding interest in the possession and manifestations of potency, but so too are the relations that a spectator enters into with the dhalang and the illusion that the dhalang creates.

Potency is always at issue in interaction, but it remains largely implicit. Speech in Java makes explicit the understandings of self and potency to which I have alluded. The Javanese language exhibits the most highly elaborated speech levels of any language in the world. Many high-frequency words in the language have two, three, occasionally as many as five or more variant forms, each of them denotatively equivalent but expressive of a particular estimation of the relative status of speaker, interlocutor, and/or a third party. This elaborate commentary on social relations, necessarily implicated in virtually every Javanese utterance, keeps a concern with social status close to the surface in every encounter. Speech and writing, further-more, are thought by Javanese to channel potency even on their own, and Javanese thinking about the nature of an individual's rela-tions with discourse—as master of or as subject to its power—illumi-nates much about Javanese conceptions of the self and potency.

Wayang is a remarkably talky art form. It is believed to tap, at least ideally, considerable reserves of potency, and it establishes relation-ships among performers, sponsors, and spectators of unusual but also telling sorts. The initial four chapters of this book are intended to ex-plicate Javanese understandings of the self, power, and language as they inform interaction, in order then, in the remaining chapters, to situate the phenomenon of wayang in an intelligible, if still at times distinctly unfamiliar, context.

If an art form can be analyzed as a set of relationships, it may still be deemed less important, and so less needful of analysis, than other aspects of a particular culture. The arts may be thought to play an only marginal role in a particular society, to stand somewhat off-cen-ter in the struggle for wealth, status, and power. Yet this provides just the reason for their interest. Whether or not they constitute a critical commentary on the world in which they are played—it is my conten-tion that wayang, at least, has no such intrinsically critical func-tion—these art forms present a distillation of cultural assumptions, an intensification of those investments that underlie all variety of ac-tion. Release from such mundane constraints as gravity and time per-mits the characters in a drama to devote their full attention to the more compelling issues of, say, honor or potency. An analyst must then try to see how the concerns that seem to motivate plot, manner of performance, and its reception resonate with other aspects of the culture in which the performance takes place.

In looking for areas of a culture in which those concerns appear, a researcher can take advantage of similarly "eccentric" phenomena. Reactions to and commentary upon irregularities in the run of events often reveal assumptions about the way things are, assumptions that "normal" patterns rarely reveal. Procedures and comments provoked by the birth of twins, to take an example common in the ethno-graphic literature, may point up assumptions about the nature of in-dividual identity, conceptions that are not revealed, because they are not challenged, when humans are born singly. I have taken this approach often, seeking to support a point by reference to Javanese comments on relatively unusual events, events that take place, as it were, on the margins of experience. In particular, I have drawn on the many comments informants made in the idiom of *kebatinan*, the great range of mystical beliefs that color much Javanese thinking about events. My point is not to reduce Javanese culture to an assortment of odd ideas about the workings of unseen forces in the world. Rather, it is to use these comments on the edges of phenomena as a kind of cultural exegesis formulated by the culture's own participants.

If I may draw a rather prickly analogy, an anthropologist must discern the import of cultural phenomena by gaining informants' associations to those facts. This means first of all recording people's comments upon their own experience. It also means observing their actions. Robert Jay has applied a useful distinction in this regard to differing levels of generalization in Javanese conversation (Jay 1969:20-29). The normatively approved values expressed at high levels of conceptualization, he notes, may be contradicted by remarks made at more immediate levels. The same point applies to people's actions as well. That what people do in Java, like everywhere else, may very well conflict with the norms they profess to hold, fits Jay's distinction between greater and lesser degrees of conceptual generality, because action is a kind of expression at the least generalized and most immediate level. It is a "statement" even more immediate and less highly conceptualized than casual remarks, and observed action can often put commentary in a fuller context. Actions, that is, are further associations to stated norms, unstated preconceptions, and often conflicting wants, all of which are necessarily both personally and culturally motivated.

A difficulty nevertheless presents itself: even if anthropologists gather something akin to psychological associations in their efforts to explicate cultural phenomena, there is no single subject in which the associations are assimilated—except the anthropologist himself or herself. This supposed gathering of material is really the generation of further associations, now the anthropologist's own, and this step immediately implies distortion. But that is my point. Distortion is a necessary feature in the process of interpreting a culture, or really, facets of a culture, all the more so when that interpretation is accomplished through the agency of one person. Analysts of cultural data can only present their interpretations in such a way as to show what sorts of evidence have suggested the connections they have made. I have tried to support my arguments about Javanese behavior by reference to the ephemeral little incidents and casual remarks that have not simply colored but in fact generated my view of Javanese culture—especially when they have startled me by running counter to my expectations. In this, of course, I hardly differ from any anthropologist. I feel constrained to point out, however, that my claim is not to present an unbiased rendering of what happens in Java, but rather to show what sense I have been able to make of the many ways in which Javanese habits suited, escaped, or confounded my biases.[2]

RESEARCH METHODS

I lived twenty months in a village I will call Karanganom in the *kabupatèn* (county) of Klaten, Central Java, during a twenty-two month stay in Java in 1978-1979. I boarded with a dhalang, to whom I have given the pseudonym of Pak Cermadikrama, and his family. My research consisted partly of interaction with the Cerma family, which was comprised of Pak Cerma and his wife, the five sons still living at home, and one granddaughter who lived with them most of the time. The granddaughter's parents, the Cermas' oldest son and his wife, lived with their two other children in a hamlet nearby. The Cermas' daughter and her husband and their two children lived in the coastal city of Semarang and visited Karanganom only rarely.

Most days I travelled to the homes of dhalang in the areas of Klaten, Sala, and Jogja, occasionally venturing to the further areas of Gunung Kidul, Wonogiri, and Bantul. These visits were unscheduled and informal. I brought snacks, as Javanese guests often do, but I did not remunerate my informants otherwise. For the most part conversation roamed freely. Dhalang are on the whole very good talkers, and this facilitated research in most respects—though it meant that all attempts to keep discussion to a specific track were doomed to fail-

---

[2] It would be disingenuous of me to pretend that my view of Javanese culture has not also been formed in great measure by Western literature about Java. My debt to previous scholars is apparent in the preceding references and in notes to the text, but I should note the particularly crucial and formative role the writings of both Benedict Anderson and Clifford Geertz have had upon my understanding of Javanese culture. Their contributions to the field are so great and so well known that I have made explicit reference to their work only when I have drawn most directly from them. But as any reader will see, their ideas have informed all my thinking.

ure. Dates to see performances followed from these visits, and I attended most performances as a guest not of the sponsors but of the dhalang. I recorded many performances, sitting among the musicians.

In Karanganom, I got to know the neighbors by informal evening visits. Silly as it may sound, the fact that the dry season hardly happened in 1978 had serious consequences for my research. It rained so many evenings that year that visits in the village were hampered. When it rains after dark in Java, most villagers just go to bed. Resident anthropologists are also subject to somnolence at such times. However, the rains did end in the usual season in 1979 (tapering off in March and April), and I was able to accomplish more visits.

While most of the research I have drawn on here was done in 1978-1979, I have also referred to observations I made during earlier stays in Java, twenty-nine months in all, in 1971-1972 and in 1974. In 1971-1972, I was teaching in the Department of Anthropology at the University of Gajah Mada. During that time, and on my return to Java after a year in Bali, I studied the Javanese language and gamelan. It was also at that time that I first became interested in wayang, though I knew no dhalang personally then. I lived in a hamlet outside of Jogja, which I have called Purwosari. I boarded at the home of an aged man, the former hamlet headman, his more vigorous wife, their thirty-year-old son (who had taken on his father's responsibilities), and a younger son of about twenty-two. Two other sons, both married, lived close by.

As is evident in the body of this text, the conclusions I have reached are drawn from the many hours of casual conversation I had with Javanese, most of whom lived in villages. While I believe that much of what I say pertains to city-dwellers as well—many of whom are newly arrived in town, and perhaps living there only temporarily—it remains true that my examples are drawn from and apply most clearly to villagers. It is also true that in both Purwosari and Karanganom most people were more syncretist than orthodox in their attitudes toward Islam. The distinction between *abangan* (syncretist) and *santri* (devout, whether orthodox or modernist) is hardly clear-cut—it is a wide spectrum, not an opposition—but I must defer to other scholars on the subject of the more orthodox Muslims in Java.

A glossary of the Javanese words that occur most frequently in the text is included following Chapter 10. When Javanese words appear in the text, only the low Javanese (*ngoko*) terms are provided, without any high Javanese (*krama*) equivalents they may have. In pronouncing Javanese words that appear in the text, the vowel written "a" in final open syllables, and in penultimate open syllables preceding final open syllables in "a," is pronounced "aw" as in English "law." (For example, the name "Cerma" is pronounced "Cermaw," and *pusaka* is pronounced "pusawkaw.") Unaccented "e" resembles an English schwa; accented "e" resembles the French sounds represented by the same symbols, "é" and "è." Unvoiced consonants are unaspirated, whereas voiced stops are very heavy. "T" and "d" are dental, whereas "th" and "dh" are palatal; "c" is similar to English "ch," as in "church"; "j" is similar to English "j," as in "jade"; and, as in German, the sounds written as voiced stops "b," "d," and "g," when they occur in final position, are actually pronounced like English "p," "t," and "k," respectively.

1. LANGUAGE, POWER, AND ASCETICISM

Formal Javanese encounter is remarkable. Among people who are not close kin or longtime associates, and to an extent even among them, face-to-face encounter requires that everyone take great care to behave in a manner appropriate to his or her relative social status, no matter what the business at hand. Vocabulary, sentiment, gesture, timing—all must be adjusted carefully in view of the responses they are liable to arouse among the people present, and in view of one's own social status relative to theirs. Such issues matter in encounter everywhere, certainly, but in Java the degree to which they have been organized in a repertoire of vocabulary sets and conversational strategies is quite awesome. To interact in Java means to anticipate, gauge, adjust for, and at times presume upon—but never unwittingly—the responses of one's interlocutors.

Yet a topic that preoccupies Javanese is ascetic exercise, and a striking fact about ascetic rigors is that they suggest obliviousness to others and to the world. Asceticism is a means, furthermore, to make oneself more impressive and less subject to external influence even in everyday affairs. This means among other things that a person who has accomplished many ascetic rigors is thought capable of controlling encounter in ways that other people cannot.

Encounter and asceticism stand as two opposite but linked kinds of action. They are logical extremes in Javanese thinking about experience. Each of them, and the way people relate them to each other, can clarify Javanese understandings of power. They enable us, as a result, to see how those understandings inform Javanese interaction in specific relationships, such as in the family, in political relations, and in the arts.

SOCIAL STATUS AND RELATIVE STATUS

To appreciate the stakes in Javanese encounter, and to clarify the present discussion, it is worth making a somewhat arbitrary distinction between social status and relative status. I will take the former, social status, as an ongoing position of greater or lesser prominence in a group, determined largely by genealogy and control over labor and/or valued resources. Such control may be due to bureaucratic position, wealth, esoteric knowledge or skills, kinship ties, etc. What I will call relative status is the degree of deference a person elicits from his or her interlocutors in the course of any specific encounter. Social status is liable to shift only relatively slowly, whereas relative status is entirely contingent upon who participates in a particular exchange. Of course, the two are intimately linked: social status determines in large measure the deference one evokes, and so one's relative status, in any encounter. Yet relative status is always contextual, ephemeral, and to some degree negotiable. Social status sets the limits within which the negotiation takes place, but it still leaves room for "discussion," as people affirm, modify, or contest participants' estimations of their relative statuses. Though social status certainly matters deeply to us all, Westerners and Javanese alike, nevertheless relative status—the degree of respect people elicit in any given encounter—arouses an intensity of interest among Javanese that Westerners, and some other Indonesians, may find surprising.[1] The Javanese language provides the clearest means by which that interest is played out in encounter.

Social status in Java is defined fairly loosely. The aristocracy in court cities attends meticulously to the ranks of its members, according to the same system of "sinking status" Clifford Geertz has described for Bali (C. Geertz 1980). Ascribed status, however, touches only a tiny fraction of the population. Instead, considerations of wealth, age, education, profession, and who one's kinsmen are determine, somewhat vaguely, a person's status. Actually, there are few distinctions with which to categorize people beyond the gross labels of nobleman, civil servant, trader, laborer, or peasant. Individuals

[1] I should point out that this analytic distinction between social status and relative status corresponds to no Javanese terms. *Drajat* ("degree," "rank") comes closest to social status as a fairly permanent social position, but it is applied primarily to clearly ranked individuals, such as aristocrats and civil servants. Other kinds of distinctions, such as among kinds of villagers (owners of irrigated land, of houseyards only, or of no land), or occupations (e.g., peasants, civil servants, or merchants), or degrees of education (ignorant people versus schooled people), implicate social status, though by no means in any clearly ordered universe of terms. To speak of the finer distinctions at issue in encounter, those that I am labeling relative status, however, Javanese would simply speak of who, in any given instance, gave and who received what specific kinship terms and what indications of respect or its opposite.

are free to try to better their social status through such stratagems as amassing wealth and/or amassing diplomas. New wealth does not necessarily win everyone's respect, at least not right away, but it certainly does raise one's social status in the long run. The father of the village headman in Karanganom, where I lived, was said to be illiterate, but had made a fortune in the tobacco business. His wealth and prestige, won through his dealings with the Mangkunagaran court in Sala, made him a very powerful personage in the area, and accounted in part for his success in procuring for one of his sons the position of village headman.

Titles obtained through membership in military or other bureaucracies have immediate implications for people's social status, winning them, for example, greater authority in community affairs. People who obtain university degrees can also bank on greater prominence, and they always append the symbols of those degrees to their names. One of Jogja's contemporary dhalang is called Ki Barno B.A., and one of the city's most famous folk drama starlets appends "Master in Law" to her name.

Social status shows not simply in people's titles. The amount of land they own, the size and design of their houses, their clothes, the kind of vehicle they use, and their ability to place relatives in good jobs—all these factors affect and reflect people's wealth, clout, and social status. But precisely because these factors are quite fluid, social status is always a bit vague.

The issue of class in Java is much vexed. Clifford Geertz points out that disparities in the size of landholdings among rural Javanese are not great enough to speak of an exploitative and an exploited class (C. Geertz 1963, 1984). His critics insist that disparities that may appear small from the outside are not perceived as such within a Javanese village, and that recent evidence points to a widening gap between rich and poor, putting the latter increasingly at the mercy of the former. (For an overview of this debate, see White 1983a). For the present purposes, determining whether class analysis applies to Java matters less than simply noting that disparities in social status do of course exist, and that they impinge on face-to-face encounter just as they do on people's access to wealth, resources, and political office.

Formal social categories, however, as indicators of social status, present an only generally differentiated assortment of individuals, who must then go about the finer business of settling upon the proper mode of encounter in any particular instance. That is, they must establish their relative statuses in the course of every exchange. When the disparities in status are great, such as when a peasant addresses an aristocrat, or when they are less relevant, such as when brothers speak to each other, relative statuses are not much open to question. However, when disparities in social status are less dramatic and therefore potentially arguable and relevant, as is true in most Javanese interaction, then relative status is very much at issue. At such times, everyone attends carefully to the degrees of deference and familiarity people evince and elicit in interaction, because these affect their own and others' perceptions of themselves.

Language and Relative Status

People attend to relative status above all by attending to the manipulation of speech levels. These make virtually every utterance a comment on the relationship between speaker and interlocutor.[2] Nothing one says can be thought to have an essential meaning apart from how it is said, and as is no doubt true everywhere, this depends on where, when, and to whom it is said. It is true, furthermore, that speakers of any language observe the same kinds of distinctions, such as formality and informality, circumspection and frankness, conventionality and boldness, that distinguish Javanese speech levels. But in Java linguistic and gestural styles have been intricately and subtly graded, so that the connotations of style are at all times present in people's minds. As a result, speech levels and their corresponding gestures take over where the rather vague categories of social structure leave off. They force speakers to make quite explicit their views of each other's relative status.

Basically, one can distinguish three speech levels in Javanese, defined by the use of several vocabulary sets. The speech levels are ngoko, madya, and krama. Ngoko is the first language level a child learns to speak. It is considered by Javanese to be simple, straightfor-

---

[2] Soepomo Poedjosoedarmo gives a thorough account of the formal rules guiding the use of speech levels (Soepomo 1968; see also Soepomo 1969). C. Geertz discusses speech levels from a more sociological perspective (C. Geertz 1960:248-60). Uhlenbeck 1978 covers a broad range of linguistic and sociolinguistic issues in Javanese. J. Errington (1981) focuses on changing patterns in the use of speech levels, especially among the aristocracy. (J. Errington [1985] summarizes much of his earlier work in a more readily obtainable publication.) Examples of the uses to which levels are put can be found in Keeler 1984.

ward, and unrefined. One uses it with intimates and subordinates, and in anger, and when joking. Krama is more elegant and polite. It is suitable for formal occasions, and in speaking to people one knows only slightly or to whom one owes deference. Madya (also called krama madya) is a less refined manner of speaking than krama, but it is also less familiar than ngoko. It is used in several types of encounter: with and among persons of low status; with people one has known a long while but with whom one is not truly intimate; and with people with whom one is close but to whom one must still show respect.

Speech levels are distinguished by the use of one or several vocabulary sets. The vast majority of words in Javanese are invariant forms. The word for "tree," wit, for example, is used without modification in all three speech levels. But in addition to this invariant vocabulary set, there are words and affixes that differ in form though not in sense, the different forms expressing differing degrees of refinement. A number of words and affixes follow the basic opposition between ngoko and krama. In speaking ngoko, one speaks of a letter as layang, whereas in krama, one says serat. There is also a limited number of words that are specifically madya. For example, "this" is expressed iki in ngoko, niki in madya, punika in krama. When no distinct madya form exists, a person speaking madya selects words from other vocabulary sets. For example, one might use layang or serat in a madya utterance, there being no madya term for "letter."

Two vocabulary sets are not linked to a specific speech level. Krama andhap (literally, "low krama") is a set indicating the humbler status of the speaker or of a third person relative to the person addressed or referred to. Krama inggil (literally, "high krama") indicates great respect for one's interlocutor or a third person. Krama andhap and krama inggil can be used when speaking in any of the three speech levels. They are not used solely in the speech level krama.[3]

Javanese themselves usually speak of speech levels not with the terms ngoko, krama, krama andhap, and krama inggil, but rather with the terms omong Jawa (omong: "speech"; Jawa: "Java, Javanese") for ngoko, and basa ("language") for any mixture of vocabulary sets, that is, any usage that includes madya and/or krama vocabulary. These terms are less precise in that they do not differentiate individ-

---

[3] There are also a very few, very crude (kasar) words, used only when speaking ngoko and only when angry or making jokes. They are ruder than the ngoko equivalents.

ual lexical items by vocabulary set. But they are more accurate in that the distinction between ngoko and all else is indeed the clearest and most important one, whereas mixtures of other terms are more flexible and more likely to shift in the course of conversations.

Although it is true that most words in Javanese are invariant, it is also true that almost all high-frequency words and many affixes have at least two different forms, so that it is virtually impossible to say anything whatever in Javanese without committing oneself to choices among available options. Vocabulary items proliferate particularly at points of direct contact between two people: in such terms as "to speak," "to give," "to request," "to order," etc. The system affords endless subtlety, and a Westerner can imagine what problems speaking can pose when a distinction comparable to that between *tu* and *vous* in French affects all parts of speech, and often provides three, four, or even five possibilities for the two available in European languages. The difficulties should not be exaggerated unduly, of course. Regular patterns emerge, and the choices usually seem obvious. Nevertheless, to have to say something in Javanese when one doesn't know what level to use gives the phrase "tongue-tied" entirely new, and nightmarish, dimensions.

Speech levels implicate relative status in two ways: in one's use of levels in one's own speech, and in other people's use of them in speaking to oneself. Ongoing social status, those more or less established positions in Javanese society mentioned above, make it possible for individuals to maintain certain assumptions and expectations about how they appear to others and how others should treat them, particularly in matters of speech. But people are concerned with the details of every encounter because how interlocutors treat them, not just how they themselves behave, affects both how they are perceived by others and how they perceive themselves. That is, even though social status sets certain parameters within which everyone operates and about which in broad terms they probably agree, the always conditional and situational nature of relative status means that it must be attended to and negotiated in every exchange.

How well people know and use refined language depends in part, it is true, on their social status. Knowledge of speech levels is by no means restricted sociologically in Java. A person of whatever socioeconomic background must know the basic vocabulary appropriate to the use of each level. However, it is true that familiarity with the intricacies of honorifics and self-humbling vocabulary, and perhaps more importantly, confidence in one's ability to use them properly, are greater among people of superior wealth, education, and/or experience in aristocratic and other high-status circles. These attributes are not necessarily all of a piece. A servant at court (*abdi-dalem*) may be very poor and have received very little education, yet his or her command of refined Javanese will be excellent. The democratization of education in Java, too, although far from uniform, has already enabled large segments of the population to gain greater fluency in refined speech than was probably the case before Indonesian Independence in 1945. However, people's social status still shows to some extent in the degree to which their use of refined speech appears easy, elegant, and "natural."

Javanese do not, however, gloss control of refined speech sociologically. Instead, they see in one's ability to use refined speech well an indication of one's sensitivity to social requirements and, too, an indication of one's self-control. In order to use refined speech well, it is said that people must know how to avoid extreme sentiments as well as crude words. They show themselves thereby sensitive to the deference others of high status deserve, while remaining unswayed by their own emotions and investments. This demonstration makes people deserving, in turn, of others' respect. A figure of authority may be highly praised for an inclination to use refined speech with people to whom he need not be so polite. Bu Cerma often said that her husband used refined vocabulary even with children. This was of course untrue, since he would have appeared silly had he done so, but the claim shows that, at the level of ideology, to use refined speech extensively demonstrates refinement, something that is almost always thought a virtue in Java.

To *basa* well (to use madya and/or krama vocabularies effortlessly) can indicate refinement—elegance, good breeding, social sensibility—as well as deference, not just because it is somewhat esoteric, but also because if one need not insist too strenuously on one's superior relative status, one shows a commitment to the Javanese ideal of smoothly flowing social relations. Still, this has its limits. No one need basa all the time, and the higher one's social status, the less compelled one is to do so.

In many situations, as I have noted, individuals' social statuses are so clearly disparate that no one feels any need to question their relative statuses. It is not debasing to show deference to those to whom it is due: on the contrary, recognizing authority proves one's own sensibility to potency and its manifestations in social order, as will be discussed below. But when status distinctions grow fine, relative status does become an issue, and the competition may grow intense. Then much care must be taken to guarantee others' deference, or at least to prevent flagrant displays of disrespect. Pak Cerma told me that when an elderly dhalang, classificatory uncle of Pak Cerma's sons, performed, the old man would very much have liked his nephews to perform in the gamelan. He never asked them to do so, though. Of course, as younger kinsmen, they should spring into action at the mere mention of his desire for assistance. But what if they did not? Then the old man would "withdraw, ashamed" (*mundur isin*), a risk apparently too great to take.

Within groups that tend to intermarry, such as aristocrats or dhalang, it often happens that two people can trace their kinship ties through both paternal and maternal lines, since kinship in Java is figured bilaterally. Then relative seniority may be disputed, since one person may be "older" if the relation is traced on one side but "younger" if it is traced on the other. The rule is to go by the closer link. That is not always clear, however, and if neither party will agree to take the humbler status—even if the matter only concerns terms of direct address—their relations may become strained. Some members of the most important extended family of dhalang in Klaten haven't spoken to each other in years because they cannot agree on how to address each other.

Indeed, terms of direct address provide a good example of how subtle and complicated the negotiation of relative status can become. Such terms are taken largely from kinship terms, but several different principles can be applied to modulate the degree of respect and familiarity implicit in how one person addresses another. This matters because the many different determinants of social status can have conflicting implications about interlocutors' relative status. For example, Pak Cermadikrama had a younger neighbor, Pak Cahyamartana. Pak Cahya was probably about fifteen years younger than Pak Cerma, and as a farmer he did not possess the prestige that accrued to Pak Cerma as a dhalang. However, although neither wealthy nor educated in his own right, owning only a small amount of irrigated rice land, Pak Cahya was a cousin of the village headman and nephew of the headman's powerful tobacco trader father. This put him in the circle of fairly prominent families in the village. He was, furthermore, related to Pak Cerma through marriage, since the Cermas' daughter was married to Pak Cahya's wife's younger brother. It was difficult for Pak Cerma, in view of all these factors, to adopt any of the usual terms, such as "younger brother" or "son," that he might otherwise have used to address Pak Cahya. It was important for him to recognize Pak Cahya's somewhat elevated social status without denying their kinship ties or Pak Cerma's own, more prestigious status. Pak Cerma's solution was to call Pak Cahya "Bang." Pak Cahya's oldest child, as son, was named Bambang. Teknonyms, terms of address and reference that name someone in terms of his or her relations to children or other offspring, are often used in Java, so Pak Cahya could be referred to as "father of Bambang" (*Pakné Bambang*). Teknonyms constitute a fairly respectful means of address, since they make it possible to avoid mentioning a person's own name, but they are still familiar, since their use implies relations with the addressee's family. Abbreviating names is also familiar: "Bang" would be a very familiar term of address to use toward someone named Bambang. But Pak Cerma used it as an abbreviated form of Pakné Bambang, striking what he felt to be just the right mix of familiarity and respect.

How one manipulates speech levels, titles and names in conversation depends, like all aspects of speech, in part on personal style. One man in Karanganom was known for his loud-voiced jokes and inordinate familiarity of manner. People would remind me from time to time not to be offended when he addressed me by an abbreviation of my name, without any title. "Pak Harja's just like that," they would say, often suggesting that he was "a bit touched." Pak Cerma often clucked at how nervy Pak Harja was with everyone. But he was pleased to point out that the man referred to him, Pak Cerma, as "the puppeteer" (*dhalangé*), failing to use the respectful "Pak," but not daring to use a really familiar term of address, let alone Pak Cerma's name without a title. In noting this, Pak Cerma pointed implicitly to his own ability to make Pak Harja acknowledge his superior relative status.

Aside from terms of direct address, certain common patterns in Javanese conversation illustrate the ways that people's relative status is negotiated in speech. When two people who are not known to each other or who only rarely meet speak to each other, it sometimes happens that one of them, speaker A, adopts a tone that the other, speaker B, finds insufficiently respectful. If so, B can indicate that fact by resisting any moves toward a more familiar style that A makes. For example, if A is speaking too familiarly in madya and ends a question with the madya pronominal negative *Senès*, B might begin his response with the equivalent krama lexical item, *Sanès*. The rest of his utterance would follow in madya, because to speak in a consistently higher degree of refinement would demean him. But the contrast between the expected madya and the krama term that B replaces it with should signal to A that B finds his tone presumptuous. If, however, A persists in his too-familiar mode, then B has no choice but to withdraw from the encounter altogether. Were he to adopt A's familiar tone in order to avoid appearing deferential, he would validate A's implicit assertions about their intimacy, and so their equivalent relative status. Were he to speak with greater refinement than A, then he would appear to grant A more respect than he deserved. Either way, B's social place would be compromised. In a public setting this would offend him particularly deeply, but in private, too, B would find A's manner unacceptable, and he would have no choice but to put a stop to their exchange.

In contrast, many Javanese relish occasions in which they garner others' respectful address. An approach Javanese often take in conversation is to recount incidents in which other people showed them great deference. Javanese almost never use indirect quotation. Instead, in relating an incident, they identify speakers and then quote them all, supposedly verbatim, with little or no gloss. A listener must rely on content, tone of voice, speech levels, and terms of direct address to figure out who is being quoted when. Confusion often ensues, but all the indicators of relative status—titles, terms of direct address, vocabulary sets, and intonation—are maintained, and these matter as much as any specific content. A speaker, A, for example, will name someone, B, and then quote him addressing A in extravagantly polite and deferential style. The higher B's status, the more prestige redounds to A. And since A is simply quoting B, he is of course not boasting, he is merely recording fact. This pretense of objectivity remains even though A may quote himself speaking in fairly normal tones, but quote B in a manner so stylized as to resemble no speech heard in Java except on the stage. Sometimes A will add a modest disclaimer, saying he doesn't know why B was so very polite.

A related way of making claims about the elevated relative status one enjoys in interaction consists of naming all the people who address one with terms of direct address expressing one's classificatory seniority. Yet another is to allude to all the people who know who one is, even though one is not acquainted with them. All these devices are claims to the superior relative status one has been accorded in interaction, as demonstrated in the deference, respect, and consideration that others have shown. Claims about one's own talents, triumphs, and special qualities also crop up in Javanese conversation, as they do everywhere. But the frequency with which one finds people constructing their own prestige out of other people's deference indicates the peculiarly operational understanding of social status and its dramatization in interaction.

Another instance of how speech constitutes relative status is a negative one: when Javanese speak with Chinese. Chinese are not thought capable of speaking anything except ngoko. This is not actually true in the case of many younger, educated Chinese in Central Java, who have fairly good control of refined vocabulary. The fact remains that when the Chinese are addressed in Javanese rather than in Indonesian, they are usually addressed in ngoko, or at most a rock-bottom version of madya. As a result, how one addresses Chinese and how one is addressed by them is practically irrelevant. Chinese are assumed, like children, to lack all sensitivity to the issues of etiquette and relative status that make the use of speech levels significant. So their speech cannot affect people's perceptions of anyone's status.

The Chinese in Java represent, actually, an interesting example of how wealth and relative status can operate somewhat independently, since their actual economic might in Java is great and the respect they elicit minimal. Chinese are perceived to be enormously rich and very powerful in their control over material resources. But they are denied any version of respect in terms of Javanese etiquette, at least in proportion to what such wealth would garner Javanese. This anomaly accounts for their usefulness. A Javanese friend who is a businessman in Jakarta explained, when I returned to Indonesia in 1983, that the enormous contracts the Indonesian bureaucracy could now give out were going to an increasing degree to Javanese rather than Chinese entrepreneurs, countering long-established patterns. Javanese bureaucrats choose to make arrangements, my friend explained, with people whose style accords with the norms of Javanese encounter. Nevertheless, this shift does not mean that Chinese are any less essential as middlemen. On the contrary, they are all the more necessary. Javanese norms would not permit a high-ranking bureaucrat to make any explicitly illegal demands upon a Javanese contractor, for example, and the latter could not make explicit offers of bribes. But there is nothing to prohibit a Javanese official from saying to a Chinese businessman, "My daughter needs braces. You know of anyone who could do it?" The Chinese man will respond, "Oh sure, no problem, I can take care of that." The Chinese can communicate such needs among parties to any contract, or take care of any special needs either party has, in return for a part of the action. As my friend noted about the hypothetical Chinese businessman in his example, "He probably has five palatial houses and a fleet of fancy cars. But it doesn't matter. You still don't have to treat him like a person." Treating him like a person would mean granting him even minimal signs of respect.

As this example of relations with Chinese makes clear, relative status does not simply affect the forms speech takes, but also what one says and how one behaves. The more respect one feels constrained to offer, the less frankly and expansively one can speak. When, in contrast, individuals enjoy superior relative status in a given encounter, they may express their opinions freely, make demands, and even impose orders. In relations among intimates of equal status, there can be much teasing and arguing, particularly if no party to the exchange is of particularly high social status. Youths can mock each other unmercifully, count on each other's assistance, and use each other's things freely. They can do so much more freely than can responsible heads of household, whose social status is higher. Village men, by the same token, can do these things more easily than high-status urban males, and women more than men. But in every case, intimates must make it clear that they are not suggesting others' subordination. They must be careful not to make familiar behavior look like the behavior of a superior.

Very few intimates, actually, even though they are of roughly equal social status, are truly of equal relative status. Birth-order among siblings, for example, imposes a hierarchy in which younger siblings address older ones with kinship terms rather than or in addition to the latters' names, but are addressed in turn by name alone and are given orders by those older siblings. In fact, it would be inappropriate to assume that intimacy means that one need not attend to one's style in Java, since all style is marked. The Cermas' son-in-law aroused considerable indignation when he sat in the front room of his in-laws' house one day on a visit from Semarang, behaving, as his mother-in-law later said indignantly, like a guest instead of like a kinsman. A kinsman would come into the private area of the house rather than sit there "as though he was waiting to be served."

If statuses were fixed and rules of speech levels' use unvarying, the correlation of speech level and status would be orderly and assured. Since that situation is obviously impossible, every encounter presents the possibility of conflict, even if much of Javanese etiquette is de-signed to obscure precisely such tension. Conflict arises when a person finds himself or herself being forced to validate another's claims to superior relative status, or worse, being made subject to another's commands. If one can instead withhold respectful speech when one feels it undeserved, one can demonstrate a capacity to remain un-moved, impervious even to the impulse to speak at all. To be forced into speech, particularly respectful speech, is a kind of submission: in registering another person's superior relative status in one's speech, a person is manipulated by context. In the face of such pressure, to say nothing is the first form of resistance.

The intense interest that styles of speech and behavior arouse in Java stems from the fact that individuals' identities, although con-strained by social status, are still open to further construction in en-counter. While social status identifies people in critical ways, defin-ing the major categories of people who enter into encounter and setting the terms of that encounter, the features of this basic mold are further specified in interaction, through the elaborate means the Jav-anese language and norms of behavior furnish every actor. A person's identity is not simply reflected in encounter. It is also elaborated through the medium of interpersonal exchange. Language, style, and social status therefore are interwoven in Java in such a way as to make social interaction an ongoing definition of relationships rather than simply a set classification of individuals. Beyond the essential defini-tions of identity that are given by gender and socio-economic posi-tion, there stands the further definition of relative status as estab-lished—always relatively and so always anew—in interaction. The self, as a result, does not simply stand prior to speech, seeking expression by means of it, but rather is constructed in the play of speech itself.

This account of Javanese encounter will remind many readers of Erving Goffman's work on face-to-face encounter (e.g., Goffman 1967). Javanese social life does indeed look like an intricately elaborated form of interaction ritual, in which all participants are concerned with how others comport themselves, how they themselves appear, and how their interaction redounds on the definition of one and all. But there are two respects in which a social interactionist approach must be supplemented. One, as I have noted in the preceding account, is to see that basic distinctions stand prior to and inform any particular encounter. Interaction does not start with neutral players. When strangers begin speaking on a bus, for example, facts about dress and manner will already have provided signals to each speaker about the other's status, and constrain the negotiation of relative status that ensues. A second factor that informs Javanese understandings of this negotiation consists of diffusely articulated but firmly held beliefs about potency. This domain of mystical forces at play in the world, *kebatinan*, is used as an idiom in which to assert the existence of an individual that does indeed exist apart from social status and encounter.

ENCOUNTER AND POTENCY

Encounter demonstrates people's status and in that demonstration, further defines them. In the Javanese view, however, the vagaries of encounter follow upon the distribution of spiritual strength or energy, what Benedict Anderson has called "the Javanese idea of power" (Anderson 1972b). Anderson writes:

> Power is that intangible, mysterious, and divine energy which animates the universe. In Javanese traditional thinking there is no sharp division between organic and inorganic matter, for everything is sustained by the same invisible power. (Anderson 1972b:7)

In order to contrast this understanding of power with modern Western understandings, Anderson adopts the convention of capitalizing the word "power" when alluding to the Javanese construal of it. I will instead, following Errington's usage in an illuminating account of similar notions in Luwu (S. Errington 1983), refer to it as "potency." The word's associations, for English-speakers, with masculine sexuality, potentates, and dangerous substances are all thoroughly appropriate. In fact, they are to be fostered, because it is essential to recall that potency and instrumental power are not really opposite or mutually exclusive terms. Potency is the grounds for the possession or loss of political authority, sexual capacity, material wealth, and other forms of effectiveness, influence, or coercive control—in a word, power—in the world. Power of whatever sort, for Javanese, is a manifestation of potency, which, as Anderson makes clear, is only of a single sort: "all power is of the same type and has the same source" (1972b:7).

Javanese colloquial usage only occasionally distinguishes among such versions of potency and/or power. There is a word, *kasektèn*, to label a specifically spiritual power. But it is rarely used in conversation. The politically powerful, the financially secure, the severely ascetic, and the sexually athletic are all referred to simply as "strong" (*kuwat*). In what follows, I will speak of potency when I wish to distinguish a spiritual or mystical concept of power, as opposed to a more material or instrumental one. The distinction, however, is always somewhat artificial: the two are not so much opposed as complementary in Javanese thinking. In fact, it is precisely the polyvalence of the concept of "strength" (*kakuwatan*) that motivates much of the politics of Javanese interaction.

The distinction between potency and mundane powers is made in Javanese, actually, in reference however not to the sort of spiritual/ temporal contrast familiar to Westerners, but rather in terms of the contrast between what is manifest and what is not. *Lair* and *batin* refer to two different kinds of phenomena: *lair* to what is perceptible to the senses and/or susceptible of common-sense explanation, *batin* to what is generally imperceptible, mysterious, and resistant to obvious explanation. The lair world refers to the waking reality that we all assume and that we can, in general, agree upon. It stands in contrast to the world of batin, that of mystical forces on the basis of which quite a different account, or accounts, of the world are formulated. To speak of individuals' "strength of batin" (*kakuwatan batin*) refers to their capacity to channel the immaterial potency that exists in the world. Such capacity is prior to, and more important than, such manifest (lair) signs of power as physical strength, material wealth, or formal political authority. Asceticism is a means of amassing this spiritual power. Encounter demonstrates the reserve of such potency that a person controls, that is, the strength of his or her batin.

The higher one's status, the stronger one's batin is assumed to be. At the same time, the greater the power of one's batin, then the greater the deference, it is thought, that one will elicit from others in encounter. The obverse is also true: if one does not command respect in encounter, that failure bespeaks one's lack of kakuwatan batin. Those who do not proffer respect may appear boorish. But if others' gestures and speech are rude and demeaning, that fact signals the inadequacy of one's own potency to compel the deference of others.

If, for example, one feels reluctant to eat in someone else's presence, one fears that one will compromise one's own dignity both by showing oneself to be subject to carnal appetite, and by showing oneself to be without respect for the other person. If another person eats too much or too freely in one's presence, one feels that one's own dignity is compromised by the other person's lack of restraint, because a person of some status should be able, by virtue of his or her impressive presence, to exert control over other people. The same principle applies to one's own and an interlocutor's use of speech levels. Others should feel reluctant to speak too familiarly in one's presence. If they do not feel this way, they have shown one to be incapable of arousing fear and respect in them. Once again, one's potency should impress itself upon those around one: if it does not, one's relative status has been impugned.

The inclination to hold people responsible for the behavior of others who are in their presence was brought home to me in the comments a man made when we were discussing a shadow play we had both seen a few days earlier. The man remarked that the dhalang, an extremely famous and popular one, was losing his powers. He cited as evidence the fact that in the course of the performance a child had yelled something out, interrupting the puppets' dialogue. My friend implied that this was not the fault of the child—children are of course likely to be unruly—but the fault of the dhalang, whose potency was not sufficient to keep the child silent.

Virtually all Javanese are concerned with issues of status and potency, though some, such as reformist Muslims, may speak of these issues in a rather different idiom than that typical of syncretist Javanese, whose comments I am relying on here. I should note, however, that a man concerns himself with his potency more than a woman does. A woman's social status and her relative status in any exchange depend for the most part on the status of her father and her husband. She must watch out for the impression of her sexual purity, however, as a man must watch out for the impression of his potency, and feelings of shame (isin) follow on the compromise of either.[4] High-status people also attend more carefully to potency than lower-status people. Low-status people are generally thought, and think themselves, too preoccupied with making ends meet to trouble themselves much with potency. But this does not mean that they do not also take it seriously, and are not liable to take what means they find at their disposal to augment their store of such potency.

Indeed, the view that kakuwatan batin determines one's status and fortunes gives rise to much discussion about the means by which an individual can accumulate such potency. Javanese have long assumed that members of the aristocracy necessarily possessed extraordinary potency. Kings, in particular, but also all people of aristocratic lineage, were assumed to possess great spiritual capacity. In other cases, God is thought to bestow potency for reasons inexplicable, which explains why some rather unlikely people sometimes rise to high position in modern Indonesia. But far more important than birth or God's inscrutable wisdom are a great variety of ascetic practices whose efficacy Javanese describe at length.[5]

Asceticism

Among the many types of asceticism Javanese value are fasting, going without sleep, sexual abstinence, doing vigil at the site of a holy man's grave or under a large tree, soaking in a stream after midnight, eating no salt on Monday and Thursday, and walking about without any goal. All forms of laku (literally, "step"), as such practices are called, are best undertaken alone. That makes them more effective tests of one's resolve. They should also be timed to suit ca-

---

[4] I will discuss men's and women's contrasting relations with potency in Chapters 2 and 4.

[5] The only explanation people could give as to why aristocrats should have greater potency than other people was that they had more time to devote to ascetic exercise. I don't believe people feel the need for such an explanation. They assume the aristocracy's superior potency as self-evident. It is still interesting that asceticism provides the only available basis for explanation, when people are pressed for one.

lendrical and other calculations. One laku called *ngebleng*, for example, consists of entering some enclosed space, usually the rice-storage area in the innermost part of the house, and remaining there for three days and nights without eating and as far as possible without sleeping. (By beginning on the proper conjunction of seven- and five-day cycles, in the opinion of some, one can in three days achieve the same results attained by fasting for forty days. This is because the numbers magically associated with those three days total forty.) As in any type of meditation, one's body heat rises, making various kinds of invisible spirits uncomfortable. These will take a number of different forms in order to tempt, frighten, or deceive a person into ceasing his practice and so failing to gain any benefit.[6] It is also believed that one's ancestors or God himself causes these spirits to intimidate the ascetic, as so many tests. Only by proving oneself resistant to temptation and fear, and able to distinguish between true and deceitful messages, does one become worthy of God's aid.[7]

Various types of divine signs, although by no means inevitable, indicate particular success in ascetic exercise. One is "like a dream, though not a dream," in which someone, usually an old, deceased relative, appears to the ascetic and gives him some instruction, obvious or perhaps puzzling and difficult to interpret. Another consists only in an image of some kind, again requiring interpretation. Superior to all other signs, however, is to hear a voice apart from any image. This is considered God's own voice, speaking without dissimulation, usually a terse phrase informing the ascetic that his rigors have been accepted.

The immediate aims that one may seek by means of ascetic exercises are many: wealth, high rank in the civil service, any kind of advancement in one's work, the ability to cure the sick, etc. But no matter what the particular request one makes, the exercises increase the potency of one's batin.

While the ideal form of ascetic exercise, forty days fasting and vigil in a cave, probably attracts few practitioners now (Javanese are con-

---

[6] Because most ascetic exercise is predicated on the fact that a person practices them alone, and because men are more likely to undertake ascetic rigors than women, I will use the masculine pronoun in this account. However, women do also practice ascetic rigors to some extent, as will be discussed below.

[7] For a presentation of ascetic and ritual practices that sticks more closely to the terms of normative *abangan*, or syncretist, commentary, particularly commentary of a rather theosophical variety, see Mulder 1983.

vinced that in the past a great many people performed it), and it is certainly true that laku are more talked about than done, nevertheless it is difficult for an outsider to imagine how much belief in the efficacy of laku affects people's daily behavior in Java. Bu Cerma spent much of the night, if not all of it, almost every night during my stay in the Cermas' home sleeping fitfully and uncomfortably on one of the chairs in the front room rather than stretched out on her bed. She did so because the discomfort was a form of laku, a way of helping to assure the safety and prosperity of the family. A neighbor was instructed by a *wong tuwa* (literally, "old person"; by extension, any person of great wisdom) to fast and remain awake for seven Fridays, that is, starting at sundown Thursday, and lasting until sundown Friday, since Javanese days start at sunset. He would drop in on us late on those Thursday nights, hoping to find someone willing to chat and so help him stay awake. Pak Cerma embarked on a similar program later during my stay. A middle-aged man and a youth in the village walked more than forty kilometers to the southern coast one *Sura* (the first month of the Javanese calendar) as a form of laku, and young men often went to do all-night vigil at the sites of holy men's graves. When a young man in Karanganom, Mas Kliwon, married for the second time following the end of his first marriage in divorce, he tried to assure the better outcome of this union by fasting and staying awake for some time prior to the wedding. Unfortunately, the ordeal caused him to become ill in the middle of the ceremony itself, leading the guests to remark that his batin was not sufficiently strong to be able to take on such a heavy laku.

The variety of different forms of laku is great. One of my most vivid recollections of fieldwork is the night I was invited to join some friends doing *laku kungkuman* ("the soaking laku"). Many people assured me that simply travelling all the way from home and family in America was a form of laku, as was charging about Central Java in the heat and the rain in search of knowledge (*kawruh*). Give or take some theological assumptions, I was in complete agreement. There is no such thing as doing too much for one's batin, though, and when I visited a dhalang one afternoon in Sura, he suggested that I join him and several friends at the spring-fed pool in the ancient capital of Pengging late that night. Pak Cerma's son, Sigit, and I did so, and all of us proceeded to take off our clothes and sit immersed to our necks in the cool water for something over an hour. Since one should think

only of God and be oblivious to all physical sensation, one must neither talk nor move when doing laku. Tropics or no, the chill was penetrating, and the mosquitoes that attacked from the neck up and the
little fishes that nibbled from the neck down added further to the
rigors. The next day, having proved my mettle, I felt quite pleased
with myself. That inappropriate complacency was suitably dispelled
when Sigit mentioned that of course we had to do it two more times
in *Sura* for the laku to have any effect. Out of a "lair" concern for my
health and physical comfort, but to the detriment of my *batin*, I
failed to do so.

By means of laku one proves one's willingness and ability to endure
privation, to resist impulses, and to act in some way outside the normal patterns of life. In some cases, such as the particularly widespread
laku of *nyenèn kemis* (from *Senèn:* "Monday," and *Kemis:* "Thursday"), which consists of eating no salt on Monday and Thursday, the
point clearly is to give up available pleasures. Another way to say
nglakoni ("to do laku") is *prihatin* ("to suffer hardship"). The obverse
is also thought to hold: that enjoying many pleasures disperses one's
potency. Bu Cerma quoted her father saying that to sleep on a mat-
tress used up one's prosperity or well-being (*kemuktèn*).

Asceticism and Sacrifice

In order to analyze the quite remarkable Javanese preoccupation
with asceticism, I will treat it as a particular version of sacrifice. The
subject of sacrifice in Java deserves attention in its own right, but for
the present purpose I will mention, only in passing, the *wiwitan* ceremony performed as a first-fruits ritual just prior to the rice harvest.
The rite can be reduced in description to four essentials: 1) giving offerings to the rice goddess, Dèwi Sri (these offerings are later distrib-
uted among officiants and neighbors); 2) cutting the first stalks and
tying them together to make up the *mantènan* ("the bride" or, according to most informants in areas outside Karanganom, "the bridal
couple"); 3) giving offerings of inedible "snacks" to lesser spirits and
pests; and 4) taking "the bride" (identified as Dèwi Sri herself) home,
in silence, and placing it on a bed in the innermost room of the house
overnight.[8]

It is apparent that in performing the *wiwitan* ritual, the harvesters

[8] For a fuller discussion of the first fruits ritual, see Keeler 1983.

proffer a share of what they wish to enjoy for themselves.[9] The procedure consists in neutralizing the competition for goods by first establishing differences in status: that of the goddess, of humans, and of spirits. By recognizing those differences and by acknowledging the superior status of Dèwi Sri, as well as the distinct status and rights of spirits, one allays their jealous pride while drawing them into safe relations of exchange. One proffers food to gods and spirits, and more importantly, one proffers to them—just as one proffers to powerful humans—respect. In return, one gains their gifts, their *berkah* ("mystically beneficent blessings"), or at least their benign neglect. Sacrifice not only acknowledges differential status; it is a gesture of respect that should at a miminum neutralize, if it cannot actually bind, its recipients.

Asceticism in Java is a form of sacrifice in which, more paradoxically, one gives up aspects of oneself in order to gain personal rewards. At the simplest, practitioners of laku give up their comforts. More seriously, they give up the satisfaction of their basic needs. Ideally, they give up all intercourse with the world. People therefore demonstrate in laku their willingness to surrender comfort and pleasure, but with the understanding that comfort, prosperity, and good fortune, although deferred, will all accrue to them in greater degree in the end. This represents a complicated form of sacrifice not just because it concerns sacrifice of self rather than possessions, but also because it implies a certain attitude toward other humans, as well as toward God. A person who enters the rice-storage area for three days—to take a somewhat extreme, but also actually practiced and certainly much idealized example—gives up not only physical comfort but also all social identity. In deprivation of food, sleep, sex, speech, and community, a person has no identity left in the world. This is a total self-abnegation before God.

I use the term "God" here because it corresponds to Javanese remarks. Asceticism, Javanese say, is an exercise undertaken in view of *Tuhan* or *Gusti Allah*. (The first term is Indonesian, meaning "lord," the second a Javanese term of respectful address coupled with the Arabic *Allah*.) Yet God is both faceless in Java and also curiously lacking

---

[9] In considering sacrifice in Indonesia, I have benefited from conversation and course work with Professor Valerio Valeri. I have, however, applied his subtle analysis of Hawaiian sacrifice in a very schematic fashion in the remarks that follow. See Valeri 1985.

in ethics. A person with evil intentions can gain potency through asceticism in order to attain those ends. To preserve some semblance of moral order, Javanese say that after his death such a person will suffer God's punishment. In the meantime, though, "God's generosity" rewards all those who do laku. So the impression remains that an ascetic really interacts not with a superhuman subject, God, but with a quantity, potency itself. And as Anderson points out, potency is amoral (Anderson 1972b:8). On the other hand, the idea of exchange that underlies asceticism, and also such phrases as "God's generosity," point to a personalized conception of God, not an intangible quantity or principle.

In any case, it is really less the nature of the supernatural agent that matters to this reading of Javanese asceticism than the nature of its relations with Javanese social life. As long as people remain engaged in encounter, they are subject to the vagaries of their own and others' speech, since they are caught up in the politicking inherent in the assertion and protection of their relative status. Asceticism, although intimidating in its own way, offers an antidote to the corrosive capacity of interaction. One need only disdain demons and temptations in asceticism. One cannot so easily dismiss disrespectful speech in interaction, because another person's ability to address one rudely already indicates one's weakness, in the failure of one's presence to compel others' respect. In instances in which status differences are great, as I have noted, an inferior's lack of respect demonstrates only his boorishness. Such people have no kakuwatan batin of their own and are insensitive to all things batin in this world. But when status distinctions are finer, another person's behavior impinges on one's own relative status, and interaction can become tense. In ascetic withdrawal, people avoid all such difficulties, while strengthening their position toward the time when they return to the fray. They hope to overcome through ascetic exercise the vulnerability to others' behavior that Javanese understandings of interaction imply.

It is not only social interaction that suggests vulnerability, however. To be subject to desire also lays a person open to external control, and the logic implicit in asceticism must be considered in light of another paradox, that of desire. Invulnerability magic, which is very popular in Java, reflects the concern to protect oneself from outside influence. Asceticism, in its requirement that one withdraw from interaction to gain potency, dramatizes the notion that everything external carries a threat to the balance, dignity, and sovereignty of the self. But to a great extent, it substitutes for the threat of external attack the threat of internal desires. The struggle is waged against cold, heat, hunger, thirst, sleepiness, fear, sexual desire, and temptation of any kind, that is, as much against one's own wants as against external agents. Yet one does ascetic exercises to gain worldly ends. One resists desire in order to see one's desires fulfilled.

The paradoxical belief that being without desire will enable one to get what one wants was neatly highlighted by an older man's remarks about rice pests. The virulent attacks of pests in Java in recent years have caused the Indonesian government to require all farmers in the lowlands to use insecticides. Insecticides are the manifest or mundane (lair) response to pests. However, the way of batin, which is the properly Javanese way, goes exactly counter to this practice. "A farmer should think to himself, 'Do as you like. Eat part of my crop. Eat all of it. It's all the same to me,' " the man said. "Then he may well be able to harvest some of his crop." Because the government directives stand, he noted, a farmer must go ahead and use insecticides. But he should do so only out of respect for the government. In his own mind, he must maintain a detached attitude.

To experience desire is to feel a lack, to sense one's own insufficiency, to become aware of an absence. To enter into relations of exchange in the world, to take part in any form of intercourse, whether commercial, or sexual, or verbal, is to admit desire, need, and dependence. Then one lets oneself be defined in terms of absences one must try to fill. Ascetic rigors overcome and deny desire. They imply resistance to lack, and in this way they suggest plenitude.

Asceticism, that is, posits a homology between desire overcome and desire fulfilled. In either case, the object of desire becomes uninvested, with the result that the gap between desire and object falls away. It is that gap, I believe, that is powerful and disturbing to the Javanese. Overcoming it, in whatever manner, releases one from its hold. In ascetic exercises, or simply ascetic attitudes, as the farmer's remarks show, desire is denied. Desire fulfilled is then substituted for desire mastered. By a kind of commutative principle, this substitution achieves the purpose that has ostensibly fallen away—and one reaps at least a part of one's harvest.

But the reward that people seek in asceticism, although it may consist in a particular goal or object, such as a good grade on an exam or a good harvest, also implies the potency that guarantees a person an impressive presence in encounter. That is, it also makes a person potent.

The Potent Self

The potent self in Java is not really what Westerners mean by "self" at all. The loss of identity in ngebleng means escaping from definitions ascribed to a person in interaction. Following that escape, a person returns to the world, now possessed of greater potency. This is manifest in two principal ways: a person is without selfish interests (*pamrih*) of any sort; and his speech is effective. That is, he is less vulnerable to his own impulses, while he is more capable of defining, or imposing upon, other people.

Pamrih implies the investments that keep a person subject to desire, and it is only through its suppression that a person becomes potent. To suppress one's wants, and to suppress (in the extreme forms of laku) one's identity, means that one is no longer vulnerable to— dependent upon, defined by—what is external to oneself in the world. In resistance to what is external stands the assurance of both one's own power over others and the satisfaction of one's wants. This is the Javanese ideal of "selfhood," a power that surpasses the vulnerability of the individual in a superior reserve of kakuwatan batin. It is a self thought to have surpassed all constraints of identity, and thereby to have become strong.

Since encounter is a negotiation of relative status effected through, as well as demonstrated in, language use, it is unsurprising that an ultimate gain of ascetic rigor, and the goal people most often mentioned, is to make one's speech take effect (*mandi*), as venom and medicine can take effect. This means that the instant one says something, it is/becomes true. God's word, of course, is effective beyond all others. But the speech of any extremely powerful person is said to mandi as well. The Sultan of Jogja is believed to be able to make a person go mad simply by saying "You're mad." People whose speech mandi are said to "borrow the authority of God."

Speech that takes effect (mandi) reiterates on the plane of language the closing of the gap between desire and its fulfillment. Powerful speech is no longer simply referential but effective. The disjunction between speech and event is overcome. This puts people in control of language, rather than subject to it, and the capacity to control language is a critical component of the potent self.

I have set out encounter and asceticism as two opposite and complementary modes of action, each informed by Javanese conceptions of potency and its effects.[10] Actually, elderly Javanese males would often tell me that the truly potent are engaged in ascetic exercise at all times. They can practice the loss of all self-interest and affect in the course of everyday life, therefore having no need to go off into seclusion to do meditation. This capacity to disengage from the world while remaining fully functional within it suggests that such a person wields control over others, yet enjoys resistance to them at the same time. As such, it is an ideal Javanese representation of individuals' interaction with the world. Yet that ideal contains within it not only a model to which one may aspire to conform, but also a prescription and standard to which one may try to hold others accountable, particularly people whose status is superior to one's own. Ideal models are never simply inspirational guides for the right-thinking, though they are often formulated in such terms. They are also polemical positions adopted by people as grounds for criticizing others, and/or as justifications for resisting other people's authority. In the chapters that follow, I will describe how people actually interact in a number of domains, domestic, political, curative, and aesthetic. Not surprisingly, self-interest, emotions, and the vagaries of events turn out to make social life far less smooth than the ideal of selfless and potent selves might imply. Nevertheless, Javanese adherence to the injunction

---

[10] The above account of Javanese ideas about status, asceticism, and speech represents something of a compromise between indigenous commentary and my own analytic view. No Javanese would agree with my claim, for example, that asceticism is a kind of reaction to the vulnerability people sense in encounter. That compromise compounds another one: the compromise between aristocratic and popular accounts of asceticism, encounter, and speech. J. Errington presents the aristocratic understanding of these ideas, a much more internally consistent and developed one, as propounded by his Solonese high-status (priyayi) informants (J. Errington 1984). People he spoke with would no doubt find the statements of many of my informants unsophisticated to the point of vulgarity. Certainly Errington's criticism of Geertz's earlier account (1960) pits a philosophically "correct" rendering against a more popular representation of the nature of the self and interaction. While admiring the elegance of the priyayi version, I still believe the vulgar version lays bare fundamental, if largely unexamined, assumptions about the nature of the self and the risks implicit in interaction.

that all face-to-face encounters be harmonious is often startling. Through it all, furthermore, people draw on assumptions about vulnerability, resistance, and potency, whether in deciding their own actions, or in making sense of their experience, or in judging and responding to the behavior of others.

2. FAMILY RELATIONS

Assumptions about the self, power, and interaction inform two kinds of action—interpersonal encounter and ascetic practices—that stand as complementary opposites in Java. These assumptions do not simply suffuse the atmosphere, however: they must be learned and acted upon. They are never systematically taught, nor are they often explicitly articulated. Instead, they are learned and applied in specific contexts, and in diverse ways. My purpose in this chapter is to show how young Javanese become familiar with these assumptions in the workings of Javanese families. In the following three chapters, I will consider how people draw upon such understandings in diverse domains: that of political authority, in the realm of village politics; that of mystical procedures, in curative and preventive practices; and that of social status, in ritual celebrations. In all these domains, the ambiguous nature of the links between potency and power gives rise to repeating patterns in the distribution, use, and manifestations of power.

Javanese acquire basic understandings of self and power first of all in the interaction among family members. Differences between a father's and a mother's roles acquaint a child with different versions of power and the different responses they should evoke. In particular, the idealization of the father attributes to him great potency (kakuwatan batin), while effectively minimizing his actual control over other members of the household. To the degree therefore that he fulfills the idealized Javanese version of masculine authority, a Javanese father protects the image of his authority while relinquishing an active role in much of family life. The avoidance relations that come to characterize relationships particularly between fathers and sons are then a model for the strategies by which Javanese deal with many figures of authority outside the family, seeking to gain by their potency while resisting any influence over one's own actions.[1]

[1] The student of Javanese culture is fortunate to have an excellent description of Javanese kinship and family relations in Hildred Geertz's monograph *The Javanese Family* (1961). Not surprisingly, twenty-five years have wrought little change in the way a Javanese family functions, for all the changes in the political and economic con-

THE FAMILY

Javanese conceive of the relationship between husband and wife in terms of his authority and her financial control. On the affective aspects of the relations between spouses, Javanese are far less romantic than Westerners. Passion is never thought really appropriate to marriage. To be *gandrung* ("mad with love") implies instability and probable sorcery. Instead, *tresna*, an abiding devotion that Poerwadarminta defines as "affection, generous feelings for another person (without desire)" should characterize the tie between husband and wife. Often, the affection seems real and the bond as strong as in any stable Western marriage. Nevertheless, the enormous warmth and solicitude that mark Javanese interaction with very small children contrast sharply with the restraint and even brusqueness that obtain between spouses.

Sexual activity is inhibited for as long as newlyweds live with either one's parents, and again as soon as there are children. Traditionally, newlyweds were supposed to wait forty days after the wedding before consummating their marriage. If the couple lived with either spouse's parents, furthermore, one of them had to sit up until both parents had retired, as a gesture of respect. An older man joked about how impatient he would become, as a younger man, knowing his new wife was waiting for him in the area of the house in which newlyweds sleep, while his father sat in the front room, lighting up yet another cigarette. "If you were lucky," the man related, "the older person said, 'You go on to bed now.' But then he'd add, 'But don't secure the door.' That was so that later the parents could look in to see whether the younger pair lay asleep close to each other, a sign they were now 'in accord,' or were still sleeping on either side of the sleeping platform." (Since Javanese usually sleep, and make love for that matter, fully clothed, modesty was not compromised by these

---

text, and some of the points I present here repeat her findings. My remarks, however, while far less comprehensive than Geertz's, focus specifically on the issue of authority and one's relations to it, giving my analysis a sufficiently different emphasis, I hope, to justify some overlap in the ethnography.

There is also some overlap with Bateson and Mead's perceptive and provocative *Balinese Character* (1942). The affinities between Javanese and Balinese culture are many. So are the differences. That child-rearing practices in the two cultures bear such similarities, while social organization, religious life, and much else differ so markedly, demonstrates once again—in a backhanded way—that culture is never reducible to child-rearing practices or any personality traits that supposedly follow therefrom.

parental checks.) A girl's first marriage may well be at an early age and against her will, so she may resist any sexual advances for a long time, and some marriages end in divorce before they are consummated.

A woman's fidelity is much stressed, but a man need only be reasonably discreet in his extramarital dalliances. Women are sometimes deeply hurt by their husbands' infidelities. Yet although women in such circumstances may garner pity, their husbands earn little censure. It is considered preferable that he go to prostitutes rather than have a mistress, since the financial drain is likely to prove much greater in the latter case. It is my impression, though, that few men have long-term extramarital affairs, preferring the occasional time with a prostitute or perhaps a quick visit to some woman in the area known to be free with her favors. That men and women often look for relatively little emotional commitment from each other may account both for this casual attitude toward men's extramarital sex, which is seen more as a threat to the household economy than to the couple's emotional satisfaction, and for the unlikelihood of such activity leading to long-term affairs.

A man's authority requires that his wife defer to him in his expectations and demands, that she address him in some degree of refined language, and that she conduct herself generally in ways befitting his (and therefore their) status. Theoretically, a woman should never contradict her husband's opinions or decisions. In practice, like anywhere else in the world, she can exercise considerable influence, whether by passive resistance, persuasion, or even fairly obvious disagreement. And she holds the purse.

Issues of financial authority frequently give rise to conflict in a Javanese family. The most common cause of divorce, and the grounds for divorce the neighbors find most compelling, is a husband's failure to keep money flowing into the household's coffers. Should a man refuse to hand over all or at least most of his earnings to his wife, he already appears irresponsible, unless his wife has previously shown herself incompetent at handling money. When a young man from another village wished to marry a woman in Karanganom, rumor went round that he had been divorced by his first wife because he gave her money only in small sums, rather than letting her take charge of his income. His new, unwilling fiancée resisted the match to the end and neighbors, repeating the rumor, tended to sympathize with her.

When people explain why polygyny is a bad idea, they invariably cite tension over the division of the man's income. Sexual and emotional jealousy between co-wives seem to strike Javanese as real but secondary problems. Tensions between female in-laws, too, usually take the form of conflicting claims to the man's property. If he wishes to give his own kinsmen money, a man must often resort to subterfuge. Mbak Tuti, recently widowed, mentioned that if she visited her brother, a civil servant, soon after he had gotten his salary, he would slip her some money, but he would tell his wife that a "compulsory contribution" had been taken out of his pay at the office.

That control of finances implies the possession of considerable mundane power by no means escapes Javanese. How to square the husband's putatively supreme authority (*kuwasa*) with the wife's role in money matters gives rise to some interesting comment among Javanese. One evening at a *jagongan* (a gathering of men held following some ritual ceremony), several men answered my questions about why women take charge of the family's finances. Their responses were phrased in terms of women's relative weakness. A man can't be bothered worrying about ten rupiahs. He'll think to himself, "Easy to go out and make some more." A woman doesn't have that option. She can't just go out and earn money. Instead, she'll think to herself, "With ten rupiahs I could buy salt and chilies." So she's more careful. And if a man is overcharged at a place to eat, if they tell him to pay Rp. 500 when he should only have to pay Rp. 250, he just pays it. He'd be ashamed to make a scene. But a woman will put up a fight.

That a man would be ashamed to protest, whereas a woman would be ashamed to let herself be cheated, sums up the contrasting concerns of men and women. A man seeks to preserve his dignity, which is an indication of his potency. When he shows himself unconcerned with mere money, when he gives way, for example, to a seller's rapacity, he demonstrates the superior ordering of his priorities. A woman makes fewer claims to ascetic detachment from material concerns, and she need not feel shame at being at the center of a scene. Her prestige depends on her keeping a sharp eye on the family's material interests. That means watching down to the last rupiah. Many men will not go into the market with their wives because they find the haggling that goes on there too demeaning. Their wives will carry on so about fifty rupiahs, it makes it appear as though the family were destitute. Pak Cerma would escort his wife to the market if she had important purchases to make, but once she began bargaining, he would go sit it out over tea at a refreshment stall.[2]

A man may happily leave household buying to his wife. He does have needs of his own, however, that require money. Clearly, it would be demeaning for a man to have to keep asking his wife for small sums of money with which to buy cigarettes, for example. To this problem, the men at the evening gathering suggested diverse solutions. One said that when a man brings home, say, Rp. 2,500, he should slip Rp. 500 into his cap before giving the rest to his wife. Then he is spared having to ask his wife for cigarette money, a gesture that would be inappropriate, indecent, or obscene (*saru*). Other men disagreed, saying instead that it was a woman's duty to make sure that her husband never ran out of cigarettes. This, of course, would obviate the whole issue, and in a particularly neat way. The man's authority instills sufficient respect/fear in his wife to keep her attentive to his wants, which he need never express. He needs only to reach for another cigarette, the supply assured by the efficacy of his power.

Not all men give up money so willingly to their wives. But if they do not, they not only encounter disapproval, they run the risk of losing it all at gambling. *Jagongan* invariably include card games played for small sums of money. On occasion, these sums escalate, and many are the stories of families forced out of their homes because of the man's intemperate gambling. I never saw anything so extreme, but I did know a dhalang who, despite his enormous popularity and considerable fee, was forced to live very simply because of the great sums he lost at roulette.

I never obtained any illuminating response to questions about why gambling holds so many Javanese men in thrall. I am inclined to believe, though this met with little agreement in Java, that men take it as a test of their potency. If wealth should flow to the potent without

---

[2] As a single Western male in Java, I was in a ticklish position when people tried to take advantage of me. For example, although bus fares are standardized, minibus fares are given to some variation. The youths who collect the fares have little status to protect and so they are not reluctant to cause a scene. They know better than to get into much of a tangle with a peasant woman: they would only waste their breath. But a wealthy, high-status, and presumably ignorant Westerner offered an obvious opportunity to make some fast rupiahs. Friends differed as to whether I should—in the interest of my dignity—acquiesce, or—in the absence of a wife to manage my money for me—argue. I argued, proving only that Westerners are, indeed, harsh and unyielding, as Javanese already assume. But whenever possible, in the interest of my dignity, I took the bus.

need of their instrumental effort, then gambling seems an appropriate sphere in which to demonstrate potency: then "chance" falls under the influence of potency, outside action. Javanese countered my suggestion, however, with the remark that the potency of one's *batin* cannot be turned to one's own material gain. This point strikes me as somewhat preachy, consistent with normative formulations but not entirely consistent with practice—but I must defer to the consistency of my informants' reactions.

In any case, a man who loses much of his family's property at gambling stands a good chance of losing his family in the bargain. No woman is expected to tolerate a gambler's misadventures, though some women stay through thick and thin. By the same token, no man is expected to be terribly careful about money. Bu Cerma said of herself that it was a good thing that she was so cheap, since her husband spent money so freely, buying friends good things to eat at refreshment stalls. Although critical, the remark indicated some pride, too, in Pak Cerma's generosity, an attribute of the rightfully high in status.

Aside from financial interests, children provide the focus of a Javanese marriage. Javanese say that the father provides for his family and makes all important decisions, whereas the mother nurtures the children. Just as importantly, a man exerts the authority that assures and maintains the prestige, dignity, and influence of the family in the community. The household is organized so as to support the father in that role, while keeping him at a remove from much that goes on in the lives of the other members of the family.[3]

Child-rearing

The first six years in the lives of Javanese children appear to a Westerner to be a continuous (though not always steady) movement from physical and emotional security to physical autonomy and emotional restraint. To Javanese, that same passage represents children coming to have a sure place in the world: becoming capable of with-

---

[3] The divorce rate is very high in Java, so that many children grow up in the absence of their biological fathers. A stepfather or other older male relative is usually close by, however, and the distinctions between male and female roles, or really, the differences between the relations a child enters into with adult men and women, are impressed upon a child in the same manner as in a household headed by a male. Nor does the presence of other kinsmen living in the house, when that is the case, seriously alter the kinds of relations I will describe in what follows.

standing the shocks and stresses of life, and becoming more aware of the rules defining interaction. At the end of this period of adjustment to life in the world, children should have acquired the emotional attitudes and the basic vocabulary of social styles that will enable them to enter into human society with an appropriate sensitivity to their own and others' status.

Javanese babies are held by their mothers almost constantly, during the first year of their lives at least. Babies can nurse at any time and will be given the breast at the slightest fussing. Even when not nursing, babies are normally held by their mothers. If she is busy at some activity, a woman will carry her baby by her side, usually supported by a long piece of cloth. Those few times when she cannot carry the child in this way, she will try to find someone else, usually a female relative or neighbor, to carry the child briefly.

The feeling that an infant should remain with its mother at all times may cause a woman considerable difficulty. Yu Paimin, a woman in Karanganom left in the lurch by the father of her illegitimate daughter, had great trouble making ends meet. She had supported herself prior to her daughter's birth by planting and harvesting in other people's fields, and by hulling rice and helping out on an occasional basis in wealthier neighbors' households. But with a baby daughter to tend to, she could find almost no employment. It was not thought proper or even possible for her to do any work in the fields with a baby on her hip. Even a servant's chores were thought too distracting from her responsibilities to her baby. If she had had a husband, she would simply have attended to the baby, and her own household, until her baby was older. Her situation was considerably worsened in that she had no relatives living in the village. A grandmother or aunt can take care of an infant in cases of real necessity, although the mother should always be close enough to be able to nurse. Neighbors are not expected to care for an infant, however, and so Yu Paimin was reduced to doing what light chores she could at neighbors' homes, applying to her brother and sister for money on the rare occasions she saw them, and accepting gifts of leftover food from neighbors. Her baby was particularly slow at learning to walk, and especially reluctant to do so once she could. Only when the baby was nearing two years of age did Yu Paimin begin leaving her at her neighbors' house for brief periods of time. There, a young mother and her children could all keep an eye on the child, freeing Yu Paimin to take on more onerous, and lucrative, tasks.

Children retain the uncontested right to be picked up whenever they wish until a younger sibling is born. They are not pressured to learn to walk, and once they can walk, they are not forced to walk when they prefer to be carried. It is said, in fact, that encouraging children to walk when they are not yet proficient at it will cause their legs to grow misshapen. If no younger sibling is born, children can continue to demand to be carried to the age of five or six. Nursing, in such cases, may continue until the age of four, and after a woman is no longer producing any milk, she may let her youngest child suck at her dry breast.

Javanese babies are held so constantly and supported even when they can walk because they must be prevented from falling or experiencing any physical disarray. Emotionally, too, they must be protected from all shocks and strains. Babies' general contentment, their resistance to disease and misfortune, and their ability to grow all depend on their being protected from any sort of upset, physical or emotional.

One must attend so carefully to babies' wishes because they are in a sense being persuaded to remain in the family. *Ngemong* means to look after children, with the understanding that one must indulge and amuse them as well as keep an eye on them. When Javanese parents refer to a child who died young, they say that the child "didn't want to be cared for" (*ora gelem dimong*). The phrase is often said in some bewilderment: here the parents had done all they could to make the child contented. Even though disease may have been the immediate cause of the child's death, vulnerability to disease is conceived of as stemming from a child's frustrated desires or unhappiness.

Infants are thought to be, as this point shows, a very tenuous amalgam of spirit and body, given over to desires and appetites that must be satisfied. Frustration and rage due to the denial of some want would endanger babies by making them vulnerable to spirits and the forces that cause body and spirit to become disjoined. Simply being in any way startled can cause these ill effects, which is why babies must be protected from any stress or upset that would cause them to be startled (*kagèt*).

How long a child receives such solicitous attention to its wishes depends on whether and when a younger sibling is born. Ideally, a woman should have both weaned the baby and begun menstruating again before having intercourse with her husband. Otherwise, in the Javanese view, the man's semen will mix with the woman's milk, causing it to be hot and smelly (*arus*, which describes anything that smells like blood or semen). This will cause the baby to become soft or weak (*lemes*), maybe feverish, and sickly. People are not always so patient, however. A woman told me that when a baby starts getting thin, its mother feels great shame because she knows the neighbors will guess that she and her husband have started sleeping together again. Many people, especially older people (of both sexes), stress that a man should go to prostitutes for a year or so after his wife has given birth, and that a woman should accept his doing so, because this is better for the baby than conjugal sex. Some men justify taking a second wife for the same reason, though most Javanese disapprove of polygyny, as I have mentioned, on the grounds that it leads to financial strains and tension between wives.

If a couple lives with either spouse's parents, I was told, the rule against sexual intercourse before a baby is weaned is quite strictly enforced. The older generation will reprimand the younger couple at any sign of renewed sexual activity. When this is not the case, observance of the rule is said to depend largely on the wife's fortitude. Sleeping arrangements in a Javanese house help the wife's cause, if indeed she wishes to resist her husband's advances. Except in the poorest families, a woman and her baby usually sleep in a curtained-off area, while her husband and any older children sleep on a wide platform. Pak Cerma told a hilarious story of how, as a younger man, he would wait impatiently until each of his many children appeared to be sound asleep, then make his way quietly toward the platform where his wife was sleeping. He illustrated the story with gestures as he told it, his arm first rising slowly, then fully extended and waving. But then he would hear his wife snap at him from behind the curtain, "Get away from here. Don't you know this baby hasn't been weaned yet?": at this point Pak Cerma let his arm fall, pathetically, to his side. Nevertheless, many babies are weaned with a younger sibling's arrival imminent.

Weaning can only come as a shock, since it is the first occasion on which children's cries fail to win them the comforting they expect. A mother may rub bitter herbs on her nipples to discourage a child from suckling, and often mother and child are separated at this time, the child sent to stay with grandparents or relatives for a few days. The child's rage and wailing win it sympathy and much attention. Javanese find it very disturbing to hear a baby cry, and the mother must work hard to resist giving a child the breast. In fact, this period is thought very trying for the mother as well as the unhappy child, and many attempts at weaning fail because the mother relents.

Once a younger sibling is born, however, separation from the mother is quite radical. It is at this time that other relatives, older siblings, and especially the father become important figures in a child's life. Ideally, the father takes charge of a child with almost as much solicitude as the mother had previously shown. It is true that if the father works outside the village, or if he shows less interest in his children, he may not take such constant charge of a next-youngest child. There does not seem to be the same insistence that a father take an interest in a child as there is that a mother tend constantly to an infant. Nevertheless Javanese males generally show remarkable patience and affection for small children.

Despite the continuity of attention all the relatives may provide, children who find themselves suddenly displaced by a newborn must undergo much disarray. When an adult daughter returned to the household where I was living in Purwasari because she had grown impatient with her husband, she brought her one-year-old daughter, Sri, with her. For several months, mother and baby daughter were in almost constant physical contact. Eventually, the woman's husband, who lived in a village a few miles away, started coming to visit. By the time she decided to move back in with her husband, the woman was several months pregnant. It wasn't long after the birth of her next child, however, that she moved back in with us. This time she brought her second-born with her. Only several weeks later did she again see her older child, Sri, who had stayed with her father and his relatives, and during the next several months, she saw the child only on a few brief visits. I don't believe anyone in her family found this shift in her attentions surprising.

The birth of a younger sibling must strike Javanese children as a sudden withdrawal of maternal support. One reaction, I believe, is a reciprocal withdrawal of affection on the children's part. Javanese children are often taken to visit grandparents or aunts and uncles and left to stay with them. They may stay anywhere from days to weeks at these relatives' homes. What struck me about children on loan in this way was how little homesickness they showed for their own parents. Yudi was about three years old when he went with his mother, older sister, and younger brother to visit his maternal grandparents in a hamlet about a mile north of his home. He agreed to stay with his grandparents when the rest of the family left, and two weeks later, his mother still could not persuade him to come home. Suddenly an "only" child, no doubt Yudi enjoyed much more attention from his doting grandparents than he received at home. It was a full month before he agreed to come back. Similarly, when Pak Cerma's daughter, who lived in the north coast city of Semarang, found herself forced to fire her servant and to leave the older of her two children, a four-year-old boy named Aris, with her parents, the boy adjusted very well. He stayed for three weeks, basking in the attention of an eighteen-year-old uncle in particular, and expressing no wish to return to his parents. Even when he did go home, he took the first opportunity to accompany another uncle back to Karanganom.[4]

That Yudi and Aris showed so little homesickness indicates how much trust they felt in their kin. And they may have found their grandparents' homes satisfying environments particularly because their own fathers, one a carpenter, the other a civil servant often away on field trips, could pay them relatively little attention. Nevertheless, the ease with which they abandoned their parents and siblings also indicated their own withdrawal of affection from their parents. I suspect that the emotional frustration caused by the loss of the mother's previously constant presence and care brought about their readiness to loosen ties with their parents, perhaps even in some spirit of revenge.

I saw no such emotional independence in any youngest children. It is difficult to imagine, for that matter, a woman parting so easily with a youngest child. The last born is traditionally expected to remain with his or her parents for as long as they live. (The parents' house and yard, if they own one, are then earmarked as that child's share of the parents' estate on their death. The rule is often broken,

---

[4] Pak Cerma's daughter was a civil servant. Lacking a servant and having to go to work, she tried leaving her baby daughter with her landlady, who lived next door, but found that arrangement unsatisfactory. Before long, she started taking the baby to work with her. Her colleagues, when I visited the infirmary in a government office complex where she worked, seemed delighted at the diversion that having a baby at the office provided.

but one of the children is expected to bring his or her spouse to live in the parents' home, and ideally, it is the youngest child who does this.) The process of weaning and of physical separation from the child is much prolonged if no younger sibling is born, and his or her demands are rarely denied.

In contrast, older children must start learning to accept the fact that many of their wants will go unfulfilled as soon as a younger sibling is born. Even though their fathers may provide them much of the attention that their mothers, now preoccupied with tending for the newborn, no longer grant them, older children must learn always to defer to a younger sibling's wishes. Whereas an American parent may go to elaborate lengths to be "fair" in satisfying several children's wants, a Javanese parent invariably blames the older child if there is a conflict of wills. As a result, older children do not present arguments or scream for justice: they give in. Toys, candy, anything that attracts a younger child's interest must be handed over forthwith, lest the younger child's cries attract an adult's attention—and sure rebukes for the older child. When a younger child does cry, older children are scolded for "not knowing how to care for [ngemong] their younger sibling," that is, for not being attentive or indulgent enough to keep him or her happy.

When children defer to a younger child's wishes, they have learned to ngalah. The word is based on the root kalah ("to be defeated"), but the initial nasalization gives the word an active and intentional cast, so that it expresses the decision on the part of a stronger or more righteous party to yield voluntarily to another. To be able to ngalah is an ability much praised in Java. That a child is expected to ngalah does not mean that at any specific point Javanese reverse themselves in their belief that a child's desires should be fulfilled as far as possible. They seem genuinely distressed at any child's unhappiness. But a younger child's contentment matters more, in view of his or her greater vulnerability, than an older one's. An older child is expected to be less subject to the ill effects of frustration and more able to cope with it.

Two of Mbak Tuti's three children illustrated the different ways in which older and youngest-born children handle situations in which their desires are thwarted. The oldest child was an eight-year-old girl, Lis, who lived with her paternal grandparents, the Cermas; the youngest child was Jaka, a four-year-old boy. When Lis was upset, she would cry quietly, seeming to expect little attention. Even when people gathered about her to ask what was troubling her, she could rarely express herself. She would fight back her tears, appearing to feel upset and ashamed of being upset at the same time. Jaka, on the contrary, could play a crowd for all it was worth. One day when his mother wanted to bicycle to the market and leave him at home with his relatives, he decided he wanted to go along. His mother said no, and he started crying. First one uncle, then another, then a third came out of the house, each offering the boy candy, or a ride out to the fields, or an ice cream. Voices grew more excited as Jaka responded to each suggestion by wailing all the louder. Soon his sisters and grandparents joined the crowd. The noise level of this business of calming Jaka grew terrific. Finally, the atmosphere having gotten quite frenzied, Mbak Tuti relented and put him on the back of her bike, muttering her displeasure as they rode off to market.

While most children must learn to indulge a little brother or sister, they must also develop feelings of *wedi* ("fear and respect") toward the environment and their elders. In light of the emphasis on maintaining children's physical and emotional equilibrium, it may seem contradictory that a parent's method of disciplining and controlling them is to snap at them in a violent tone (*nggetak*) and often to voice a specific threat. Tigers will get them if they wander far from their mother. They'll get left behind if they don't come along at once. Every Westerner in Java hears mothers taking advantage of their presence to tell children, "Watch out or the Dutchman's going to get you." A popular threat these days runs, "Watch out or I'll give you a vaccination." A man who had recently returned from Sumatra told his son who would not stop crying and go to sleep, "I'll go away and leave you again." Another threat particularly rich in psychological overtones is, "Watch out or I'll circumcise you." I have often seen Javanese mothers let children begin doing something—play with food being prepared, or get into anything they shouldn't—without reacting in any way, then suddenly snap at them with remarkable vehemence. The delay heightens the drama: the effectiveness of the reprimand must be thought to depend on its vigor, which is justifiably greater when children are in the thick of mischief rather than just getting near it. That is, the mother (or any adult) wants to startle the child. Presumably, the force that being startled carries, in Javanese eyes, is precisely what makes it seem to them the most effective means of instilling proper behavior. It is perhaps similar to the way a Westerner to whom the thought of child abuse is abhorrent will strike a child quite vigorously for running out into the road.

These threats grow more frequent and intense the more independent will and movement a child shows. They seem intended not just to make children behave, but also, it appears to an outsider, to make them fearful of any new place, person, or situation. For example, small children discover that if they wander about while their mother does the washing at the spring, she will suddenly burst out with some reference to what evil lurks in the place. These thunderbolts of warning and rebuke foster children's wariness about action of any kind. I believe it is the parents' ambivalence toward children's increasing autonomy that causes them to make these rather infantilizing threats.

Yet such threats, however vehement, never materialize, of course, as children eventually learn. Javanese parents are extremely reluctant ever to strike a child, and so beyond a threat there lie only more threats—or perhaps capitulation to a child's wants. Since if children, especially youngest ones, doggedly persist in their demands, they will usually obtain satisfaction, many children learn simply to disregard verbiage. One day a young woman was spooning food into her four-year-old son's mouth. The youngest of the children, he was used to being indulged in this, as well as in many other, ways. He spied his mother's paring knife on the table and started playing with it. His mother told him twice to stop playing with it. When he persisted, she finally took the knife from him and put it beyond his reach. The boy walked away from the table, refusing to eat anymore. His mother gave in and handed the knife back to him.

Nevertheless, one sees in most children a particular reaction to their parents' verbal attacks on their behavior. It might be called passive desistance: children simply stop what they are doing. They neither resist their mothers nor appeal to them. It is as though they have heard nothing, they register nothing, but having lost all interest in what they were doing, they look away. When, for example, a child suffers rebukes for trying to keep candy from the clutches of a younger sibling, he or she will simply let the younger child get the candy, offering no further resistance.

This pattern of silently withdrawing from action in the face of conflict or criticism characterizes another crucial area in children's development of feelings of fear/respect, namely, in their acquisition of refined speech. As discussed in the preceding chapter, the system of speech levels is complicated, and no one (with the exception of children born high in the aristocracy) is expected to have full control over it at least until adolescence. Parents start teaching children some refined words almost as soon as children can speak, however, by speaking for them and forcing them to imitate their words and intonation. So during the first year and more of their lives, children are addressed and begin speaking exclusively in ngoko, in which the terms relating to speaker and addressee are usually undifferentiated. However, when an older relative or guest addresses a child and the child answers in ngoko, the mother will correct him or her, substituting the respectful forms, which the child must repeat.

Since most of these new forms are aurally completely unlike the words children have previously learned, their first reaction is likely to be complete confusion. But before very long they learn that if they imitate their mother's words and her highly exaggerated (drawn-out and therefore refined) intonation, huge praise will be bestowed upon them. The pattern then turns into a great game played by mother and children when any other adults are present. Eventually, though, the fun wears off, as greater demands are placed on children to speak properly, but less attention is devoted to teaching them how to do so.

From about the age of five or six, children should use some measure of refined speech in addressing their father and other adults aside from their mother. Failure to do so evokes contemptuous corrections. Children's usual reaction is once again to fall silent, look away, and disengage themselves as much as possible from the scene. (This silence is liable to evoke another rebuke, or the crude epithet, "Goblog!" ["Idiot"].) Most children, by the age of six or so, have grown very leery of interaction with adults outside their immediate family. When addressed by adults who are not close kin or well known to them, they will answer in a single word or phrase, usually mumbled.[5] Within the family, too, they may grow less voluble, particularly with their fathers. The increasing pressure on children to use refined

[5] Yuni, a girl aged four when I moved into Purwasari, was a particularly close friend of mine during the two years I lived in her grandparents' home. Every day she came to look at picture books, one or two younger brothers in tow. But when I returned to the village after a year in Bali, Yuni, now in school and aged seven, would not speak to me. My extravagantly high status (as an adult Western male) and the problem of how to respond to it had become clear to her, and though I lived next door for another five months, Yuni and I were never again such chums.

speech with their fathers, as well as with other adults, while not a sudden development, nevertheless undercuts the warmth and trust that have built up between them and their fathers since the birth of a younger sibling. It is surprising, actually, how quickly the affection Javanese males show small children falls away once children need to start learning the proper attitude and behavior of respect.

Javanese children are taught to distrust the physical environment and their own impulses. To move about on their own, and to taunt, evade, or otherwise upset a younger sibling, risk arousing parental reprimands and threats of their withdrawal of support. When even words children have previously used unself-consciously grow increasingly, and what must seem to the children erratically, unacceptable, then their environment, desires, and language all prove suspect, far less trustworthy than these had previously appeared. The result is that children experience fear in many situations. The physical and social environments have both come to appear dangerous. It should be understood that fear is not, for Javanese, something one tries to help children overcome. Children *should* feel afraid in the dark.

The specifically social fear children must evince in the presence of their fathers and of non-kin is the first understanding of *isin* ("shame") children gain. The acquisition of isin is considered by Javanese the crucial element in a child's emotional development. Children must become hesitant to express their own wants or to impose their wishes on any situation that includes their superiors. They should come to know that in such people's company they must appear self-effacing, and that they must address those elders in refined Javanese, demonstrating thereby that they feel fear/respect (wedi). They also show thereby that they are "aware of shame" (*ngerti isin*) and have an awareness of how much they must be careful in the presence of others, particularly in the presence of people who are not close kin. That is, their behavior shows that they have become aware of their vulnerability in interaction.

Shyness and timidity, which is what isin means in reference to a young child, are highly esteemed by adults, even if they chide children for such reactions. When, for example, children are told by their parents to introduce themselves to a guest, according to Javanese etiquette they should step forward, extend their hand, and say their name. Most children will instead cling to their parents, hiding their faces, or go scampering off. The adults say, "*Kok isin!*" the *kok* expressing surprise and some derision, as though the children were silly to act so fearful. Yet children must sense the approval implicit even in this ostensible dispraise. To say of children that they have no awareness of shame (*ora ngerti isin*) is, in contrast, unequivocally critical.

To what, it may be asked, are children vulnerable? To the conflicts, first of all, that seem inevitably to arise between their own impulses and the demands of their parents. But beyond that there is much children must learn about interaction, namely, the importance of status, its determinants, and its constraints. Children learn first that there is a difference between kin and non-kin (*wong liya*), with whom their relatives act more formally than with kin. Then, as they grow older, they see that receiving deference matters as much as giving it, that controlling others' behavior is as significant as controlling their own. Their education in what it means to be able to conduct themselves properly consists in deepening their appreciation of how interaction defines them, and of how inappropriate behavior—their own or others'—will make them isin.[6]

Young Javanese who learn to overcome their own impulses begin to understand how to negotiate relative status in encounter. They thereby initiate the consolidation of their own status, since in becoming sensitive to others' positions, they begin to learn how to demonstrate and protect their own, through their own and others' deference. Of course, no one except a few elevated aristocrats can expect to exert much personal authority over others in encounter at least until marriage. Still, an adolescent male who looks askance at a nine- or ten-year-old acting bold or impertinent in his presence shows that he already knows that he is vulnerable to the implications of others' actions, not just his own.

The first way that a child can exert any "control" over others' actions may only be negative: in resisting any control others may wish to exercise over him or her. But this ability to resist others' com-

---

[6] In the absence of wedi and isin, the ill effects of frustration on a young person are still to be feared. If children insist on having something, if they have not yet learned to feel isin about demanding it, then their wishes must be gratified. A young man in Karanganom was unruly and demanding from early childhood. His father told me, in bewilderment, that he and his wife had responded by being especially indulgent to him. The father seemed to feel that satisfying their son's wants should have made him docile and sensible and so able to develop feelings of wedi and isin. Yet he had only grown worse.

mands or wishes, as a kind of guarantee of one's own sovereignty, is an essential component of status. High status consists at the very least in one's imperviousness to manipulation, and others' deference consists at the very least in their recognition of that resistance. A boy, especially, first asserts his own status in the family in just such a negative way: in his escape from the household.

The activities of boys and girls begin to differ clearly after children are six or so years of age. Patterns of avoidance between father and son are sometimes already apparent at this point. The son adopts a wary attitude toward his father, in contrast to the spontaneity and affection that marked their relations earlier. Of course, this is a question of degree: some sons remain close and relaxed with their fathers. But the constraints of deference more often introduce circumspection and distance into their relations. At the same time, from the age of about six at least until he is a teenager, a Javanese son enjoys considerable independence. If his family is poor, he will have chores to do, such as taking ducks out to feed in the fields. If his family is wealthy enough to own livestock such as water buffalo, or if, less wealthy, they have rights to such animals' use, then he will spend much time taking them out to graze, and bathing them. For the rest of the time, being too young to do much work in the fields himself, or to get any other sort of work (except perhaps selling snacks), he and his cohorts enjoy the run of the village. When they appear at home, boys may well be expected to attend to younger siblings. But they can leave again soon without much trouble. It is the memory of this period, when they were herding boys, that arouses the greatest nostalgia among middle-aged Javanese men. They recall it as a time when they were subject to no constraints whatever.

When he gets older and stronger, in his teens, a Javanese son will be expected to do harder chores, such as working in the fields. If his father does other types of work, such as making and firing bricks, a son often joins his father in that work. Or he may seek other kinds of employment, as a petty trader or peddler of snacks, or at whatever jobs are available in the area. He may continue this work until marriage and after.

However, the situation becomes complicated when, as often happens in Java today, the son attains a much higher level of education than his father did. Then there is some feeling that the son cannot be expected, or in any case will not be forced, to do heavy labor. As long as the son is in school—which can be a very long time, since by stay-ing back, switching schools, starting over, etc., getting a high-school diploma can see a man well into his twenties—the priority of school-work over labor goes uncontested. Even if a son does not get a high-school diploma, but instead falls along the wayside in junior-high school, he may resist attempts to press him into work. This is partic-ularly true when his family is, by village standards, relatively well-off. Sons in a landless family, or in a family with only a tiny amount of land, have no choice but to find work to supplement the family in-come. In the rare cases in which they manage to continue school be-yond the elementary level, they can pay for their schooling only by working, perhaps as farm laborers. Tarno, a sixteen-year-old youth in Karanganom whose parents had only a tiny plot of rice land but many children, won universal praise because he managed to continue his studies by working every afternoon after school and weekends. How-ever, sons whose parents can afford to pay school fees are less likely to respond to pressure to bring money into the household, or to help in their father's work.

A girl enjoys less freedom of movement. She will be expected to help her mother cook, wash dishes, do laundry, fetch supplies from nearby stalls where basic commodities are sold, and of course tend younger siblings. But she, too, can wander about the hamlet, even if burdened with a little brother or sister on her hip, and play with friends—and their little brothers and sisters. Few girls get as much schooling as their brothers in Java, except in wealthier families. Even if they do go to school, girls are expected to devote much time to household chores. Notions about the proper age for a girl's first mar-riage are changing, but traditionally a girl aged thirteen or fourteen was considered old enough, and at nineteen or twenty, if no marriage plans were set, there was cause for alarm. Although there is a general consensus among villagers that if a boy is smart enough and rich enough to go on to high school or even college, he should do so and put off marriage until he is established in some job, there is less agree-ment about whether a girl should place her schooling over marriage. When an intelligent and attractive girl of sixteen resisted engage-ment to a suitor from another village whose parents had protected her father in the aftermath of the coup of 1965, neighbors tended to side with her. She should have been allowed, they said, at least to finish junior-high school. On the other hand, when the hamlet head in

Purwasari agreed to marry a twelve-year-old girl his aunt had found for the purpose, he and his relatives all scoffed at the idea that the wedding should be put off a year, until the girl had finished elementary school. In this case, the girl's wishes prevailed and the engagement was never announced. In the former case, the unfortunate girl was obliged to marry her clearly less gifted suitor.

POTENCY AND POWER IN THE HOUSEHOLD

Throughout the period from when children first learn respect and refined language until their marriage, they must evince a properly deferential attitude toward the father. A man's status defines that of his wife and children and so it determines much about the treatment they receive from others.[7] At the same time, a man's wife and children must show him the respect that demonstrates the impressive force of his presence, which follows from his potency. This presence must be seen to prevail upon his immediate family if it is to exert any influence over others. Pak Cerma and his wife were much scandalized by their neighbors, Pak Cahya and his family, because even though Pak Cahya was cousin of the village headman, his children did not speak to their parents in refined language. At the very least, Pak Cahya should have insisted that they do so in public. The same inclination to make family interaction a demonstration to the public showed in Bu Cerma's habit of addressing her husband in a fairly high degree of refined language when guests were present, especially if the guests were from a different village, whereas otherwise she spoke to him in a rather minimally refined mix. She explained that she did so in order to make it clear to others that she feared/respected (wedi) Pak Cerma.

Even when not in the public eye, family members interact in such a way as to protect the image of the father's authority. This explains

---

[7] This point was impressed upon me when I asked about the cecala, the youth who goes to each house in a hamlet inviting the family head to attend a ritual ceremony (slametan) about to take place. The youth need not be a member of the sponsoring family. He is simply a low-status youth of the hamlet. When I asked if any of Pak Cerma's sons was ever cecala, everyone laughed and said, "No, you've got to note who the father is." As sons of a dhalang, Pak Cerma's sons were of too high a status to be cecala, even for their own family's slametan. It would be unseemly for them to be people who take orders (konkonan), and especially for them to have to show the exaggerated deference that is built into the cecala's conventional message.

in part avoidance patterns between fathers and sons. Ideally, a son's obedience should be assured by the fear/respect that he feels for his father. When I asked people what it meant to say that one must fear/respect one's father, they usually answered without hesitation: Told to do something, one must be willing to do it (*Dikonkon kudu gelem*). In practice, the relationship takes on a rather different emphasis. A young boy certainly does jump when his father tells him to get something. But in the overall pattern of avoidance, the son demonstrates his respect more by what he does not say and does not do. He waits until his father has eaten, or at least until he is mostly done with his meal, before taking any food.[8] He speaks in some degree of refined speech to his father, and he does not say what he thinks his father might not be pleased to hear. He is careful not to cross his father's will overtly. In some cases, this submissiveness has serious consequences. When a dhalang's elderly father was taken to the hospital, the doctor explained that surgery to remove gallstones was necessary. Although the dhalang consented, his father insisted that he be taken home. The dhalang obeyed, and his father died soon after. When I asked if he couldn't have refused to take his father home, the dhalang said that he feared/respected his father. His tone made it clear he felt he had had no choice but to comply with his father's wishes.

For his part, the father is usually careful to avoid contests of will. This means that he avoids imposing demands on a son if he feels there is much risk his son will disobey him. Several men in Karanganom expressed displeasure with their sons who never helped them out in the fields. These men said their sons' character or disposition (*watak*) was simply like that, so what could they do?

If even a grown son makes great demands, his father may feel curiously obliged to meet them. Late in my stay, a dhalang I was visiting asked if I was going to sell my motorbike. When I said yes, he asked his teen-age son, who happened to be passing through the yard, if he wanted my bike. "Nope," he answered, "I want a bigger one." His father, who had just been bewailing the carnage on the highways, said resignedly that he would have to find his son a bigger bike.

---

[8] Except for some families in town, Javanese families do not eat together. Women cook rice one or two times a day, and side dishes are kept available so that family members can eat when they like. Adult men are usually served meals, but they do not eat together except by coincidence, and then somewhat uncomfortably.

(Some Javanese attribute young Javanese males' fatal lust for big motorbikes to Japanese sorcery.)

Javanese deeply disvalue open conflict, and so if a son does not fear/respect his father, disciplining his misbehavior presents great difficulties. A youth in Karanganom named Parto was a problem to his parents from the time of his childhood. By the time he was a schoolboy, he had taken to stealing money from the wardrobe where his mother hid it. His father told his mother that from then on they must keep all money locked in a special storage space. Nothing was to be said to Parto about it. The eruption of unpleasantness in the household was thereby prevented. His brother also told stories of how his money and clothes disappeared, the latter sold off for quick cash. But he had tired, he said, of reprimanding his brother. In what seemed a tacit agreement, Parto's parents and brothers all came to accept that anything they neglected to lock up Parto would steal. That is, everybody had to be careful, alert, on guard (*sing ati-ati*), an attitude Javanese always think praiseworthy, and at the same time, conflict was avoided.

Outbreaks of conflict must be avoided because they would indicate the father's lack of potency. The powerful presence of any figure of authority should be such as to prevent disturbance within his domain. Since conflict of any sort would inevitably incur his wrath, everyone else should fear expressing hostility openly. Pitched battle, particularly if it engaged the father, would radically undermine his authority by demonstrating his inability to keep other family members under the constraints of respect. Any occasion that caused the father to raise his voice in anger might well show that his speech was not effective (*ora mandi*), that it was not sufficient to maintain perfect order. Such an event would undercut the impression of his potency greatly.

Tension and conflict do arise, of course, in a Javanese household. The father's authority is insulated from the family, at least partially, however, by the nature of the mother's role. The mother takes responsibility for those areas, finances and chores, most likely to give rise to conflicts with children as they grow older.

Conflicts in the Cerma household illustrated this distribution of roles. Of Pak Cerma's six sons, three were still in school during my stay in Karanganom. One was twenty, another eighteen, and the third son was twelve when I first moved in. Few were the mornings when I was not awakened by the sound of Bu Cerma excoriating all three of them for asking for money before they left for school. School fees, books, a desire for snacks or, in the case of the oldest of the three, the basic masculine need for cigarettes, all were grounds for their requests. The sons' laziness and irresponsibility, and the family's financial straits, provided Bu Cerma grounds for denying them. The sons became alternately plaintive and contemptuous in response to their mother's abuse. Bu Cerma complained, in the low growl with which Javanese express displeasure, but interspersed with occasional shrieked epithets, that the sons had no notion how hard it was to get enough money to eat, let alone keep everybody entertained. Other young men worked, why couldn't they? In the end, she often came across with some very small sum, perhaps fifty rupiahs, more often twenty-five. Even in Java, such sums wouldn't buy you much, and the sons would complain in turn—sometimes as they picked coins up off the floor where their mother had thrown them. Pak Cerma maintained complete silence through all this, often withdrawing to another part of the house until the scene was past.

Bu Cerma's behavior highlights the regular pattern in Javanese households whereby the woman saves, spends, or distributes her husband's earnings as she sees fit. Children in other families can sometimes expect more indulgence from their mothers when they ask for money, but they know that it is to their mothers that they must apply. As a result, one of the most volatile points in family interaction is effectively removed from the father's concern.[9]

[9] Certain circumstances exacerbated the tensions about money between Bu Cerma and her sons. For one thing, the family's finances were not, by Javanese standards, so desperate. The family owned one quarter-hectare (one *pathok*) of irrigated rice land and rented another *pathok*, and Pak Cerma performed often enough to supplement their income somewhat. When a real need came up, Bu Cerma could go sell gold jewelry at the market in town. (When, for example, the opportunity arose to buy her late father's gamelan from her stepmother, Bu Cerma came up with the sum of Rp. 400,000, about US$1,000 at the time, within a couple of days.) But Bu Cerma had seen many hard times, first as a girl, when her mother, sister, and she were left to fend for themselves after her father took a younger wife, and again after 1965, when Pak Cerma was imprisoned for eighteen months and then forbidden to perform for several years. Even if the family appeared well-off now, Bu Cerma knew better than to let the family's wealth dissipate in pursuit of petty pleasures. Never did she buy meat for the family's meals, or let anyone's skin get used to the feel of good cloth. Her tightfistedness was considered exaggerated by her neighbors as well as her sons, as she was well aware, but she countered proudly that unlike many wives of political prisoners, she had

Pressing teen-age sons into doing chores can also present problems, and here again the mother often takes charge. I have already mentioned that several fathers complained of their sons' reluctance to help out in the fields. The most serious quarrel to take place in the Cerma household during my twenty-month stay there turned on just this point. The incident itself and Pak Cerma's comments about it point up masculine and feminine ideas about parental authority, and it is worthwhile relating the incident in some detail.

In a poor family, as I have said, a young man rarely has any choice but to work, either with his father or outside, to help keep the household economy in order. But any status claims the family makes cause difficulties about a son's employment. Agricultural employment is appropriate for sons in such families only if they work the family's own land. For sons to hire themselves out on a wage-earning basis would demean the entire family. It may not seem obvious to the sons that they should work even in their own family's fields, for that matter. Pak Cerma's sons were not at all quick to help their father work the family's rice fields. They were educated, and further, they preferred to see themselves as aspiring dhalang rather than farmers. The distinction between wong tani ("farmer," but the word has connotations of our "peasant") and dhalang ("puppeteer," but the word has some of the glory of our "artist") was clear to them, and they did not wish to obscure it by doing agricultural labor.

Actually, although Pak Cerma worked hard in the fields, in conversation he often contrasted farmers and puppeteers, including himself among the latter and indicating some disdain for the former. He was fond of citing the time his father had given up land-use rights accorded him by the village with the proud remark that he was no farmer, he was a dhalang, with better things to do than to go out to the fields. Bu Cerma was less taken with this categorical distinction. When one son balked at the suggestion that he go out to do some weeding, claiming that he didn't know how to weed, she snorted, "What do you mean, the son of a farmer and you don't know how to weed?" Yet on occasion even she was pleased to dismiss the neighbors as so many ignorant farmers. So although not as impressed as her husband and sons were with the responsibilities their dignity entailed,

managed to keep her family going without selling off land or the house during her husband's imprisonment.

she too fostered that sense of the family's particular status that kept the sons' fingernails long.

Nevertheless, the sons' attitude toward working in the fields was always a source of some friction with their mother, and it caused something of a flare-up one noontime. For several days one weeding season, Bu Cerma, never a slouch, was particularly busy out in the fields. She made several remarks to her five sons that they should help. One of them managed to get himself out there a few times, but Bu Cerma was not satisfied. Finally one day she, her husband, and three of the sons all happened to gather in the kitchen at once. Pak Cerma had just returned from town, Bu Cerma from the fields. Bu Cerma made several comments to the effect that she expected help in the fields. Pak Cerma eventually said that she shouldn't go on about it then. Bu Cerma persisted, however. Exasperated, Pak Cerma laid down his spoon and fork with some force and left the table. This gesture may not strike a Westerner as dramatic, but in Java such a clear sign of displeasure on the part of an adult male of some status is very startling. Bu Cerma was furious with her husband and sons alike, and in a common Javanese expression of rage, she stopped talking to them all for several days.

When Pak Cerma talked with me about the incident, he put all blame on his wife. For one thing, Bu Cerma was wrong to talk of any touchy subject when he had just returned from some distance away. A person who has travelled a ways is in a state of pollution or danger (*sawan*). He may have seen something unpleasant or disturbing. "To put it in the manner of mysticism," he added, "spirits are still clinging to him." This means that if you speak to him boldly, he is liable to get angry. It takes about a quarter of an hour for this condition to pass. Pak Cerma was forced to leave the table in order to become calm and without tension (*tentrem*). Furthermore, Bu Cerma should not have broached a difficult subject while her husband was eating. An argument then makes people unable to absorb their food, and it does not turn into flesh. Finally, she was wrong to give the boys orders because boys (Pak Cerma used the term *bocah*, roughly equivalent to our "kid," any person not yet fully mature) are liable to talk back, to answer rudely (*mangsuli*). They lack understanding (*ora ngerti*), implying that they are neither aware of their obligations nor fully in control of their speech. So it is up to their elders, when they want to give them tasks, to be patient, accepting, even indulgent (*sabar*). But

Bu Cerma is a difficult woman and she went ahead with all her talk, leaving Pak Cerma no choice but to leave the table.

Pak Cerma delivered this account very much in the style of a respected elder (wong tuwa)—and within earshot of Bu Cerma, for whose enlightenment it was clearly intended. (The advantage to having an anthropologist in the house in Java is that you can tell him things in a loud voice that you couldn't say to other people, but that you would nevertheless like them to know.) Bu Cerma's self-imposed silence permitted her to register no reaction whatever. In the days following this incident, she threw herself into her work even more vigorously. She restored communication with the family only when they all went off to a performance Pak Cerma gave at the end of the week. At such times, feelings of family solidarity ran high, and the petty aggravations of farm work could be forgotten.

The remarkable fact remains that Pak Cerma did not blame his sons for failing to help in the fields. He blamed his wife for running the risk of making displays of disorder and disrespectfulness break out in the household—and in his presence. The sons' failure to help out was a function of their immaturity, and that immaturity meant that they might talk back. An elder's duty is to exercise such judgment and discretion that a young person has no occasion to speak rudely. Rude words spoken to, or even just in the presence of, the head of the household are highly distressing, since, as mentioned above, such open conflict indicates the father's inability to maintain order within his home. Bu Cerma had quite simply sacrificed concern for Pak Cerma's dignity, and with it, the peace and well-being of the whole family, in favor of her wish to get help in the fields.

If controlling sons' behavior is so problematic, what then is to be done in cases of a son's serious breach of conduct? Some Javanese fathers will curse or even strike their sons when sufficiently provoked. The most highly approved method of reprimanding young people, however, is to speak to them, quietly and at length, making them conscious of what they have done and so arousing in them the proper feelings of shame. In this way, they are "led along" (dituntun)—as one walks alongside a bull or a bicycle—the path to proper behavior. This treatment invites no arguments, no denials or retorts. Of course, one must wait until the incident has passed and emotions have cooled before adopting this approach. Then the instruction, as it is called, can have its full effect. Not incidentally, the older person's authority then stands unchallenged, proving the efficacy of his speech.

Such moments, when the father can bring the full weight of his authority to bear upon a son in displays of his, the father's, judiciousness and superior wisdom, fulfill Javanese notions of the father's commanding presence. Nevertheless, it is the extreme nature of such cases that elicits the father's response. In day-to-day affairs, as the handling of money matters and chores indicates, children are more liable to come into contact and conflict with their mother than with their father. They are also liable to be in closer communication with her generally. The mother is more likely to be at home anytime during the day, and to be in the kitchen when someone comes in to eat, so she is more likely to keep abreast of what everybody is doing. More importantly, communication is freer with the mother, and both contact and conflict much easier, because no one need be so concerned with her dignity. A few sharp words between mother and child from time to time do not hold the implications that tension between father and child does. A fight over fifty rupiahs with her does not have many repercussions in the rest of life. A man's anger, on the contrary, is frightening because the family's status and well-being depend on his equanimity. Anything that causes him to feel anger or shame implies the dissipation of his potency, because all extreme emotions disperse such spiritual power. It also demonstrates the inadequacy of his potency to prevent whatever aroused his wrath in the first place.

Javanese views of women fit this distribution of roles within the family. It is a general consensus among Javanese, male and female, that women have little potency. As a result, they lack both the coolness necessary to resist angry outburst, and the stake in maintaining a calm demeanor that concern for one's potency implies. Female neighbors occasionally engage in verbal and even physical fights. While Javanese find all conflicts upsetting, women's fights are taken relatively lightly. Women are like that. So although both ideology and behavior reveal latent hostility between fathers and sons in Java, as I will discuss shortly, Javanese are more conscious of and and speak much more freely of friction between mothers and daughters. Tensions between mothers- and daughters-in-law, and among sisters-in-law, are always assumed to exist, no matter how well they may be dissimulated. In every hamlet, some women will stop speaking to each other (nengnengan), sometimes for months or even years. These facts need not even be dissembled, because women's spats have so little social resonance.

A woman is not uninterested in status and power. She watches carefully for signs of deference or presumption on the part of her neighbors and guests. But particularly when at home, as I have said, she need attend much less carefully than her husband to her own dignity. To put the distinction somewhat boldly, the mother operates in terms of a more material understanding of power: who holds the purse and who's willing to yell. The result not only keeps her in firm control of the family finances, it also keeps her husband's authority insulated from the petty strains of family life.[10]

It is differences children observe between their father's and mother's authority, and the kinds of behavior that each of them insists upon, tolerates, or rejects, that teach children not just what it means to be a man or a woman in Javanese society, but also what it means to be mindful of one's own and others' status. First, in learning that they must fear/respect their father, and must demonstrate that attitude in their speech, whereas with their mother they can maintain a much more casual tone, children first recognize the distinction between kin and non-kin. Javanese would reject out of hand the suggestion that the father becomes to a degree assimilated to the category of non-kin by this distancing. After all, the definition of "other people" (*wong liya*) is that they are not bound to one by kinship ties. Yet the guardedness children come to adopt toward their father already sets the pattern for their responses to non-kin, particularly to those of high status.

Secondly, in seeing the distinction between a father's and mother's area of greater jurisdiction within the household, a child begins to see that power can be conceived of in different ways. The mother's power is overt. She tends to the family's obvious, external (lair) needs, such as food and money. A man's power is at once more subtle and more impressive. It is his potency (kakuwatan batin) that commands deference, which controls other people's behavior, and at the same time determines the family's condition, that is, its fortunes and status. The extent to which a man develops or even concerns himself with his

---

[10] No doubt my view of a Javanese household is colored by the particular personalities of the members of the Cerma family, the family I observed most closely. Bu Cerma was a bit feistier, Pak Cerma a bit more serene, than many Javanese of their respective sexes. Yet I believe their somewhat exaggerated character traits only made patterns common to many Javanese households that much clearer.

Ki Dhalang Sarwadisana in performance

Ki Sarwadisana, at far left, manipulates the puppets on the screen. The *dhalang* moves Semar's arm while two other *punakawan* (servant-clowns), Nala Garèng and Pétruk, look on. *Near left*, Ki Sarwadisana pauses to sing a *suluk*.

A *wayang* usually requires at least seven musicians. The *dhalang* subtly signals which *gendhing* he wishes them to play. The drummer (*near right*) times his playing to highlight the puppets' moves. Many musicians, such as the *slenthem* player (*far right*) and the *bonang* player (*above*), tend to become sleepy when the *gamelan* isn't playing.

Invited guests sometimes sit on chairs, sometimes on floor mats. They are served drinks and snacks at tables. A fair number of men sit outside as uninvited spectators, watching the performance on the puppet side.

Members of the *gamelan*, or percussion orchestra

potency varies individually, and some women show an interest in developing their own spiritual power. Yet as an assumption about what underlies the phenomena of social life in Java, potency remains preeminently a masculine concern.

The third point children learn as they mature in a Javanese family is that status, and the potency that underlies it, must be protected. I have argued that roles in a Javanese household are organized in such a way as to insulate the father from conflict, and that this guards the image of his authority from contradiction or challenge. I would suggest, furthermore, that in learning that other people's behavior has such implications about one's status—or more concretely, in learning that a father's status depends in large part on the behavior he elicits from his wife, children, and others—young Javanese come to understand their father's, and so eventually their own, vulnerability to interaction. They come to understand how relative status is constrained in encounter, and how very much it matters.

There is one circumstance in which the concern for potency and status loses all significance. Very small children provide Javanese adults opportunities to express a range and especially an intensity of feelings rare in interaction among adults. This is because relative status pertains so little to young children. As soon as children develop an awareness of how persons fit into differential sets, they must make their behavior conform to the requirements their own and others' status imply. An adult's behavior toward them must also shift. Very young children do not yet understand etiquette, however, and their behavior can hardly be labeled respectful or disrespectful. Also, their dependence is total, and dependence is a version of respect. Even a high-status man, therefore, need not be so restrained with very young children, because their behavior cannot compromise his status. Neither he nor they are susceptible to feelings of shame (isin). Some Western males shed self-consciousness and reserve when playing with children, but others, especially when confronted with a baby, grow anxious, thrown off by the apparent lack of social conventions. Javanese males seem remarkably relaxed around children under five and often appear happiest of all when playing with infants who cannot yet speak.

Potency and Fathers and Sons

Relations between father and son are problematic because as a son matures, he seeks to establish his own identity and sovereignty. This is not simply to impute adolescent rebellion to Javanese teen-agers, however. Careful avoidance of open conflict precludes much of the paternal assertion of authority, and adolescent reaction to it, that can make life in an American household, for example, so tumultuous. On the contrary, the pattern of mutual avoidance and the son's use of re-fined language often grow increasingly marked as the father ages. Nevertheless, both behavior patterns and certain beliefs about po-tency indicate an ongoing tension in father-son relations, suggesting that a son poses a potential threat to the status and well-being of his father.

Javanese believe, as mentioned above, that if a man and his wife have intercourse while a baby is still nursing, the father's semen will mix with the mother's milk and cause the baby to grow sickly and per-haps die. This belief indicates hostility between father and a child of either sex even while the child is still an infant. Such hostility later focuses more specifically on a male child. Mothers and siblings often play with a baby boy's penis, causing him to have an erection. This practice stops as the boy gets to be about three. Adolescent and adult males, however, will tease a boy by reaching to pull at his penis and saying, "*Kacuk!*" (*Kacuk* means "penis," but is used to refer to a boy's penis, not a man's.) The boy brings his legs together and squirms away unhappily. Ostensibly a game, this pattern must appear to the boy openly hostile. By the age of five or six, a boy learns to respond defensively to any older male who approaches him too intently.

Javanese believe it inauspicious if a child is born on the same birth-day (*weton*, the conjunction of five- and seven-day calendrical cycles) as either of its parents. They are particularly concerned when a son's weton coincides with that of his father. In such cases, one of them is thought likely to grow sick or die (*kalah*, "to be defeated"). Javanese say that such a son should either be sent to live in another family, or should by magical means have his weton "changed." In this belief, Javanese appear anxious that a son will replace his father, or that the father will weaken or kill his son. While the avoidance that characterizes their relations already implies some sense of potential conflict between them, when a son takes so "personal" an attribute as his father's weton for himself, the suggestion of competition be-comes too intense and some disjunction, either physically separating father and son, or magically distinguishing their weton, becomes necessary.

There is a similar effort to distinguish fathers and sons in their respective stores of mystical knowledge (ngèlmu), consisting of magical
formulas (aji-aji and rapal), arcane lore, and knowledge of various ascetic and mystical practices. Ngèlmu can be translated most generally
as "knowledge" or "wisdom." It contrasts with ilmiah, "science." The
latter may be difficult and obscure, but it confines itself to the external world, as understood by and subject to everyday relations of cause
and effect. It is what one learns about at school and what Westerners
have such a knack for. Ngèlmu, on the contrary, deals with all manner of things which are not susceptible to obvious analysis: formulas,
spirits, sorcery, asceticism, vows—in a word, all things that are tied
to the operations of kakuwatan batin. A youth in his late teens may
begin to develop an interest in ngèlmu in the form of invulnerability
magic. As he achieves adult status, his interests should diversify. The
great spiritual potency of an old man accounts for his ability to remember and deploy this esoterica. But people assured me that a man
could not find a guru (a teacher of ngèlmu) in his father. The particular bond of respect and loyalty that ties a student to his guru, a bond
highly idealized in Java, is distinguished from that between father and
son.[11] Granted, Javanese also idealize a son's relationship with his father when they insist on a son's obligation to fear/respect his father,
and to support him in his old age. But the conventional image of the
young man given guidance and strength through the teachings of a
guru stands at a remove from family relations. In fact, the special status of the bond between guru and student, while likened normatively
to that between father and son, differs from that relation because it
fills in conscious and positive affective ties that are lacking among
males within the family.

I was given various justifications for the need to distinguish between guru and fathers. Most important among them was the notion
that the son might not be strong enough (ora kuwat) for his father's
ngèlmu. Trying to assimilate ngèlmu beyond the capacity of one's
own spiritual potency causes confusion, madness, and even death. A
guru will know to introduce ngèlmu to his student by degrees, and to
take proper ritual precautions along the way. The student then suffers
no ill effects. A father, however, will not know to gradate his teach-

[11] On the bond between guru and pupil, see the Introduction in Anderson 1972a.

ings in this way, and even a famous guru is thought unwise to teach his sons.

This need to distinguish the roles of father and guru repeats the concern implicit in the need to distinguish fathers' and sons' weton. Ngèlmu is an important part of a man's authority because its possession, like his impressive aura, both constitutes and demonstrates the potency of his batin. Were a son to share the ngèlmu of his father, the latter's superior authority would be challenged and the conventional distribution of roles would be undermined. The belief that the father's ngèlmu would overpower the son, like the belief that his semen would cause ill effects to a nursing baby, seems to cover hostility aroused by the son's potential capacity to substitute for, that is, repeat and replace, the father.

At a certain point, the distinction between father and guru diminishes. This is when the father nears death. Possession of certain varieties of ngèlmu, particularly magical formulas (aji-aji) that grant their user invulnerability, is believed to prolong a person's death agonies. The pain continues excruciatingly while the person longs for death but, being too potent, cannot die. Some informants called this "God's tortures," punishment for having arrogated to oneself, through esoteric knowledge, powers rightfully exercised by God alone. An older person avoids such pain when he throws out (ngguwak) or casts into water (nglabuh) such ngèlmu. Informants' accounts of how to do this varied. Almost all agreed that a man could go to the banks of a river at night, give offerings to spirits, repeat the magic formula, and then announce, "I am throwing out this formula." In this way, while he might still remember its words, he would no longer be able to use the formula to its intended effect. (One goes to a river to do this so that the formula will be carried downstream and into the southern sea, considered the home of many spirits.) But there are other means of ridding oneself of ngèlmu. A man grown old and weak can call his favorite son over to him and teach him a formula. The son can then use it, whereas his father, whether he remembers the words or not, will no longer be able to do so. The formula's energy (daya) will no longer be subject to the older man's control. The repetition of the ngèlmu between father and son necessarily means the father's loss of control of it.

A guru also teaches magical formulas. Unlike a father, he need not wait until he is approaching death to do so, because he will be able to exercise the formula himself even after he has taught it to someone else. A guru, that is, need see no loss to himself in his student's gain in power. Still, people commented, "They say a guru gives his students branches but keeps the trunk for himself," meaning that a guru wouldn't give out his most powerful formulas. In general, guru are known to be somewhat secretive and difficult. The suspicion that they, too, are holding back suggests that some sense of competiton also exists between a guru and his students. Yet that competition comes out much more obviously in the case of fathers and sons. Only when the father's imminent death makes competition irrelevant does it become possible for a man to act as his son's guru.

Father and son can cooperate in the domain of ngèlmu most fully only after the father's death. Dreams and visions obtained through ascetic exercise often take the form of one's late father's image making some statement or offering some advice. For example, if a person is considering buying a Javanese sword (kris), often believed to be endowed with magical properties, he must test (nayuh) it to see whether he and it are compatible. This means that he sleeps with the kris next to him, usually after engaging in some form of fast. During the night, an older person should appear and say something like, "I want to stay with you." This divine sign (ilham) means that the kris is a good match (jodho) and will bring him good fortune. The older person is often one's father. Whether or not the sign is really communicated by the spirit of one's father was a point much vexed among my informants. A majority seemed to feel that this was probably just the form taken by the power of the kris in order to convey its message. The point remains, though, that the paternal image, if not the father "himself," becomes the source of counsel and ngèlmu, a role the living father might assume ideally but in practice assumes only rarely.

The annual ceremony of nyadranan, in the lunar month of Ruwah, presents an idealized version of father-son relations, now assimilated to those that obtain between a person and his ancestors. At this time, all Javanese should visit their ancestors' graves to pray and give incense and flowers (ngirim) to their ancestral spirits. In return, the spirits of the dead grant the living peace and prosperity. It is difficult to go to the graveyards of all one's ancestors, but it is essential to visit the grave sites of one's parents. (One can also pray at one's ancestors' graves at other times during the year, but in Ruwah it is a responsibility one must fulfill if at all possible.) The living affirm their respect, while their parents' spirits direct their beneficent influence (berkah) to the good of their children. This exchange maintains the relationship between them in life, but it is possible not in spite of but really because of the gulf now separating them. In fact, one must not appeal to the spirits of the dead until the full course of funerary rituals has been completed, at the time of the ritual on the thousandth day following a person's death (sèwu). The disjunction between father and son in life, which consists in the son's respect and the father's distance, has then become translated into a disjunction in realm and time following the father's death.

Intimations of tension between fathers and sons are common to so many cultures that it may seem superfluous to illustrate the point once again in the Javanese case. The interest in doing so lies in observing the particular domains in which Javanese behavior makes such tension apparent. That conflicts we deem oedipal seem to be played out in Java in the stress on appropriate speech and gesture, and in the disjunction of weton and ngèlmu, shows how importantly these figure in the definition and mediation of selves.[12] A father's identity and potency depend on the maintenance of certain critical disjunctions: between his own and his wife's roles, between his own and his children's—particularly his sons'—weton and ngèlmu, and between the impression of his superior potency and their subordinate status. The latter impression is constructed out of his own and their studied patterns of interaction and avoidance. As children grow up in a Javanese household, they understand from just these patterns the nature of authority and how to deal with it, that is, how to defer to, benefit by, and/or elude it. Similar patterns then mark their relations with other figures of authority, among them the village headman, the territorial spirit, and the dhalang. In fact, as the following chapters are intended to demonstrate, all mediations of self and other in Java, whether that other is a person, an aesthetic impression, or any type of sign, are colored by these contradictory impulses to depend upon and to resist what is external to the self, through its simultaneous idealization and control.

[12] For an extended discussion of the cross-cultural implications of oedipal relations, see Parsons 1969.

3. VILLAGE POLITICS

If in Javanese families potency should concentrate in the person of the father, in larger realms, such as the village and the state, potency should concentrate in males of similarly elevated status. Efforts to protect and magnify impressions of a leader's potency, efforts to benefit by it, and efforts to escape any control it might imply mark political relations in these domains much as they do in the family. As a result, in all these political relations, the paradoxical concept of quiescent power influences everyone's behavior.

That there is a politics implicit in the relations between a dhalang, his sponsors, and his audience will be the burden of later chapters to establish. It is worth looking first to the more obviously political domain of villagers' relations with their village headmen, in order to trace the ways in which the ideology of potency and the circumstances of village life actually meet on the ground.[1]

The king who exercises great power in his slightest gesture represents a recurrent image in Javanese culture, one that might be termed a dissembled center. As Anderson has pointed out, the conventionalized description of the good king endows him with such attractive power that subjects and foreigners alike submit voluntarily to his suzerainty, while enemies are easily defeated in battle by the superior strength of his batin (Anderson 1972b). This ideal view makes the king a strong, vital, and authoritative center, one toward whom all others submit, whether in allegiance, obeisance, or helpless subjugation. However, the same image suggests the king's necessary stasis. In contrast to a less powerful person, who must exert himself strenuously to attain any end, such a king need do very little. Should he need to exert himself obviously, he demonstrates a lack of potency. So his power must always be in a sense absent: evident in the condition of the kingdom but never demonstrated in coercive action. This is, of course, an ideal view, not a description of how kings in Javanese history have attained and kept the kingship. Yet the re-

[1] An ethnographically more detailed version of this account can be found in Keeler 1985.

lations between figures of authority and their subordinates in Java are all colored by this idealized conception of power.

Like Javanese princes, and like Javanese fathers as well, Javanese village headmen must concern themselves with the impression their authority makes upon those around them. It should impose order and respect upon the people subject to that authority without requiring any overt, coercive action. A truly potent headman need never resort to such action, just as a truly potent prince need never do so. In practice, of course, this ideal of a serenely potent leader is rarely fulfilled. On the contrary, village headmen (*lurah*) and villagers enter into diverse alliances and conflicts, in constant renegotiation of their relations. Nevertheless, the ideology of potency informs the behavior of both lurah and villagers.

Some lurah choose to make claims to potency in terms of ascetic action and/or communication with spirits; others ground their authority in more mundane definitions of power, based on their control over labor and material resources. Yet most presume the obeisance of villagers, and they do this in ways suggesting that they believe their title should entitle them to the respect granted powerful figures. Villagers, for their part, try to hold their lurah to the ideal of a potent, but largely quiescent, center, protective rather than coercive. They seek to tap his power, while at the same time restraining it, in a characteristically ambivalent approach toward and avoidance of any powerful figure. As a result, the ideology of the potent center colors everyone's views of political action in Javanese villages. Nevertheless, it hardly does so uniformly. Like any set of assumptions, those about potency and its manifestations contain ambiguities upon which villagers play in pursuit of their own purposes, stressing now one, now another element in the system as suits their needs.

Villagers want very much to see in their headmen powerful leaders. But powerful in this case means first of all potent, and endowed with the qualities—generosity, even-handedness, and a paternalistic regard for people's welfare—that such potency implies. Bureaucratic power as exercised at higher levels of the government, such as in obtaining government funds allocated at meetings at the *kabupatèn* ("regency") level, and for that matter, personal wealth, also impress villagers. To an extent, these are seen as concomitants of potency. More crucial, however, in the view of most villagers, are other reponsibilities a headman should be able and willing to fulfill: to give material aid to people holding ritual celebrations or who are in distress; to assure harmony among neighbors; and/or to protect villagers from outside influence, whether mundane or mystical. In fact, a headman, like any elder, who can cure the sick or stave off spirits' attacks fulfills expectations of his potency especially dramatically and effectively.

What we would call "aggressive leadership" within the village, in contrast, in which a headman makes demands upon people in the name of improvement and progress, is seen as a deflection from the ideal of an effective but non-coercive authority. If the headman's potency was sufficiently great, there would be no contests of will: people would submit voluntarily to his benevolent guidance. If there is discord, this reflects poorly on the headman's potency, which is proved insufficient to assure harmony. As Wilner has written,

> the traditional authority figure . . . [is] hopefully perceived by his subjects as benevolently paternal; or is so treated in the expectation that he will so respond to their perceptions of him. . . . Paradoxically, exerting overt force tends to diminish presumptive authority in constituting a tacit admission that it can no longer be taken for granted. (Wilner 1970:271-72)

Since at times there is very likely to be tension between villagers and their headmen, although headmen as well as villagers are aware that coercive action compromises the impression of their potency, certain stratagems must be adopted—by both villagers and headmen—to obscure at least partially the contradictions that arise between idealized image and action. One such device is for a headman to make the people who surround him "the heavies": to give them the task of carrying out his wishes and so acting in the rough, intimidating manner that would contravene impressions of the headman's potency were he to behave in such a way himself. Schulte Nordholt provides a good example of this in his account of elections in six Central Javanese villages:

> [The] candidates themselves take little or no part in the campaign. They leave this to their *jagos* [lit., fighting cocks; here, campaign workers]. The latter can on the one hand make promises and dole out gifts, and on the other hand be *kasar* (rough, crude in behavior and speech) and if necessary intimidate people. (Schulte Nordholt 1982:122; my translation)

A related device, one that I will illustrate below, draws on conventional gender roles. As described in the preceding chapter, Javanese often contrast men and women in terms of their differing relations with potency and money. Ideally, men concern themselves with potency and their dignity; women concern themselves with the more obvious and less prestigious matters of money and children. Villagers follow this conventional distinction when they represent a headman as potent and magnanimous as compared with his rapacious wife. In their eagerness to stress this contrast, as well as to blame a headman's henchmen rather than him for heavy-handedness, villagers appear inclined to idealize their leaders. They can maintain trust in the essential benevolence of a headman even as they excoriate his wife and subordinates.

Yet if villagers do wish to see in their lurah a powerful center, capable of assuring harmony and prosperity in the village, they also find ways to resist his power. They multiply the numbers of powerful people with whom they enter into relations, thereby reducing the degree of dependence they have upon any one of them. Just as important as the felt need for a powerful center is this impulse to diminish the authority of any single center, thereby protecting oneself from inordinate infringements upon one's own status and sovereignty.

A fundamental tension, therefore, colors all political relations in a Javanese village. Villagers draw on the idea that a figure of authority should be, to use Clifford Geertz's phrase, an "exemplary center" (C. Geertz 1980), not a coercive agent, in order to try to insulate themselves from direct or material pressures. At times, those in positions of authority also draw on this understanding of potency to shield themselves from the demands and conflicts of political action. Yet, as I have said, Javanese villagers also show a real desire to find in their headman a figure of authority upon whom they can depend. It is this effort both to rely on a headman's authority, in some ways, and to resist it in others, that gives Javanese village politics their particular tone, and in some cases puts just about everybody at cross-purposes.

These ambiguities in village political relations are highlighted by the national regime's current efforts to modify village life through agricultural development projects, increased schooling, changes in political procedures, etc. Headmen are often caught between the bureaucracy's expansive demands and villagers' wants. In addition, headmen and villagers all develop new expectations and wants as consumer goods flood the market and definitions of prestige and status in Java shift. This does not mean that conceptions of spiritual potency and the powerful center, or centers, evaporate. Rather, they are construed in new ways, as they apply to new contexts.

The relations people entered into with their headmen in three villages in the area where I did my research illustrated all these tensions and contrasts. The headman in the first village I will discuss, Karanganom, fulfilled the conventions of a potent leader least effectively, and was by far the least popular and least respected of the three. The second headman was greatly admired as a potent elder. The third had found an effective and original mediation of "traditional" and "modern" versions of leadership.

PAK LURAH KARANGANOM

A *kalurahan* is an administrative unit, usually translated "village," made up of several hamlets. At the time of my stay there, Karanganom had a population of close to three thousand inhabitants. The former lurah was removed from office in 1965, due to some sympathy he had shown for communist-affiliated organizations. A powerful tobacco trader in the area was able to make his nephew "caretaker" lurah, and the trader's son was later elected.[2] It was this son who was lurah during my stay in the village.

Pak Lurah presented himself, to any assembly as well as to an outsider, in such a way as to emphasize his interest in modernization. Soon after his election, he supported several irrigation projects in the kalurahan, some small-scale (improving water conduits to the fields), one large-scale (the construction of a dam and waterworks connected to it). Indeed, when compared with the accomplishments of other Javanese lurah, Pak Lurah Karanganom's record looked good. He was active and energetic when other lurah in Java are simply ineffective. In concerning himself with irrigation, building projects, and village

---

[2] At the time of my fieldwork, a lurah was elected for life, although there was some talk in Jakarta of making the post subject to periodic election. For information on how individuals campaign for office, see Schulte Nordholt (1982). Frans Hüsken details the ways in which privileged families maintain their control in rural areas in Java (Hüsken 1983).

appearances, he had truly earned his reputation as a *lurah pemban-gunan*: a development-minded lurah.

Yet the people of Karanganom were decidedly unhappy with their lurah. It was said that if a new election were held, Pak Lurah would not be reelected. In speaking with inhabitants of the kalurahan about their dissatisfaction, I became aware of two quite different kinds of complaints: one concerned Pak Lurah's honesty and tact in fulfilling the role of modern lurah; the other, more important one, concerned his failure to satisfy more traditional expectations of an important figure.

Pak Lurah's handling of the village finances was one area that caused much discontent. Pak Lurah was rich and getting richer by the day. There was virtually no public scrutiny of the village finances: at the annual village meeting a lot of figures about income and expenditures were trotted out, and that was that. But although it was easy to see why people would grumble about probable corruption at the village office, public sentiment on the subject fell very far short of outrage. It seemed to scandalize people less that Pak Lurah should be growing so rich in questionable ways than that he failed to use that wealth in ways they thought appropriate. Munificence is considered an essential trait in any person of authority or wealth in Java. People are quite willing to disregard the circumstances in which wealth is accumulated, provided that it then continues to circulate. Much of the disaffection with Pak Lurah Karanganom stemmed from his refusal to redistribute his wealth.

A lurah has at his disposal a system of patronage. He can manipulate it to maximize the number and kind of obligations people owe to him. Or he can use it in stricter financial dealings. Pak Lurah Karanganom opted for the latter. For example, in renting out the village treasury lands each year, since the land-rent was paid in advance, Pak Lurah guaranteed that a certain sum of money entered the kalurahan coffers. He also guaranteed that only the richest people in the kalurahan were able to benefit from the use of those lands, because only the very wealthiest residents had the capital to pay such a sum in advance. Had Pak Lurah been willing to sharecrop the land, something that he had promised to do during his campaign but that he later found too difficult to monitor and too disruptive to budgetary planning, he would have been able to bestow the favor of land use on whomever he pleased. Since there were, as elsewhere in Java, many landless families in Karanganom, Pak Lurah could have put many people in his debt by distributing and manipulating land-use rights to the village treasury lands. He would then have been able to draw on their services in a number of ways, following the traditional pattern by which a Javanese official maintained a following. Even if he did not choose to sharecrop the treasury lands, he could have had his own fields sharecropped. For the most part, though, he chose to have his own land worked by wage-laborers on a daily basis. This was the most financially advantageous way to have irrigated rice fields (*sawah*) worked, since the amount expended on labor and capital input fell below the value of the rice a sharecropper would take as his due, at least as long as the harvest was reasonably good. Sharecropping land, that is, could provide a form of relief for poor people in the village. It would at the same time permit particularly exploitative relations beteen the lurah and the poor. Pak Lurah chose, for the most part, to avoid both possibilities in favor of the greater cash profit obtained by using hired daily laborers. But in doing so he frustrated the expectations of many poorer people in the village, who anticipated a greater share in the lurah's considerable means.

The difficulties over patronage that arose between Pak Lurah and the inhabitants of Karanganom reflected in part his impulse to keep his relationships clear-cut and businesslike. Daily-wage labor minimized his obligations to people while assuring him a maximal profit. The villagers, or some of them, would have liked to see their dealings with him more socially embedded. Patron-client relations would have not only given them a share of the yield of Pak Lurah's lands; they would also have permitted the villagers to presume upon his munificence. As luxury goods become readily available in Java, however, cash displaces patronage as the end sought from one's investments. Pak Lurah's prestige as well as his pleasures depended on the huge sums necessary to maintain him and his family in the opulent style of the new consumer society. So he was anxious to obtain the maximum cash income he could, at the expense of traditional images of the patron. Actually, for much the same reason, a subordinate was increasingly likely to opt for opportunities for cash employment, rather than the long-term security of patronage ties.

But people did not seek only financial advantages in their dealings with Pak Lurah. Certainly, his extravagant wealth made them covetous. A lurah's responsibilities as "father" of the community, however, go farther. Here again, Pak Lurah was often found wanting. He failed to fulfill the role of judicious, evenhanded, and paternalistic figure people look for in a lurah.

That his authority could, indeed, exert a powerful influence over people was brought home to me the morning the terrible news came that Pak Cerma's oldest son had just been killed in a motorcycle accident. In the anguish and weeping that filled the house, neighbors kept assuring the family that Pak Lurah was on his way, and his arrival with his wife a few minutes later had a noticeably calming effect. Pak Lurah could "take responsibility." This meant of course that he would take care of arrangements with the morgue, the police, etc. But aside from such practical concerns, his presence as an important person, an authority, and albeit young, a paternal figure, was reassuring. Even his much-resented wife could be seen to bring some comfort to the grieving women by her mere presence.

The capacity and willingness to take responsibility is thought a distinguishing characteristic of the truly powerful. Most Javanese are frequently at pains to disclaim responsibility for anything they do or say. In repeating an opinion people feel to be tendentious or simply outside the purview of their control or experience, they are likely to dissociate themselves from it, saying, "That's just what I've heard. I don't know if it's true or not." Appointments can rarely be considered definite; work is never guaranteed. And one reason so little authority is ever delegated in a Javanese office is that few subordinates want to wield authority. Whenever authorization for something is needed, the better part of bureaucratic valor is to add documents to the pile awaiting the attention of the office's head—and to tell the suppliant to come again some other time. In this way, people forgo claims to power of their own. They also avoid the risk of being held accountable for any consequences their words or actions might have.

In contrast, those rare individuals willing to answer for their own words, to recognize their responsibilities to their kin and subordinates, and even to acknowledge their liability for those people's actions—such individuals are clearly in possession of unusual resources, both material and spiritual. To act coolly and effectively in the face of trauma also shows that a person can take responsibility, as Pak Lurah did at the time of the Cermas' bereavement.

But to take responsibility should also imply that a person is ready to use his authority—and resources—for the benefit of the powerless.

In this respect, Pak Lurah proved himself lacking. A poor older woman, Mbok Paira, estranged from her relatives and living alone, suffered a snake bite one day while digging for crabs in the *sawah*. By the time she finally called to the neighbors for help several hours later, her arm had swollen and become stiff. When someone suggested taking her to a doctor, the old woman demurred, so Pak Lurah had her taken to a curer known for his ability to cure snake bites. A week later, news came back to the village that Mbok Paira was weak and that her hand was rotting away. Her relatives, happy to leave her in someone else's care, and somewhat fearful of contravening the curer's instructions, could not be persuaded to do anything for her. Neither could Pak Lurah. Everyone's refusal to get involved was due in part to the fact that whoever fetched Mbok Paira from the curer would have to give the latter some money. Pak Lurah justified his inaction on the grounds that it was up to Mbok Paira's relatives to take responsibility for her care. But many people felt it was at just such times, when relatives were squabbling among themselves, that his intervention was needed. Pak Lurah's loss of interest in Mbok Paira's condition after the initial crisis was past was seen as a refusal to take responsibility for the welfare of the poorer members of the community, those, precisely, most in need of a "father."

Pak Lurah's failure to follow through came back at him in another incident that was a serious blow to his prestige. A few years before my stay in the village, a poor young woman, Yu Paimin, whose parents were dead and whose brother and sister had left the village, became pregnant by a middle-aged man from the adjoining kalurahan, Pak Tomo, who was married and relatively well-off. Although he would normally have been forced to marry a woman he had gotten pregnant, Pak Tomo was able, with Pak Lurah's assent, to avoid marriage by promising to give Yu Paimin child support. He gave her one small payment and that was the end of that—until he started coming to her place again a couple of years later. Yu Paimin felt powerless to refuse him, but she notified some youths, the sometimes unlikely upholders of public morality in a Javanese village, of his visits, and they captured him. Pak Lurah made a great show of outrage and packed him off with the police summoned from town, saying that Pak Tomo had made it clear that he would not abide by village rules and so he, Pak Lurah, was forced to turn him over to higher authorities.

Imagine, then, Pak Lurah's dismay when Pak Tomo turned up at

home again two days later, with no charges against him, no promises
to keep toward Yu Paimin, and no evidence even of bodily injury. It
didn't take people long to conclude that Pak Tomo had put some of
his wealth at the disposal of one or several of the higher authorities
to whom he had been referred. Pak Lurah kept a stony silence on the
matter, in my presence at least, but his prestige was clearly compromised. People said that he should never have let Pak Tomo off from
marrying Yu Paimin in the first place. At the very least, he should
have exerted pressure on Pak Tomo to pay her (difficult as that would
have been to do). Having failed to follow through after the original
incident, Pak Lurah had in this second one given up all jurisdiction
and left Yu Paimin worse off than before.

I believe Pak Lurah had taken a calculated risk. By linking his position directly to the governmental hierarchy, he had taken a particularly modernist position. A more traditional response would have
been to keep the affair as local as possible. But Pak Lurah meant to
stress that he was a link in the great chain of the entire bureaucracy,
not just the highest authority in the village. He wished to show that
behind his authority stood the authority, quite awesome to many villagers, of the supra-village government. His tactic failed because the
hierarchy failed to exert the authority upon which he had relied to
strengthen his own position.

In the villagers' view, however, Pak Lurah had compromised
impressions of his potency in several respects. If he were truly powerful, no one would have dared to come tomcatting in the village in
the first place. Once apprehended, Pak Tomo should have felt constrained by Pak Lurah's authority to marry Yu Paimin, or at the very
least, to abide by the deal Pak Lurah had made with him. Finally, by
sending Pak Tomo out of the village for punishment, Pak Lurah had
in effect declared himself unable to impose his authority upon Pak
Tomo, and had brought shame down on the village in the bargain.

The incident epitomized contradictions in Pak Lurah's position.
He stood caught between a modernist image of a lurah, which he fulfilled with erratic dedication, and more traditional expectations of
him. By modernist I mean not only "modernizing," concerned with
agricultural and economic innovation and the administration of government programs, but also "rationalizing," relatively detached from
the social implications of his position. In part, his difficulties
stemmed from his youth. Still in his mid-thirties, he simply did not

win the respect that a man twenty or thirty years his senior could as-sume. If he remains lurah, it is possible he will grow into the role. But his problems stemmed as well from his own inconsistencies. Often he wished to disencumber himself of claims on his support and resources, while at other times he tried to take advantage of the prerogatives his title granted him. He disappointed people because he neither dem-onstrated the benevolent interest nor provided the dignified guidance that people expected in times of distress. The result was great disaf-fection and whispered criticism—and high hopes that the post of lu-rah would be made, as the Indonesian government has considered making it, subject to periodic election.

As a final note, I must mention one side of Pak Lurah's life, appar-ently the most compromising, that seemed to win him considerable support. Marriage is an important means by which Javanese families seek to maintain or better their social status, and to concentrate their political clout and material wealth. Marrying into a family with aris-tocratic titles still offers some attractions in Java, but sheer wealth also holds much to recommend it. Soon after his election, Pak Lurah, still a bachelor, had made an excellent match with the beautiful and stylish daughter of an extraordinarily wealthy man from another kalurahan a few miles away. Bu Lurah distinguished herself from all other women in the village by her half-closed eyes, elegant clothes, and heavy, but by village standards subtle, make-up. Her manner was coquettish in the style of city women, and indeed she had attended high school in Jogja. The impression she made on villagers of a spoiled young thing was evident in the many stories villagers told against her. These impugned her virtue in slanderous ways, and em-phasized her cheapness. It is true that a woman is expected to manage her family's finances carefully. Her financial shrewdness should ena-ble her husband to avoid any obvious concern with vulgar money matters, which would compromise his dignity. But a wealthy, high-status woman is also expected to help people out in times of need. Bu Lurah, it was said, refused to do so. That few loans are ever repaid in Java excused her not in the least. Typical was a villager's comment that if he wanted some money, back in the days when he was doing tasks at the village office, he was careful to apply to Pak Lurah, not his wife. Bu Lurah would give him some laughably small sum, or re-fuse him outright, whereas Pak Lurah would have been ashamed to be so cheap. In this way, the couple fulfilled a conventional contrast between a woman who lets no one squeeze a rupiah out of her without a fight, and a man who cares more about his dignity and social harmony than mere money.

Actually, any discussion of Pak and Bu Lurah, even if it started out in criticism of Pak Lurah, ended up by contrasting the two in Pak Lurah's favor. After making wild claims about Bu Lurah's infidelity, people would invariably end up expressing sympathy for her husband's suffering. They would discuss his petty ailments, how pale he looked, and tired, and then mutter something about the troubles that he bore in silence but that inevitably took their toll. And they would praise Pak Lurah for his patience. Patience is a cardinal virtue in Java, valued to a degree quite unusual in the West. It is a trait deemed especially laudable in a man—women are thought less capable and also less needful of having it. In attributing the quality to Pak Lurah, people once again cast him in a stereotypical role, that of the long-suffering husband whose strength and wisdom just suffice for him to keep on despite the outrages committed by his wife. It was in fulfilling such conventions that Pak Lurah was perceived to possess those qualities—patience, judiciousness, dignity, and generosity—that people in Karanganom wished of him. Whereas in discharging his official duties Pak Lurah disappointed people by his inconsistent and even suspect behavior, being neither generous with the fruits of office nor fastidious in the avoidance of corruption, he won sympathy and respect for waging the time-honored struggle against feminine baseness and wiles.

PAK LURAH PASAHAN

While people in Karanganom found much to criticize in their own lurah, they expressed great respect for the lurah of an adjoining kalurahan, Pasahan. This respect was shared by the people I spoke to living in that kalurahan. What distinguished Pak Lurah Pasahan from Pak Lurah Karanganom was his ability to appear possessed of great potency.

Pak Lurah Pasahan was much older than his counterpart in Karanganom. The son of a scribe in the employ of the Dutch, he started working as a low-level civil servant in the area in the 1920s. After spending a few years in a kalurahan office in the hills far from town, he was named assistant to the lurah in Pasahan in the 1930s. A few years later, he took over when the previous lurah retired under a cloud of corruption charges. In 1979, he had been lurah for thirty-four years.

Pak Lurah could point to almost no development projects he had initiated. True, two new schools had been built in the kalurahan, but one of them was financed with federal funds. It is also true that Pasahan was a much smaller kalurahan than Karanganom, with a very small treasury. Nevertheless, I believe the real reason for the lack of projects was that Pak Lurah Pasahan had little interest in such matters. He blamed popular apathy as well as the kalurahan's limited funds for the lack of progress. He cited the years it had taken to accomplish even minor improvements on the kalurahan office as evidence that people were unwilling to cooperate on kalurahan projects. When I asked others about the lurah's achievements—even people such as schoolteachers who were most likely to be enthusiastic about government projects—they were quick to excuse his poor record in development, citing the same reasons Pak Lurah himself did.

Pak Lurah Pasahan enjoyed great prestige for reasons quite unrelated to village development projects. He was famous not for his political administration, but for his ascetic practices and his ability to communicate with spirits. People liked to repeat the phrase, one applied to any renowned ascetic in Java, that "he bathes every *Sura*," that is, only once a year, in *Sura*, the first month of the Javanese calendar. This indicates an ascetic's tolerance for great personal discomfort. People also pointed out that Pak Lurah slept extremely little. Either he napped in the evening and then was up for the night, or he stayed awake until two in the morning. And he never slept inside the house. He ate very little and embarked on all manner of fasts. Most of the time he could be found sitting on a wall above a culvert alongside the main road.

I am not sure that Pak Lurah Pasahan really spent so much time sitting on that wall, but it is noteworthy that people often mentioned it when speaking about him. Pasahan straddled the Jogja-Solo highway on an extremely hazardous curve. The angle was just sharp enough that vehicles coming from the west were likely to enter the curve too fast and fail to hug the northern side of the road. Particularly when the road surface was wet, or late at night when drivers had gotten sleepy, terrible accidents occurred. Inhabitants of the area saw in these accidents the work of the territorial spirit (*dhanyang*). Javanese believe territorial spirits to be very ambiguous beings, both protective and threatening. In Pasahan, whenever the dhanyang was sighted, in the form of a large snake crossing the road, people understood that a victim would soon be lost to the spirit. But Pak Lurah had a special relationship with the territorial spirit that enabled him to protect the village's inhabitants from the spirit's desire for human victims. It always appeared to Pak Lurah and obtained his permission before doing the deed. Pak Lurah acceded to the spirit's request, but with the stipulation that it not take any inhabitant of Pasahan but rather someone from some other area. After any fatal accident on the road, the story always spread that Pak Lurah had previously met with the dhanyang and reached such an agreement.

In addition to this special power over the territorial spirit, Pak Lurah Pasahan was credited with the ability to cure illness and, like any respected older person, to provide mystical support to people. People who had suffered an injury, youths about to take exams at school, anyone facing a particular need or challenge, were all likely to come to Pak Lurah Pasahan to ask for his beneficent mystical support (berkah). For example, when a young man in the village was facing his final exams in high school but appeared listless and incapable of studying, his mother brought him to Pak Lurah to obtain his berkah, in order to enable the youth to study effectively.

Pak Lurah Pasahan did not, as far as I know, exhibit any particular largesse in the form of food or entertainments given the people of his kalurahan. Sitting on his veranda in the evening, one was unlikely even to be served any tea, a rare deflection from Javanese etiquette, but one that people glossed as an ascetic rigor. It was true that he lived very simply, although some women in Karanganom told me that he was plenty rich because his wife lent out money at usurious rates. Once again, the contrast between the righteous male and his unprincipled wife only strengthened the man's virtuous image.

Pak Lurah's great prestige depended on his ability to foster an impression of spiritual authority. That is, his largesse was perceived to consist in giving not material reward but berkah, the protection and security that his potency enabled him to provide. At the same time, his authority did not imply any unwanted intervention in people's daily lives—no village beautification program, no "compulsory contributions" for special projects, in a word, no activism. In this way, Pak Lurah Pasahan fulfilled precisely the functions that the Javanese hope for in any person in whom there inheres a fair concentration of power: maintenance of order, and provision of a font of beneficent influence, but without any demands made in return other than the demand for respect.

PAK LURAH KENTHUNGAN

Pak Lurah Pasahan could bank on traditional images of authority because, after thirty-four years in office, he was himself something of a tradition. A young, newly installed lurah such as the lurah of Karanganom did not enjoy that kind of prestige. But another young lurah in the same area, Pak Lurah Kenthungan, had found an interesting device for bridging the gap. Like Pak Lurah Karanganom, Pak Lurah Kenthungan attained his post in the wake of the events of 1965-1966. In his case, too, his father's influence in the area, notably among district political officers, enabled him to be named caretaker lurah, after the removal and imprisonment of the previous lurah. He was later elected permanent lurah.

Despite his father's orthodox religious views, as a young man Pak Lurah Kenthungan had developed quite a reputation as a rowdy. His father had given him a big old German motorbike in the days when few motorbikes were on the road, and he had proceeded to terrorize the one street in town. He was also said to have been quite a womanizer. As is imputed to any headstrong Javanese youth, he was said to have studied invulnerability magic assiduously. Such magic, in contrast to the wisdom sought by older Javanese males, is thought dangerous, because it encourages its possessor to engage in many fights. As a phase in a young man's life, though, interest in such magic is considered normal and even admirable. It was claimed that Pak Lurah had even travelled to Ponorogo, known throughout Java as a center for occult practices, to learn more magic. People believed that Pak Lurah's son's slight mental retardation stemmed from his father's studies of magic. Pak Lurah must have learned a magical formula too shortly before sleeping with his wife, or perhaps recalled such a formula at the moment of ejaculation, and the potency of the magic was too much for the foetus. Such are the dangers of pursuing mystical knowledge.

Pak Lurah's most visible achievement since he had become lurah was to organize a *jathilan* troupe. Jathilan is an art form in which a group of men dance while carrying horses made out of plaited bamboo. The musical accompaniment consists of only a few instruments, with an insistent drumbeat. Eventually, some of the men go into trance while two clowns, named Penthul and Tembem, dance among them. There had been a jathilan troupe in Kenthungan in the 1920s. The troupe stopped performing sometime in the thirties, and by the early seventies only two old men who had participated in it were still living. Nevertheless, Pak Lurah conceived the idea of "maintaining" the tradition. He invited two instructors, old men with mystical knowledge, to come from another kalurahan and train the new troupe. They did so, but neither became the troupe's leader, as would usually occur. This role was reserved for Pak Lurah himself.

In addition to training the musicians and dancers, the instructors directed Pak Lurah and other members of the troupe in the business of persuading spirits to enter the horses. It was these spirits who were believed to enter the dancers' bodies and cause a trance in performance. Attracting them required fasting and doing vigil in the cemetery of the hamlet in which Pak Lurah lived. Eventually, a spirit appeared to each dancer charged with the care of a horse. All the spirits, and in addition to them Pangéran Palémbang, a powerful old man who was buried in Kenthungan long ago, appeared to Pak Lurah. It was Pangéran Palémbang who gave orders to the other spirits. He was, in a sense, Pak Lurah's invisible counterpart.

The troupe's instructors also taught Pak Lurah a series of magical formulas by which to summon and, more importantly, to dispel the spirits at the time of trance. Pak Lurah, however, found these unduly long and complicated and substituted for them a single phrase from the Koran, which he used in all contexts. The theology of the whole performance was, in fact, quite streamlined. God enables people to perform various startling feats in jathilan, Pak Lurah told me, in order to give evidence of the power of faith.

In the old days, the jathilan troupe was hired to perform at ritual celebrations, particularly to precede the wedding party when the bridal couple moved from the home of the bride to that of the groom. (Apparently it was decided beforehand whether the dancers would go into trance or only dance. Trance entailed a higher fee.) Today things are quite different. On one or, in peak season, two mornings a week, a group of German tourists comes to the village to see the performance take place. I saw one of these performances in 1979. On a small, grassy field, eight or nine dancers began moving, quite slowly, to the drumbeat in roughly identical patterns. After several minutes, they picked up the horses and started dancing with them. The music grew faster and louder, and after about half an hour, some of the men were on the verge of trance. During this opening section Pak Lurah stood inconspicuously on the sidelines, talking with his friend Pak Lurah Karanganom. But as the tension grew, Pak Lurah Kenthungan readied himself for action. He took up a whip, cracked it dramatically, and strode in among the dancers. While they danced, he cracked the whip at their heels. Soon four men were in a trance, and under Pak Lurah's direction they proceeded to perform a variety of remarkable acts. One ate broken glass, another needles. One man broke open a coconut with his teeth. Pak Lurah leaned a crowbar against one man's neck and had him push against it. Pak Lurah also whipped several of the men. At the conclusion of the performance, the men had to be taken out of trance by the two clowns and Pak Lurah, while the other dancers sang a song.

Pak Lurah Kenthungan's reputation as a "modern" lurah was considerable. The fact remained that in a small kalurahan with little irrigated rice land, he had been either unable or uninterested in carrying out many agricultural and other development projects. Instead, he had made a name for himself and the kalurahan by finding a way to tap into the tourist market. He was often invited to attend meetings in Jogja on how to attract more tourists to Central Java and what to do with them once they got there. He had been invited to go to the World's Fair in Osaka and to take along two members of the troupe. (The two he chose were his cousin, not a participant but an administrator of the troupe, and his son, who was too young to be in it. Presumably no one in Osaka knew the difference.) Nothing in Java symbolizes prestige and success more than a trip abroad, and the event was often mentioned in conversations about Pak Lurah. It is also true that although Pak Lurah, as leader of the troupe, received a good portion of the fee paid by the tourist agent, he passed on to each of the players at least the equivalent of a day's pay in return for about two hours' labor.

It would be silly to claim that Pak Lurah Kenthungan had found any solution to the real problems presently facing the people in a Javanese village. Tourism does not offer lasting or reliable relief from the underemployment that affects almost all Javanese peasants. Nevertheless, he had lit upon an ingenious way to shore up his authority, integrating roles—as a possessor of magic and as a progressive administrator—that won him respect. In several ways, in fact, his identity and behavior represented a shrewd compromise. Raised in a devout, orthodox Islamic family, he had good credentials in the face of rising Islamic activism in Java, but little personal involvement in the tradition. Such an involvement would have antagonized many syncretist villagers. His exploits as a young man impressed people, in retrospect, as the exuberance of an exceptional person, and his reputation for seeking magic supported his claims to meeting up with spirits in the cemetery.

In taking on the role of head of the jathilan troupe, Pak Lurah Kenthungan had secured for himself the ideal position as its director and bursar, and as the person responsible for contact with the spirits. That contact enabled him to direct the spirits as they took possession of others. But Pak Lurah never abdicated the dignity and authority of an elder. That he could perform various hair-raising acts upon those men's bodies and finally cast the spirits out implied that his potency was exercised over spirits as well as men, that spirits, too, had to submit to him. So he elicited the particular awe that possession and trance states cannot help arousing, especially in a society where consciousness and self-control are so much stressed. Yet he maintained his own distance from these unruly phenomena. Furthermore, of course, he caused a novel, even quite extraordinary effect every time one or two huge white busses drove into the village and disgorged a number of large, strangely clad German tourists. Pak Lurah's ability to attract these unusual visitors could hardly strike the villagers with less force than his ability to control invisible and mysterious, yet in many ways more familiar, spirits.

THE LURAH AS A FIGURE OF AUTHORITY

Javanese assume that officials are corrupt until proved otherwise, and they resent any interference in how they choose to run their own lives. At the same time, however, they are in no way comfortable with ideas of anarchy. The need for authority in order to maintain an even and untroubled social environment is never questioned. Those people who wield some form of power, whether spiritual, bureaucratic or material, are viewed as mainstays upon whom all must depend. The problem lies in how one wishes those superiors to exert their authority and how one wishes to define one's relation to them.

The range of behavior characteristic of Javanese lurah is certainly not exhausted by the three headmen I have discussed. There exists in particular a very different kind of authority figure: the abrupt, energetic, direct, and unrefined one. In the Javanese arts, such figures are sometimes ridiculed, but they are often much loved and admired by the populace. In politics, the popularity of the Indonesian Communist Party in the early sixties stemmed in part from its leaders' reputations for honesty, frankness, and willingness to appear openly hostile, qualities that contrast with the discretion and allusiveness of refined behavior. More recently, military figures who have acted in a decisive and even arrogant manner have won respect. People seem to feel that anyone who can risk offending so many people and arousing such hostility must be spiritually strong: otherwise, he would fear revenge-takers. In the late sixties and early seventies, especially, the militaristic style, intimidating, manipulative, and *disiplin* ("disciplined"), was evident in soldiers and bureaucrats alike. I have concentrated attention on another conception of power, that exemplified by the respected elder, because as political repression wanes people try to normalize their political relations by falling back on safer models. Some young people speak of the need for more innovative leadership. Other people, recalling the excitement and then the terror of the sixties, want only that things be uneventful and calm (*slamet, tentrem*). Actually, the pressure on lurah to play the part of respected elder may well be greater now, in the aftermath of the sixties, than it ever was before.

By stressing that understanding of power that sees it evidenced in the unruffled harmony and prosperity of a village's inhabitants, rather than as demonstrated in the activity and directives of its leaders, villagers try to balance off their wants: to insulate themselves from political pressure while gaining by the power—spiritual, financial, or whatever—that political authority implies. They try to make of political authority a potent center, rather than a coercive agency.

It is not that villagers want idle lurah. They want such signs of development as new schools, electricity, and improved irrigation. They do not feel bold about agitating for any particular project, but they hope that their lurah will arrange to have such projects implemented on their behalf. They believe that he has access to channels through which government funds and matériel flow, and they hope that he will be able to direct some of that flow into their kalurahan. It is in this and similar concerns, those whose scope surpasses the confines of the kalurahan, that a person is most likely to look to the lurah for help. The lurah can intervene on a person's behalf in dealing with officials from town, or from another kalurahan, or in dealing with any foreign person. In such cases, his authority is felt to be protective and paternal. As lurah are fond of saying, a lurah is called Bapak, "Father," because he is father to everyone in the village.

Of course, that paternalism has its limits. One lurah told me that when the killings began in the fall of 1965, many politically compromised men came running to the kalurahan office for shelter. He took them all in—and then turned them over to the military. In his own view, he had discharged his responsibilities fully, granting the men protection from the "wild actions" taking place in the village, while in no way obstructing the government's pursuit of its own purposes. When he quoted himself telling the men, in low Javanese, that they were right to come to him, and that now they must be calm as they submitted to the wisdom and authority of the government, he spoke in tones similar to those of a father speaking to his children.

The lurah acts as a paternal figure once again when he exercises authority over beings who do not stand outside the limits of the kalurahan but rather outside those of the visible world. It is precisely because spirits are at such a remove that the lurah's power over them is highly valued. His authority is then wielded not over oneself, but over some other object and on one's own behalf. At this point, when, say, Pak Lurah Pasahan made deals with the territorial spirit to spare the village's inhabitants, or when he granted a young man about to take an exam the benefit of his mystical influence, he was assimilated to the category of a respected elder.

A person who contravenes this conception of a figure of authority, on the other hand, is likely to arouse disapproval. Pak Lurah Karanganom did just this with all his projects. I have mentioned that he won respect only insofar as he fulfilled another conventional image, that of the patient husband. This image is also related to that of the respected elder, since the contrast betwen men's and women's roles also turns on the contrast between a reserved authority, ideally characteristic of older men, and a mundane and obvious control that is exercised by women over such things as money and material goods.

A village headman is liable to believe that as a center of power, his authority should be unquestionable and unquestioned, that he should win both the compliance and trusting respect of villagers. They should assume that what he chooses to do is in the best interests of everyone, as children should assume about their fathers. Nonetheless, when villagers try to keep their headman to a particular understanding of the powerful center, one that stresses his potency but discourages his activity, they construe his role in such a way as to try at once to restrain him and to release themselves from his control.

These generalizations should be qualified according to the social standing of different inhabitants of a village, as Frans Hüsken's work on the links between kinship ties and control of wealth and political power in Javanese villages makes clear (Hüsken 1983). It is true that some people in Karanganom would have liked to enter into more substantial patron-client relations with their headman. These people were poor and of low status: they were willing to enter into dependent relations in return for material gains. As I have mentioned, however, in Karanganom relations of economic and social dependence such as sharecropping proved far less common and less durable, and they fit into a less extensive context of relations, than I had anticipated.[3] Instead, more "businesslike" arrangements, such as daily wage-earning agricultural labor, implying fewer commitments on either side, appeared predominant. In large part, this was due to the reluctance of Pak Lurah (and other wealthier villagers) to take on the responsibilities of a patron. Increasingly, though, even poor people in Java seem liable to prefer to keep their relationships short-term, and other less

---

[3] Hüsken's findings on sharecropping contradict my own. He states that sharecropping has increased in the village where he did research in the Pathi regency (Hüsken 1979:147). He gives three reasons why, for landholders in that area, sharecropping is more advantageous than other arrangements: it costs them less; it minimizes their risks, since if the crop fails they pay out nothing; and it maximizes their political control. He notes that sharecropping arrangements have progressively reduced the sharecroppers' portion of the harvest, to as little as one-ninth or even one-twelfth of the yield. In Karanganom, there is some evidence that sharecroppers now receive a smaller share than they once did, but the least I ever heard of was one-fourth of the yield. Jean-Luc Maurer reports findings similar to my own in the area of Bantul, located like Klaten in the Principalities, and suggests that this is a consistent contrast between the north coast and southern central Java (Maurer, personal communication, March 1984). But it is difficult to explain at this point the great contrasts among tenancy arrangements in different areas of Java. These are, for that matter, only some of the many complicated variations in labor patterns to be found in Java, as White has demonstrated in a recent paper (White 1983b).

indigent Javanese are still more likely to seek a discreet relationship with authority. They thereby keep a certain distance from the powerful center.

To grant someone respect in interaction and to enjoy the privilege of applying to him for various boons, and yet to remain free of other obligations to him outside encounter, is to find just such a political, or politic, middle ground. Respect enables a person of lower status to interact in the mode of exchange without any necessary material loss. This is not to say that Javanese value goods over status, rather that they consider respect rendered to be as valuable as goods or services received. Respect in language and gesture balances a system of exchanges and assures that there will build up no completely one-sided relations of creditors and debtors. That a person of authority and/or wealth should give gifts without stinting seems only proper, considering his abundant resources. His inferiors dispose of the resource of style. The respect they proffer registers, validates, and in so doing contributes to the creation of high status. High status, therefore, does not necessarily grant control over labor or resources: it does not necessarily enable its bearer to impinge unduly on others' lives beyond the context of encounter. The hierarchy of status relations may be an organization of exchanges of a sort, but it is hardly an order of command, even if some lurah would like to make it one.

A person believed potent (a wong tuwa) repeats, at a lower level of magnitude, the idealized image of the exemplary king at the top of the Javanese hierarchy. In both cases, that of the king at court and that of a wong tuwa in a village, authority should impress itself upon others through the disinterestedness, dignified bearing, and impressive aura of the person in a superior position. These qualities prove that that person possesses a great reserve of potency. And it is through the exercise of the beneficent influence such potency puts at his disposal, rather than in an active intervention in people's lives, that any figure of authority should exert himself. The fact that the elderly Pak Lurah Pasahan held the position of lurah, for example, was taken as evidence of his potency. But he did not wield the power that office gave him in ways people did not wish. Rather than an instigator of action or propagator of change, he became, or remained, a conduit of potency, which is what both a respected elder and an exemplary prince in Java should be.

If respect for the powerful center can be taken to imply both claims upon it and a certain release from its control, further distancing takes place when centers multiply. Anderson has stressed that Javanese conceive of power as homogeneous (Anderson 1972b:7). That is true, and it explains why Javanese can treat a leader's control over people, spirits, and the world as somehow all of a piece. Nevertheless, it is also true that individuals' capacity to channel and manipulate power can differ in significant ways, and those differences make it possible to counter the concentration of authority in one person. In contrast to the inclination to make a variety of demands upon a headman, efforts to domesticate his authority fit a tendency to distribute kinds of authority among several different persons. So, for example, a man enters into agreements to provide labor to several different landholders (who in turn employ a series of different laborers); he seeks guidance on ritual procedures from one authority but finds a teacher of mystical wisdom in someone else; and he may go to yet others for cures from sickness, advice about dreams, or any other mystical need. Loyalty certainly develops in these ties. Still, there seems a pervasive impulse to limit the nature and intensity of any single bond. By recognizing authority in a variety of distinct figures, people limit the degree of authority they acknowledge in—and the degree of dependency they feel upon—any one of them. If one must respect an official for the political clout he wields, one can nevertheless deny him the respect granted a curer, who in turn can lay no claim to the particular prestige of the religious official, or the dhalang, or the aristocrat.

This dispersion of authority among several figures fits the Javanese concern, really just an aspect of their understanding of idealized power, to maintain what could be termed their personal sovereignty. This is a concern to demonstrate and assure one's own status by remaining impervious to external influence of any sort, including political influence. The higher people's status, the more carefully they try—and the more frequently they manage—to avoid others' control. The poor and low-status are much less capable of resisting influence and constraints. Yet people of all estates, although they may attempt to tap others' power, try to do so without incurring obligations to the sources of that power, because to be subject to obligations suggests that one's own status is insufficient to resist them.

Javanese villagers, in sum, exhibit a consistent ambivalence toward power. Their criteria for judging a headman's performance reflect simultaneous desires to benefit materially and mystically by his power and to defend themselves from it. I do not mean to say by this that the Javanese idea of potency is a deliberately falsified construct, cleverly designed to box a headman in. On the contrary, Javanese deeply wish to find in a headman, as in many other figures, a person they believe truly powerful, one who can indeed provide them with the sense of well-being such power assures. The very lack of strong formal organization in Javanese society heightens the need to find in a superior a guarantor of stable, protective, and dependable order. Yet it is true that, in everyday life, the implicit theory of potency as an attractive and compelling, rather than coercive, force, undergoes some modification. In particular, the idealization takes on a defensive coloring, becoming as much a sanction against some actions as a support for others. Such shifts in emphasis are the fate of any ideology when it appears not as an ideal formulation but as an assumption acted upon in the world. And the idealization and particular context are mediated variously. The headmen of Karanganom, Pasahan, and Kenthungan demonstrate a range of possibilities within which a village headman in Java today is likely to act. But all three men were judged with reference to certain conceptions of how authority should be exercised, conceptions that are also at issue in the family, as discussed in the preceding chapter, and in mystical beliefs and practices, as will be discussed in the following chapter.

4· POTENCY, POSSESSION, AND SPEECH

A powerful figure in Java suggests the possibility of protection, well-being, and prosperity. He thereby invites voluntary submission. In return for the style and, to some degree, the services indicative of deference, an individual wins some assurance of the powerful person's material and/or mystical support. However, ideological precepts and practical patterns of avoidance show distrust of the impulse to compromise one's own sovereignty in dependence upon or submission to a powerful figure. At the same time, such figures may resist people's attempts to put claims upon them. I have discussed the nature and workings of such ambivalence in relations between fathers and other family members, and between lurah and villagers. Kebatinan, all the beliefs that concern potency and the imperceptible world, present Javanese with alternative sources of assistance when special needs or aims arise, and these are the subject of this chapter. I will begin, however, by discussing popular notions about territorial spirits (dhanyang), since these epitomize the conflicting Javanese reactions to power.

DHANYANG

Contradictory feelings about any concentration of power external to oneself became especially clear to me in the wildly dissimilar remarks people made about territorial spirits (dhanyang). These comments were inconsistent from one person to the next, and even within a single person's remarks. Whether every household and every topographical feature, such as a spring or a large rock, has a dhanyang was mooted. People agreed that every contiguous cluster of hamlets has its dhanyang, and probably each hamlet. The spirits that inhabit a large tree or thick cluster of bamboo, which are sure to be inhabited because they are imposing and frightening, may or may not be deemed worthy of the title of dhanyang, but places of great impressiveness, such as a mountain, a large spring, or a palace, are assumed to harbor powerful dhanyang. The much-loved and very powerful wayang figure, Semar, is called the dhanyang of Java (*dhanyang tanah Jawa*). Whether or not a village's dhanyang can be identified with its first settlers (*cikal bakal*) was also disputed, though the identification was often made. A related issue was whether or not a dhanyang is the spirit of a once-living person. A few informants identified the dhanyang of Java's great volcanoes as the spirits of the Hindu-Javanese gods, banished there on Java's conversion to Islam. Others said instead that the spirits of Java's nine Muslim proselytizers (*wali sanga*) inhabited those peaks. As for the houseyard, some among those informants who attributed dhanyang to every yard identified them with the miscarried foetuses that are buried outside the front door.

Vagueness about the origins and distribution of dhanyang is less surprising than the contradictory impressions of their intentions. Many people expressed the rather starchy view that dhanyang are tutelary spirits who do only good, or at most harm only those people who deliberately provoke them. Numerological calculations (*pétungan*) that try to make a ritual coincide with a day (one out of three) when the village dhanyang are "awake" and so are able to fend off external threats imply the dhanyang's benevolent interest in the village's inhabitants.[1] Much talk and behavior, however, indicate other views.

The dhanyang of a village often appears to people, as it does in Pasahan, in the form of a very large snake. "You can tell it's not a real snake because of the way it moves and the fact that it's not afraid of you," one man said. Its appearance is usually thought to bode ill: it has been affronted in some way. Failure to make all the requisite offerings in the proper manner on ritual occasions will arouse a dhanyang's rather peevish wrath. One must stay on its good side and avoid speaking of it too boldly. Yet although respect is certainly in order, and some people said that of course one used refined language (basa) to the dhanyang, others answered my questions about this in a way

[1] The three possible conditions of the dhanyang make up a formula (rapal) that one repeats, counting it off against the number mystically associated with the day on which one proposes to hold a ritual. An auspicious day's number will count off such as to end on "awake." On the other two days the dhanyang are "having intercourse" or "asleep." This is the only context I came across in which dhanyang were identified as plural and a couple. Javanese nouns are not marked for number, and pronouns are marked for neither number nor gender, so such issues are always somewhat vague. What the formula suggests about dhanyang need not correspond to actual conceptions about them in any case. Formulas are not explanations or descriptions: they are tools.

best summed up in one man's words: "Oh no, you wouldn't use re-fined language with the dhanyang. Then it would start getting up-pity."

People sometimes attributed overtly hostile impulses to a dhan-yang. These ranged from causing traffic accidents, as in Pasahan, to hiding a valuable brooch of Pak Lurah Karanganom. The snake that bit Mbok Paira was generally believed to have been a dhanyang. Then again, when travelling, one can request the protection of one's own village's dhanyang and even ask its good offices in contacting the dhanyang of the village of one's destination. This protection, like the assistance one requests of one's ancestors, suggests the benevolent in-fluence of a person of superior status. Indeed, people sometimes refer to their ancestors collectively as their dhanyang.

A few informants accounted for the contradictions in the behavior of dhanyang by distinguishing between "settled" dhanyang (*dhanyang tetep*) and "wild" dhanyang (*dhanyang liar*). In this way, they applied to them the general Javanese suspicion of anything that lacks a spec-ifiable location. Some people distinguished dhanyang according to their status and used this to explain the discrepancies in their behav-ior: high-status dhanyang are benevolent, but among their underlings are some that are irresponsible and hard to control. One man ex-plained that lesser dhanyang sometimes bother or trouble people, but that important ones have submitted to the king (*wis tundhuk karo ratu*). The comment implies that great and well-behaved dhanyang enter into the rules of hierarchy that order Javanese society. To be submissive to the king is in a sense the prototypical sign of social ac-countability in traditional Javanese ideology. Yet even important dhanyang are suspect. Several people mentioned that the dhanyang of the palace in Solo fear/respect (wedi) the king when he is present but must be carefully propitiated to prevent mishap in the king's ab-sence.

The simultaneously protective and threatening nature of the dhan-yang focuses ambivalent Javanese reactions to any concentration of power, and in this regard the instance of the palace dhanyang is par-ticularly telling. This dhanyang is thought especially powerful, be-cause the palace is the residence of a man in whom great kakuwatan batin inheres, and no average dhanyang would be able to live in prox-imity to such concentrated potency. The dhanyang's status, there-fore, complements and also demonstrates the power of the king. Yet it also evokes the possibility of disaster: if the restraint of the king's presence is removed and the dhanyang is no longer bound by the constraints of hierarchy, then it may use its power destructively.

The palace dhanyang constitutes a counterpart to the king, one that lives in the invisible realm of spirits. (Dhanyang are often described as marshalling armies of subordinate spirits, just as the king marshals human soldiers.) The ideal king—like the ideal father, the ideal guru, and the ideal lurah—is without selfish or aggressive impulses of any kind. He is the apex of order. Nevertheless, the paired figures of king and palace dhanyang actually exemplify the equivocal nature of any concentration of power. That is, the idealized view of power as potency sees its concentration manifested in a hierarchy of individuals joined in voluntary submission to the protective king. In the dark side of the dhanyang, however, lurks the impression that in this stable order there inheres competition, conflict, and the threat of violence as well. Although neither king, lurah, father, or guru is believed given to hostile impulses, behavior and ideology point in each case to a deep-seated distrust of their authority.

MAGICAL MEANS AVAILABLE TO THE POTENCY-DEFICIENT

Because concentrations of potency are always equivocal—potentially beneficent and potentially threatening to one's own integrity and status—finding ways to benefit by such potency outside oneself is always problematic. Asceticism represents the ideal way to accumulate potency, increase one's status, and attain one's ends in Java. Not everyone, though, has the stamina to practice ascetic rigors consistently. In fact, very few people have such resolve. For the many people whose reserves of potency are low, various means are available by which to make up for their own batin's deficiencies. Among such means, to "seek wealth" through a compact with a spirit is thought perverse; to consult a magic specialist or other respected elder is found eminently respectable; to visit a medium is believed efficacious but suspect; to make a vow is thought risky and unpredictable in its effects. In each case, people trade some degree of their own sovereignty by submitting to an external authority, in the hope of attaining some end. And just as asceticism augments power by making people exempt from the power other's speech might have over them, and by making their own speech effective in the world, so these alternate sources of power are defined in large part by reference to language.

Seeking Wealth

In contrast to asceticism, which is a version of sacrifice said to be directed to God, Javanese conceive of another, monstrous form of sacrifice, in which one gains selfish ends by making secret deals with spirits. This Faustian practice is usually called "to seek wealth" (*golèk pasugihan*), and the spirits with which one traffics are called *inthuk* and *buta ijo*.[2] A person goes to some special spot, usually in a cemetery, summons a spirit, and strikes a deal with it. In return for providing people with great wealth, the spirit will take the lives of their children and other kin. An alternative or additional effect is that people will become the spirit's slaves after death and join the armies of Nyai Rara Kidul, the dread goddess of the South Sea. Bu Cerma explained, "They say the *inthuk* hops on your shoulders and says, 'Okay, I supported you all those years. Now you support me.' " Whereas any wealth one gains from ascetic exercise comes directly from God and therefore implies no one else's loss, wealth gained from an inthuk comes out of the hands of other people. If people come home from the market with less money than they thought they had, they realize that an inthuk has gotten away with some of it and taken it to its clients. Any person who enjoys particularly good fortune, especially sudden good fortune, will be said to have gotten an inthuk. Neighbors, Bu Cerma said, had whispered such things about her and her husband when Pak Cerma was such a successful dhalang in the early sixties, especially after the death of their five-year-old daughter. Having reported this in hurt and outrage, she went on to state as common knowledge that the people with a little store up the road enjoyed the services of a *buta ijo*.

To seek wealth (*golèk pasugihan*) perverts relations of exchange. In fact, it is a demonic version of asceticism, a negative form of sacrifice that contrasts with asceticism's positive form. Instead of suffering hardship in order to reap eventual rewards, it implies enjoying material pleasure at the expense of those people whose money is stolen and of those kin whose souls are snatched. One does not win potency

---

[2] The latter term means "green monster," but I found no way to distinguish the two kinds of spirits except in name.

with which to assure the well-being of family and suppliants, as in asceticism, but rather sacrifices other people to gain one's own pleasures. At the same time, one indebts oneself to spirits. So rather than insulating people from spirits and obligations, to seek wealth binds them to spirits in perverse ways. In particular, the parody of patron-client relations that inheres in the spirit's servitude takes a monstrous turn in the reversal of roles after death.

Magic Specialists

Appeals to respected elders (wong tuwa) and magic specialists (*dhukun*) for assistance in matters of kebatinan are culturally approved and very frequent. Any person thought to have much potency is a wong tuwa. The term, as previously mentioned, means literally "old person." It can also mean parent, or any relative of one's parents' generation or older. Then again, it can refer to quite a young person, even someone younger than oneself, if he is thought to have substantial kakuwatan batin. (I use the masculine pronoun because most people to whom one goes for assistance are male; women would not usually be thought potent enough for such work. The exception is *dhukun bayi*, women who double as midwives and as magic specialists before, during, and after childbirth.) *Dhukun* are those people who have set up shop: they are recognized as experts and people come to them for assistance frequently. The slightly commercial look to this makes the term *dhukun* equivocally marked, slightly demeaning in some people's view, whereas the term *wong tuwa* is unambiguously positive in connotation. But almost everyone in Java, with the exception of some among the most highly educated reformist Muslims, has occasion at some point to consult a dhukun. This may be to inquire about mystically auspicious dates for a ritual, to win someone in love, to improve one's profits in trade, to seek a cure for sickness, to ask for clues in a search for lost or stolen goods, to assure success in one's studies or a bid for higher bureaucratic rank, or in pursuit of many other needs.

The procedure is usually roughly as follows. If a couple goes to a dhukun together, on arriving at the dhukun's house, the woman goes to the kitchen to give the dhukun's wife small gifts of food that guests take their hosts (*olèh-olèh*). A man sits in the front room, which is where public business is conducted, and his wife eventually joins him there. The man lays an unopened pack of cigarettes on the low table around which he and his host sit. Underneath the cigarettes he conceals some money. (During my stay, a Rp. 500 note was the usual sum given.) As in all polite encounter in Java, a visit is likely to begin with considerable amounts of small talk while visitors and host are served sweet tea. Only slowly do the visitors approach their purpose. As they do so, their voices may drop to a whisper, and references to individuals are obscured by the use of kinship terms and pronouns rather than names. The dhukun can respond in any of several ways. He may fulfill their request for assistance by using incense, magical formulas, and other paraphernalia, perhaps in the presence of his visitors, often instead in the innermost part of the house. Most dhukun also give ritual prescriptions to the visitors. The latter excuse themselves soon after. If no other people are waiting to see the dhukun, one visit can last, what with all the preliminary chatting, a couple of hours. If there is a line, however, or if the dhukun has other things to do, he may treat his visitors with much the same brusqueness many Western doctors display, hurrying his guests to come to the point in a manner few Javanese hosts would otherwise dare to assume.

A dhukun usually enjoys some prestige and receives greater deference than many other people of similar wealth and age. That becoming a dhukun represents one way to gain prestige and improve one's status was made clear by an incident in Purwasari. An older man, Pak Murti, had risen to high rank in the Dutch colonial administration. He and his wife both had ties to the aristocracy, and they had moved into, or really to the edge of, the village from town only after Pak Murti's retirement. They had been sufficiently well connected, politically agile, and lucky to find their son employment in the Jogja tax office. But although Pak Murti had the quiet, self-effacing dignity of some high-status Javanese males and was much respected for it, his only son Nur obviously felt superior to his peasant neighbors and was heartily disliked. He was apparently no more politic in his work. His conceit and irresponsibility eventually cost him his job at the tax office, and while his father despaired of finding him another post, Nur started spending his time with a young but noted dhukun, an army officer stationed nearby. This friend began holding regular hours, receiving visitors at the Murtis' home, and soon Nur had set himself up as a dhukun as well. (His father was just Dutchified enough to be somewhat dismayed, but also religious enough, in a syncretist Javanese understanding of religion, to be impressed.) The respect Nur garnered as a result was not that, based on aristocratic title and/or high office in the civil service, to which the *priyayi* ("aristocrats," and more recently, any high-status people) are accustomed. Yet it maintained the distinction between him and the neighbors, which was probably the point.

To maintain their prestige, dhukun and wong tuwa of any sort must never expressly demand payment for their services. To do so would prove their cupidity and selfishness, traits that would necessarily vitiate all claims to potency. When in the early seventies an amazing percentage of the Javanese populace was betting avidly on the national lottery, many people stressed that a dhukun could not place such bets. If he did, his potency would immediately disappear. In fact, he would show himself, in his desire for mere money, without potency. However, a dhukun can assume that gifts of snacks, cigarettes, and cash will be given him by those requesting his assistance. Furthermore, people always mention that if a dhukun enables you to make money at your trade, say, or gain any other goal, of course you'll "remember" that fact and give him some money or other gift in thanks. Though represented as a spontaneous gesture of gratitude, I suspect there exists some belief that failure to complete the exchange in this way might provoke mysterious retaliation. In any case, as in sacrifice, one cannot impute lack or desire to a dhukun or wong tuwa. Yet one must acknowledge his status through tribute.

The success or failure of a dhukun's ministrations depend in part on his potency, and in part on whether or not he is compatible (jodho) with his suppliant. The issue of compatibility admits of little discussion. A suppliant's firm belief in a dhukun's or wong tuwa's potency is always deemed a *sine qua non*. Without it, no efforts will succeed. But beyond that, one can only wait and see. Whether or not someone is compatible with any particular dhukun can be determined only retrospectively, by whether or not his advice and ministrations worked.

The capacity of dhukun and other wong tuwa to cure the sick takes on special importance when someone suffers possession by spirits. In such cases, the wong tuwa is often asked to come to the patient to dispel the spirit. In children, sudden fevers and seizures of any sort are usually attributed to spirits. In adults, possession is usually manifested in wild speech and uncontrollable action, occasionally in sustained silence or fainting. Raving words and silence alike are attributed to the spirit, who is said to have taken its victim's voice.[3] The wong tuwa is able to defeat the spirit provided his batin is stronger. If the spirit is less potent (*kalah kuwat*), then it fears/respects (wedi) the wong tuwa, and when the latter demands to know who it is and what it is after, the spirit answers meekly and truthfully (still using, of course, the victim's voice). It may then explain that some human's (unintended) slight provoked its attack. Often, there is no clear cause. In any case, it is pressured by the wong tuwa to express some request, usually for some kind of offering. The satisfaction of this request should suffice to rid the person of the spirit. (If the patient has a relapse, it may be said that several spirits took possession of the person, simultaneously or in turns.) A mute spirit (*dhemit bisu*) is considered particularly dangerous and hard to deal with, since then it is more difficult to ascertain its identity and make it articulate a particular wish. However, a particularly potent wong tuwa may not even need to enter into dialogue with a spirit. The strength of his presence may be such that the spirit flees at his mere approach.

When Javanese speculate on what impels spirits to take possession of people, they often attribute to them the characteristics of naughty children or dissatisfied and rather ill-mannered adults. For example, a spirit may feel hungry or thirsty, so it takes possession of someone in order to force people into giving it offerings, which are its food and drink. It may simply be feeling lonely, or perhaps impish, or insulted by some human's thoughtlessness. That spirits are so bothersome and truculent follows from their origins. They are the spirits of stillborn babies, or of people who died suddenly, violently, and "before their time," before the time appointed by God. (The theological inconsistency, between God's omnipotence and the contravention of his wishes suggested by someone dying "before his time," never seemed to bother my informants.) Such people were frustrated by death, they were not yet ready to quit the world when they lost their human identity, and God will not yet accept them into heaven. Their still-human desires keep them roaming the world, though they lack the physical body that would make it possible to satisfy those desires. Most tryingly, and most crucially, they lack voices. In taking possession of people, they acquire voices with which to speak, and so to mystify,

---

[3] The usual word for spirit here would be *jim*, *dhemit*, or *sétan*. All are unambiguously churlish beings and likely to bother humans, in contrast to the more complicated and higher-status dhanyang.

taunt, or order people around. Eventually, they are forced to express some very specific, and modest, desire, and the little escapade is over.

What happens to spirits' victims in some ways parallels the vicissitudes of spirits. People susceptible to spirits are those who have experienced frustration, anger, loss, and other strong negative emotions that lay them open to attack. Spirits penetrate them, depriving them of all active command over their voices and bodies, and they become passive spectators, driven by foreign but now internal agents. The key term is frustration: like spirits, these people are often affected by the strength of their own longings.

A young married woman in Karanganom, Mbak Painah, was possessed by spirits, and the virulence and persistence with which the attacks recurred caused her relatives enormous trouble and worry. She and her husband had gone through their property trying to cure their small child's illness. Included among the goods they gave up was a gold necklace Mbak Painah much prized. The child died despite all their efforts, and neighbors believed that Mbak Painah's vulnerability to spirits' attacks was attributable both to her grief and to her disappointment at the loss of the necklace. In addition to calling in wong tuwa, her relatives decided to buy Mbak Painah a new necklace in order to enable her to regain her equilibrium.

All these relations between the three agents—spirit, victim, and wong tuwa—turn on changing relations to voices. Whereas spirits seek to acquire voices, a wong tuwa uses his voice to drive a spirit from its victim's body, forcing the spirit into reasonable communication. This first step, which coerces the spirit into locating and naming itself, marks the critical shift between the spirit's autonomy and its submission. Spirits use language, but in ways beyond human control, often beyond human understanding. The ravings of a person who is possessed (kepanjingan: the word is an impersonal passive form of a root meaning "to enter") must be transformed by a wong tuwa's potency into interpretable speech. By specifying a particular wish, a spirit is forced into exchange: doing so disempowers the spirit.

The spirit world is normally beyond human perception, and spirits are not under the sway of normal language. A wong tuwa's speech, however, forces them into submission. So the victim's weakness is figured in the radical separation of consciousness and voice, whereas strength is figured in the perfect efficacy of the wong tuwa's speech. In the first case, people's voices escape them altogether, to their peril.

In the second, the wong tuwa controls both his own voice and the second one, that seized by the spirit. Potency means both self-control and control of others. But as in interaction among humans, that control means above all the ability to control people's voices and actions through the effectiveness of one's own speech.

The importance of voice is that it is the point of intersection between batin and the world. Batin is a constituent element of the self that is not subsumed in interaction: the potency of a person's batin can be sensed only through its effects. Language, as an old puppeteer was fond of saying, "is the messenger of *batin*," and voice is the instrument of language. Voice, therefore, is the means of expression in the manifest (lair) world of the imperceptible realm of batin. The transformation one seeks in asceticism is from having to use language to express deference and desire and remaining vulnerable to others' speech, to being in a position to manipulate power and language in the same breath. It is for this reason, I think, that when Javanese describe a dhukun, wong tuwa, or any other authoritative figure of great potency, they may exclaim over the allure of his person, the fear and respect aroused by his presence, or the instances in which he has proved himself invulnerable to attack. Invariably, however, they state that "the sound [of his voice] is potent" (*uniné mandi*). Rather than enter into perverse dependence upon spirits, he uses his potent speech to exert his authority over them.

Mediums

To Javanese, wong tuwa and mediums (*préwangan*) differ radically. The former are highly respected, whereas the latter are much maligned. It was extremely difficult for me to collect information about préwangan, particularly to observe them directly. People were so anxious to steer me away from them that they would not reveal where any were to be found. The idea of "disinterested" questions is foreign to most Javanese. If I wanted to locate préwangan, clearly I wanted to avail myself of their services. Rather than have a hand in my perdition, friends would invariably launch into an explanation of the uselessness of consulting préwangan. During two years of fieldwork, I managed to meet only five, three of them clustered in a single village in the mountains and locked in such intense rivalry that I was able to speak at length with only one of them. (As with all things suspect and scary, I was assured that préwangan hardly existed in Central Java—and that East Java was crawling with them.)

Yet people go to préwangan for the same reasons that they go to wong tuwa, and the procedure of a visit and the provision of small gifts are also much the same. Préwangan summon a spirit, usually a particular spirit familiar, in some cases any one of several, and become entered or possessed by that spirit. (The word for possessed is again *kepanjingan*, as in the case of a person possessed involuntarily.) Suppliants speak directly to the spirit, or perhaps through the offices of an attendant, and state their particular needs. The spirit may give instructions, ritual prescriptions, or more general advice. Eventually, it signals the end of the audience, either by saying, "Fine, that's enough," or by departing from the préwangan's body. Afterwards, the préwangan usually declares complete ignorance of what has transpired and must be informed of the spirit's remarks.

The bad reputation that préwangan have does not diminish the impression of their efficacy. Even if préwangan are subject to disparaging remarks, their transparency to spirits makes consultation with them particularly effective. Rather than relying on the mediating ministrations of a wong tuwa, a person who consults a préwangan communicates directly with a spirit, clearly present because it is speaking.

Indeed, people flock to préwangan. A particularly famous préwangan, called Bu Dhukuh (*dhukuh*: "hamlet") because she was the widow of a hamlet headman, lived in a village that is very difficult of access, on Gunung Kidul, the great limestone shelf southeast of Jogja. On an auspicious day, despite the miles of difficult roads that lay between the village and town, minibus after minibus drove up full of people who then sat in a large front room, like people at a bus terminal, waiting their turn for an audience.

The contradictory contempt for the person but awe of a préwangan's capacity was apparent in the case of old Mbah Harja in Karanganom. Though physically feeble, he was still considered a potent wong tuwa. Among the claims made for his powers was the fact that late at night, especially on auspicious ones, he sometimes spoke as though delirious (*ndleming*). These words were taken to be the words of spirits that had entered Mbah Harja, and people tried to make them out. The practice suggested Mbah Harja was a préwangan, but no one would permit me to label him such. People in Karanganom insisted he was a wong tuwa who, as it happened, was occasionally entered by spirits. The effort to protect Mbah Harja from the term préwangan indicated the antipathy felt toward such people as a class, even while the fact that he was sometimes possessed contributed to the old man's fame.

Préwangan are defamed on many counts, principal among which are three: that they have neither potency nor esoteric knowledge (ngèlmu) of their own; that by dealing with spirits they indebt themselves—and perhaps their clients—to those spirits, with dangerous results; and, incorporating both of the preceding two points, that they are simply empty vessels for spirits. As one man put it scornfully, "A préwangan is like a slit-gong with a bee inside it. As long as the bee is there, it buzzes [mbrengengeng], but once the bee leaves, it can only make its usual noises of thang, thung."

A wong tuwa gains power over spirits through ascetic rigors, and the potency of his batin, therefore, derives directly from God. That is, he taps into power itself. Préwangan take a very different tack, not consciously channeling potency but instead giving over their bodies and voices to spirits. Their amnesia and the change in their manner of speaking indicate their absence, which permits the substitution of the spirit's presence. While some informants thought it possible to become a préwangan through ascetic exercise, most stated that it is purely fortuitous who becomes one. People become préwangan if and when some spirit decides to borrow their body and voice. Ascetic exercises, in this view, would only scare spirits off, because they give a person "contents" (isi, often used to mean esoteric knowledge [ngèlmu], and also potency [kakuwatan batin] in general), whereas a spirit seeks someone who is "empty" (kothong) and "uninhabited" (suwung), that is, without potency.

Whereas a wong tuwa can drive off spirits by the potency of his batin, préwangan can do so only by pitting their spirit familiars against the attacking one. The outcome depends entirely on which spirit is more powerful and of higher status. So where a wong tuwa forces a spirit to submit to the rules of human encounter—language and exchange—préwangan simply encourage conflict in the realm of spirits (alam panglémunan). Spirits, furthermore, always demand their due. Just as a suppliant always provides gifts to a wong tuwa, so préwangan, it is assumed, must promise their assisting spirit some reward. And here, as in deals struck with spirits in order to gain wealth, there press forward images of dead babies and the armies of Nyai Rara Kidul.

If potency can be known only in its effects, and those effects are most compellingly achieved in speech (or a potent silence), then abdicating one's voice means giving up the primary instrument by which one asserts one's own potency. When Bu Dhukuh absented herself to allow the spirit of her niece, Ndhuk Supien, to speak, she forswore any claims to manipulating potency in her own right. This is probably why her brother-in-law, who controlled interviews with Bu Dhukuh, spoke of Ndhuk Supien as "the one who cared for" (*sing ngemong*) Bu Dhukuh. I have mentioned the word *ngemong* in reference to parents' and older siblings' responsibilities to care for a child. The usage here is inverted: the child cares for (*ngemong*) an adult. The formulation is possible, I think, precisely because Bu Dhukuh ceded her own place to her niece and in effect became a child—without potency, status, or voice.

This cession seems to me precisely what a father seeks to prevent by not teaching his son esoteric knowledge (ngèlmu). That fathers should behave in a manner exactly opposite to Bu Dhukuh touches on the issue of gender and préwangan. Many Javanese seem to think a majority of préwangan are women. I have no idea of actual percentages. What is of note is that many people, though by no means all, felt it to be a fact. Since, as already mentioned, Javanese pronouns are not differentiated by sex, it was difficult to investigate the issue without pressing a perhaps irrelevant point. Some informants did think it irrelevant; others thought women were more numerous. In any case, none thought men more numerous than women among préwangan, whereas males are both thought to, and clearly do, predominate numerically among dhukun and other wong tuwa.

The view, or prejudice, that a majority of préwangan are women, fits the conventional understanding of women's nature, because a préwangan is deemed a *wadhah*—a vessel for the spirit who takes the human voice—just as women's wombs are described as vessels for their husbands' semen. (Both notions, of women as wadhah and of préwangan as wadhah, converge in the belief that many préwangan are women whose miscarried children's spirits have become their spirit familiars.) Many people, as I have said, travel great distances to visit préwangan out of the conviction that a spirit's clairvoyance surpasses any human's. Yet the low regard in which the spirit's human vessel is held repeats the attitude toward women's limitations: that they lack esoteric knowledge (ngèlmu) and that they cannot control their consciousness or their own voice. Préwangan gain a particular kind of power just as an involuntarily possessed person does. In giving up their voices, préwangan acquire potency by becoming apparently disjoined from it. That is, the contravention of their own presence diminishes their personal status, in the eyes of many. Yet however one conceives of this compromise of the integrity of a person's body and voice in subservience to a spirit's control, it is potent. Lacking power, préwangan, like women, and in many cases *as* women, can make their own voices powerful only by putting them at the disposal of more powerful agents. In so doing, they play on their marginality to gain some form of power.[4]

The people who condemn préwangan also distinguish between gaining potency from God and obtaining it, as préwangan do, from spirits. Yet the vehemence with which all these contrasts are drawn—and wong tuwa, not surprisingly, stress them especially vigorously—seems to me to stem not from préwangans' abdication of voice, nor from the nature of the power they wield, nor from other contrasts between préwangan and wong tuwa generally, but from their affinities. An ascetic absents himself from the world, perhaps even physically removing himself from people's sight, in ascetic exercises. Préwangan absent themselves by breaking the link between consciousness and voice, in seances. The point, to make oneself

---

[4] In alluding to marginality, I of course invoke Victor Turner's important work on the subject (Turner 1969). It is worthwhile in that connection, however, to note certain aspects of the Javanese case that diverge from his analysis of marginality in Ndembu and other societies. Asceticism might be seen as a kind of liminal stage in Java, and dhukun, and especially préwangan, are marginal figures. In each case, extraordinary powers devolve upon a person who surpasses the conventional limits of social life and normal human routines, precisely as Turner suggests typical of "marginal figures." However, Javanese do not speak or allude ritually to pan-human values, or any existential person apart from role and social structure. I have said that asceticism's effectiveness must depend on an individual's capacity to abandon particular identity. Wong tuwa, dhukun, and préwangan all play on their ambiguous implication in, and their capacity to surpass, ordinary social life. But the interstitial moment of ascetic exercise, and the marginal positions of elders, magic specialists, and mediums, do not imply affirmations of any human solidarity or common values in Java. Status distinctions among humans not only go uncontested; practitioners of ascetic exercises and the people who consult with marginal figures often seek to get ahead in the competition for status in the world. They do so without referring to any notions about the joys of fellow-feeling.

"empty" (*kothong*) and so a purveyor of powerful signs, is essentially similar. The word for empty, *kothong*, can carry exactly opposite implications and value judgments in Javanese: it can be used to describe someone who is empty of investments and so potent, or empty of potency and so vulnerable. This ambiguity in its meanings stems from the underlying paradox of the potent self: that a potent individual must be totally selfless, without an individuating self, and without selfish interests (pamrih). In either case, that of wong tuwa or préwangan, a person suppresses the self in order to become a vessel to powerful speech. A wong tuwa denies comforts, wants, and needs, whereas préwangan deny everything but the physical presence of their body. Whether the powerful voice that then speaks is deemed "one's own" or "a spirit's" is something of a supplementary gloss.

Préwangan are scandalous, however, because they suggest that the opposition between the presence and absence of a self *cannot* be overcome. Instead, the terms can only be temporarily reversed, through the medium of voice. The préwangan becomes absent, the spirit present: the removal of the first is the prerequisite to the second. Potency, therefore, depends on the establishment of the lack of a self; the self's absence is the precondition of potency's presence. The wong tuwa, in contrast, makes rather more grandiose claims: to be at the same time something more (potent) and less (individuated, selfish) than an individual self.

Wong tuwa and préwangan both profess that in their speech, their suppliants can attain plenitude—meaning, foresight, and the fulfillment of their desires. They themselves seek nothing, and in seeking nothing, support the impression of their self-sufficiency and potency. It is telling that an accusation invariably made against préwangan by dhukun, against dhukun by préwangan, and in fact, by all experts in kebatinan against each other, is that while the speaker demands and even anticipates no payment whatsoever, the other party or class demands money on the line. This is equivalent to asserting their powerlessness. But it does so by imputing to them desire, limits, lacks. If a person trades speech for money, then clearly that speech has no contents (isi), because potent speech cannot emanate from an unfull (desiring) source, and so it can be of no help to anyone else.

Vows

There is, however, a kind of speech that is deemed, or at least hoped to be, potent, yet that arises out of impotence: vows. Whenever I asked people about vows (*kaul* or *nadaran*), they would speak to me instead of the release from vows (*luwaran kaul*). Poerwadarminta glosses *luwar* by *oncat*, "to get free, to escape," and *ucul*, "to come untied, undone." To *ngluwari* means "to let go free," but it can also mean "to pay off a debt," that is, to free oneself from a debt. In the context of vows, it means to carry out what one had vowed to do, but the expression implies that one thereby frees oneself from the vow, or better, loosens the bonds of the vow.

The critical ritual gesture at a *slametan* (a ritual meal) held in fulfillment of a vow (*ngluwari kaul*) consists of untying a *kupat luwar*. *Kupat* are rice cakes made by cooking rice wrapped in braided coconut leaves. A *kupat luwar* is a young coconut leaf tied into a knot such that when two people grasp it at either end and pull, the knot comes undone. The knot is called *tali bali* (*tali*, "knot," "tie"; *bali*, "to return"), and the untying signals a return to the condition prior to the making of the vow, that is, to being without bonds. My informants' immediate and unanimous impulse to speak not of making vows but of fulfilling them suggested a certain anxiety about vows, one that release from them, or in this case, talking about such release, could alone assuage. (I will use the words "fulfill" and "fulfillment" to refer not to attaining the goal sought but rather to carrying out, or fulfilling, the obligation one had taken on.) I believe that anxiety depends on the notion of bondage that vows establish, and that their release (*luwaran kaul*) undoes. To get at that understanding of vows, I will give a fairly lengthy account of my own efforts to research the subject. I see no other way to elucidate the peculiar Javanese notion of vows as a kind of binding non-contract.

Sendhang Selirang is a pond outside of Kutha Gedhe, near Jogja, to which people often vow to go if their wishes are attained. (Marketplaces, grave sites, and the zoo are other very commonly cited goals in such outings.) One day neighbors in Karanganom, Pak Marta and his wife, took their grandson, whom they were raising, to Sendhang Selirang. He was now three, but in infancy he had been so sick that his grandmother became desperate with worry and made a vow to take him to Sendhang Selirang if he survived. This occasion of fulfilling the vow was festive: the grandparents, who were quite well-off, chartered a minibus and filled it with relatives. After making the necessary ritual gestures at the pond, all of them spent the day at the Jogja Zoo, coming back to the village full of stories about the fabulous things they had seen. Curiously, few of those stories had to do with

Sendhang Selirang. When I asked questions about the latter, the Martas told me that two turtles, Nyai Kuning ("Lady Yellow") and her consort, used to inhabit the pond. They are no longer visible but presumably their spirits are still about, and it is to them that one gives offerings. Yet Pak Marta and Bu Marta each assured me that in making the vow, Bu Marta had not made any promise to Nyai Kuning. Nyai Kuning had had no part in curing the sick boy. As a matter of fact, Nyai Kuning knew nothing about the vow until they showed up that morning to release themselves from it. What Nyai Kuning did was to witness the act of *ngluwari kaul.*

Every step of the way, from pronouncement (or only thinking) of the vow to its fulfillment (such as in the trip the Martas made to Sendhang Selirang), admits of a great range of variation, and I was given contradictory comments about each of these steps. I find this ethnographic richness rather trying, but it is interesting to note precisely where Javanese ideas on the subject are most consistent and where they are most likely to vary. The two points people had perfectly clear were that: 1) a vow that went unfulfilled would cause its maker great misfortune; and 2) the fulfillment of the vow had to be witnessed (*disekseni*), and the person who acted as witness had to attest verbally to having seen the vow fulfilled. Less clear was: 1) to what agency a person appealed in making a vow; and 2) what agency insisted on its fulfillment and punished all lapses.

Vows are made in a great variety of circumstances and to many different ends. Often, the latter are no different from the needs that prompt a person to do ascetic exercise and/or consult with *wong tuwa* or *préwangan.* People who wish to pass their exams, or to get a job in the civil service, or (since vows can be made on others' behalf) who wish any of those things for a relative, can make a vow that they will *angsum dhahar* (literally, "offer food"), that is, hold a slametan with offerings made to God and to ancestral and territorial spirits, and perhaps also hold a performance of some sort, if they see their wishes granted.[5] In the discussion that follows, however, I will focus on what seems to be the classic instance of vows, the one I encountered most frequently and on which people seemed most interested to comment: a vow that if someone survives a particularly grave illness, then one

---

[5] To avoid inappropriate implications about vows and gender, I will speak of "people" and "their" vows. However, it must be understood that vows are made by single individuals, not groups or even couples.

will either invite him or her on some outing, or hold a performance (usually a wayang). Fulfillment of such a vow also involves a slametan at home, plus offerings made to the dhanyang and other spirits at the place to which one travels. It is usually fulfilled only years after the desired end has been attained, and if it includes a performance, it may be combined with other ritual celebrations (*nduwé gawé*), such as a son's circumcision.

Many people remarked that pronouncing a vow usually follows only after all other attempts at cure have failed. Parents who have taken their ailing child to a series of docters, to dhukun, and to any wong tuwa they know of, yet still see their child's condition worsening, may suddenly find a vow pass their lips. The spontaneity of the act is much stressed. A person cannot decide to make a vow; it is not a strategy he or she adopts. It is, as one person put it, the "bubbling up of one's *batin*."

The formulation of the vow itself is often cited as follows: "Child, if you get well I'll take you to have snacks [*midhang*] at the market in Prambanan." Or, ". . . I'll take you to Sendhang Selirang." Or, ". . . I'll invite Pétruk of Such-and-Such Village [meaning, a particular dhalang] to perform here." The words may not be addressed to the child. Often they are addressed to no one: the first phrase is simply put in the optative subjunctive, "May my child get well and I'll. . . ." Although the verb in the second phrase may suggest a pleasurable outing or performance, informants did not conceive of this as a way of persuading the child to get well. After all, the child may be too sick to hear or too young even to understand the words. The efficacy of the vow does not lie in any immediate effect on the child's state of mind.

I attempted to find out what agency responded to or intervened on behalf of someone who had pronounced a vow. However, my attempts to fit vows into some version of contract were rejected by most of my informants. A vow, they insisted, was not directed to any agent: it implied striking no bargain. Yes, there are situations such as what I described in the Western practice of praying to saints for assistance: namely, to go to some person's grave, a holy man's or a king's, and to make a request, accompanied with a promise that, should it be granted, one will bring flowers to the grave, burn incense, or some such. That is called nenuwun ("to plead"). Vows, however, are different. If I persisted in demanding to know who cured the child (or brought about whatever the desired end), then of course eventually I was told *Gusti Allah* (God), or sometimes the dhanyang. In the case of the latter reply, it was difficult to ascertain whether it was the dhanyang of one's own village or that of the place to which one vowed to go that interceded on one's behalf.[6]

Dhanyang do figure importantly in ideas about vows, but not as agents with whom one strikes bargains. When one makes a vow, then one's words (*uni*, literally, "sounds") have been, as several informants put it, "written in the world" (*katulis ing jagad*). A person becomes bound by those words. Releasing oneself from such bonds must be done in the full cognizance of the dhanyang where one lives and (if one's vow is to go on an outing) where one goes. It is the dhanyang who can attest to the fact that the release from the vow (*luwaran kaul*) is truly complete (*sah*), that one is truly free from the vow. *Sah* means "completed, good," as in "to make good one's debts." When something is sah, no party involved can make any further claims upon any others.[7] Humans must also be party to this event. One must hold a slametan at one's house, inviting members of one's ceremonial exchange group and the religious official (*modin*), who explains that the gathering is in fulfillment of a vow. When one goes on an outing, one must also buy food and announce to the seller that one has come to the place in observance of a vow. At some places, including some markets, there is a keeper of the keys (*juru kunci*) to whom one gives offerings for the dhanyang, plus a little money. The seller or *juru kunci* must then state formally that he or she has witnessed one's fulfillment of the vow. "So you can't tell some pretty girl who'll be *isin* and just giggle and say nothing," Bu Cerma remarked. "Then it wouldn't be *sah*."

Some informants said that if one fails to fulfill a vow, it is the dhanyang who imposes punishment in the forms of diminishing income,

---

[6] One informant managed to come up with a complicated system of messages relayed among dhanyang, but I couldn't help feeling that this Pony Express of territorial spirits was the direct result of Western pressure.

[7] A dhalang made this clear to me when he spoke of a performance he had given at the palace in Jogja. If he performed at a private home, he said, he received a fee of Rp. 150,000 for one night. At the end of the palace performance, he was given Rp. 5,000. He had no interest in such a trifling sum, he maintained, but the organizers would not hear of him not taking the money. By accepting it, and signing for it, he made the transaction sah. "That means you can't complain about it (*mboten kénging grenengan*)," he explained. The gloss neatly captures the neutralization of debt and feeling that making something sah should accomplish.

sickness to oneself or one's kin, and other misfortune such as Javanese usually ascribe to mystical influence. "After all," as some people put it, "here the *dhanyang* has been looking forward to all those good things to eat [the offerings to be made at the slametan], and you act like you've forgotten all about it." Even though dhanyang may enforce the commitment, however, it does not bring about the vow's goal. The effectiveness of a vow, people often repeated, is just *ndilalah*—it just happens.

The word *ndilalah* probably refers, etymologically, to God. In popular speech, though, it has no such theological overtones. Some informants did speak of God as the agent to whom the maker of vows appeals, and by whom the wish may be granted. Since a vow need not be, and actually very rarely is, addressed to God, however, this account strikes me as something of a *deus ex machina*. Furthermore, implications of exchange in ideas about ascetic exercise are explicitly discounted in discussion of vows. God may look with favor upon an ascetic's pleas for some end in view of his rigors. But such rigors are irrelevant to vows. As one man said, "If Pak Marta has been doing a lot of ascetic exercises and then makes a vow, and I haven't done any and I make one, it is just as likely that my vow will succeed as his." Potency does not pertain to the efficacy of vows.

The notion of contract or exchange, in sum, seems curiously diminished in Javanese understandings of vows—at least in their making, if not in their "loosening." Another point that obscures reciprocity about vows is that the obligation to fulfill a vow remains even if one's wish is not achieved. If people make a vow during a child's illness but the child dies, then they do not fulfill the vow by going on an outing, or whatever thay had promised. Nevertheless, they must ask the religious official (modin) to include reference to the vow when he dedicates offerings in the funerary slametan. Then the vow has been released (*diluwari*), and that fact has been witnessed by one's guests as well as by the dhanyang and God.

I have described the progression from the pronouncement of a vow through its fulfillment. To appreciate the nature of a vow's logic, however, one must consider the secrecy and anxiety that vows usually imply. People stressed the anxiety a person experiences about a vow once made, and they attributed that anxiety to two causes: that one would remember one's obligation, and that one would forget it. To see one's end attained pursuant to a vow makes people pleased but uncomfortable. They know that they "have words" (*nduwé uni*, from *nduwé*, "to have," "to own"; *uni*, "sound," "words"), or "have speech" (*nduwé ujar*, from *ujar*, "speech"). They cannot feel really at ease until they have fulfilled the obligation. This is because they are "fearful of their own voice" (*wedi karo swarané dhéwé*), knowing that "there is nothing so effective as one's own voice" (*ora ana sing mandi kaya swarané dhéwé*). To dream that one is being pursued by a great snake is a reminder that one has left a vow unfulfilled.

As long as makers of vows remain mindful of their pledge, they are not likely to experience any ill effects apart from this anxiety. It is in the nature of humans to be forgetful, however. Eventually, putting off the ceremony until they have some other ritual need (thereby saving on expenses), until they have some extra funds about, or until they find themselves less busy, people are liable to forget that they have outstanding vows (*nduwé uni*). Years may go by without mishap, but in time misfortune begins to plague a person who has left a vow unfulfilled. Should a child fall sick, one may suddenly recall having made a vow during some earlier illness of that child. But even then one may be completely forgetful of it. If one goes to a wong tuwa for help, the latter may discern that an unkept vow lies at the root of the trouble. "You're suffering from your own speech" (*Kowé kena kandhamu dhéwé*), one man quoted such a wong tuwa as saying. If the wong tuwa is particularly prescient, he may be able to say, "It was at such and such a time. You were sitting facing this particular direction." Most of my informants said, however, that the wong tuwa could not recover the content of the vow itself. Only the maker of the vow could do that. And if he can't, as one man put it, "You're in trouble, eh?" (*Rak cilaka ta?*).

Makers of vows run special risk of amnesia in light of prejudices against either writing a vow down (a possibility my informants, literate but not accustomed to keeping written records, found thoroughly bizarre) or revealing it to anyone else. Once, when his son was sick, Pak Paira vowed that he would hold a wayang at the time of the son's circumcision if the boy pulled through. It was years later and only a few days before the circumcision was to take place that he revealed this fact to his wife, causing Mbok Paira enormous difficulty getting the money together and making arrangements for it in time.

There seems a general tendency to keep a vow secret until one feels ready to fulfill it, perhaps because secret speech often seems more potent as well as more dangerous than revealed speech. Not everyone is as private as Pak Paira was about vows they have made, but in all the conversations I had on the subject, no one ever told me of a vow that remained unfulfilled. Instead, people assured me that all the vows they had ever made were now completed (sah). Some people denied they had ever made a vow, only eventually admitting to having done so once or twice.

The secrecy that tends to surround as yet unfulfilled vows may be linked to the obfuscation of exchange that vows suggest. The power of a vow must lie in part in its nature as a concealed exchange: it is speech that may or may not be addressed to anyone, may or may not even be spoken, may or may not be effective, yet that will, if not loosened, turn back upon its source, causing him or her misfortune. A vow is one's own speech (uniné dhéwé), but with the peculiar twist that it is directed to no listener and that its meaning binds oneself, not others. It is also a secret deal: its secrecy makes it dangerous, since no one will be able to help one recall it; and the very vagueness about who or what hears and notes a vow makes it all the more imposing. Perhaps it could even be linked to "seeking wealth" (golèk pasugihan), with the critical difference that one puts one's future in hock, rather than signing away one's own and one's kin's souls. In any case, the importance ascribed to the public nature of the release from the vow (the luwaran kaul)—that it be witnessed, that the witness attest to the fulfillment of the vow, and that the witness accept some form of remuneration—this emphasis must depend on its opposition to the private and (in a way I will explain in a moment) almost perverse nature of the original statement. The public ceremonial of luwaran kaul replaces the shadowy contract of the vow with clear, completed, and so neutral transactions. It replaces a vague exchange with two other, more ordinary types of exchange: the long-term and sanctioned exchanges among all members of a hamlet ceremonial group that the slametan brings into play, and the momentary and so particularly clear-cut exchange with a seller at a market.

The point remains, however, that most of my informants would not allow that vows represented a version of exchange or contract of any sort. If a vow is not a bargain struck with God, or with the dhanyang or other supernatural agents, what effect can its maker hope to have over events? The most obvious answer, and one that I believe true in outline, is that its effectiveness depends on a magical homol-

ogy similar to the one I have suggested in discussing asceticism in Java
(see Chapter 1). Faced with a situation they cannot control, people
set up, parallel to it, a situation they can control. The intention to
accomplish one action, an intention it is within one's own capacity
to carry out, suggests a conjunction between intent and fulfillment
that is to be repeated (before the fact) in the conjunction of goal and
its attainment in the crisis at hand.

These general remarks can be phrased to fit the Javanese context
more closely. People who make a vow find themselves subject to an
intense desire. Release from a vow, or projection of such release in
measures it is within one's capacity to take, repeats (once again, before the fact) release from desire. The power of vows then lies in the
definition of a wish and its attainment on the one hand, and of
speech and its fulfillment on the other, as disjunctions that can be
and are bridged. In this respect, the logic of vows resembles the logic
of asceticism.

Allusion to mastery and its lack, however, points to what distinguishes vows from asceticism as well. When people spontaneously
voice a vow, they express a commitment, thereby making themselves
subservient to their own words. But these are no longer their own
words. They have been inscribed in the world. They contrast precisely with the ideal form of speech, speech that is effective (mandi), in
which the world submits to one's own power and that submission is
manifested in the world's instantaneous conformity to one's speech.
Rather than resisting language, as in asceticism, and becoming capable of manipulating it, in making a vow one delivers oneself over
to it: one promises to make one's own actions conform to speech. To
say of a vow that the words are effective (mandi) does not mean that
they are effective over the world. They are effective, quite the opposite, only in reference to oneself. Practitioners of ascetic exercises
give up their voice as a form of self-mastery and give up self in order
to gain some mastery over the world. Makers of vows give up their
voice and self-mastery—because commitment impinges on a person's
freedom of action, and that is a loss of self-mastery—in return for immediate gratification. They must then take responsibility (tanggung
jawab) for those words.

It is worth noting, in contrast, that situations in which Westerners
feel bound by their own speech, such as making arrangements with
another person, imply less compulsion in Java. All dates are easily

broken. People who arrange to meet a friend at a particular time may see him or her appear eventually, or they may not. If not, the next time they run into each other the friend may come up with an excuse, but he or she may simply say, "It didn't happen" (*Ora sida*). People who are left waiting are not expected to become impatient, nor disappointed, certainly not angry. Such reactions would demonstrate their own lack of self-control, a lack for which their friends cannot be called to account. People can be called to account, they are responsible, for their words in encounter. They should seek to assure a pleasant exchange of chat, banter, and—among intimates—even sarcastic teasing, and they should avoid obvious expression of displeasure, criticism, or refusal, except when they are of much higher status than their interlocutor. They are not responsible, however, for anything that happens outside encounter. Another person cannot "hold them to their word" because their word does not stand apart from a particular context. It is not appropriable by others. They can be "held" only to their style. Pak Cerma's son Sigit was asked by a group of high-school girls to teach them gamelan. He didn't much want to but agreed, rather than saying no "and disappointing them." A time was set up for them all to gather at the school one Tuesday. Sigit had no intention of going, he told me a few days beforehand, and sure enough, at the appointed time he just sat about at home. He had avoided an unpleasant encounter by agreeing to go, and an unpleasant task by failing to. And like a great many things that "don't happen" in Java, that was the end of that.

If a figure of authority takes upon himself responsibility for important tasks, he proves his power by this willingness to take responsibility (tanggung jawab). To *have* to take responsibility for others' wishes or commands, however, means that one is subject to them. In making a vow, one obliges oneself to take responsibility: one puts oneself in servitude to one's own speech. The danger in a vow's secrecy is that the words will prove impossible to recover, yet, let loose in the world, their power over oneself—uncontrollable and controlling—will remain. The element of perversion lies in the fact that these words, one's own words (*uniné dhéwé*), do not appropriate power but let the world expropriate oneself.

In abandoning control of their own actions, even if only in a specialized sense, people who make vows compromise their sovereignty. To make a vow puts them in a dependent relationship: they abandon any pretense to mastery over the situation at hand, in voluntary but binding submission to what informants called variously (and in many cases indifferently) God, dhanyang, the world, or nothing in particular. It is not the identity of the master but the fact of subservience that makes vows compromising, and yet, through that very compromise, effective.

PATRONS, SPEECH, AND AUTHORITY

Two issues then converge in the subservience implicit in vows. One concerns patrons and clients, the other fathers and sons.

In Java, people who are without means have traditionally held the option of throwing in their lot with a person of superior wealth, status, and power. In so doing, they compromise claims to status they might make on their own. Any such claims they would then make would have to be phrased in terms of their privileged relations with some powerful figure. When I spoke to Mas Sulis, Pak Lurah Karanganom's night watchman and factotum, he lay much stress on the fact that he alone sharecropped Pak Lurah's land. This turned out not to be true. Pak Lurah granted Mas Sulis more favors than any other person in the village, but a few other men worked plots of his salary lands (*lungguh*) at times. They, too, however, minimized the number of people who enjoyed such opportunities, reserving for themselves the prestige of a special relationship with Pak Lurah. In this way, a fact that was essentially demeaning to their status, their dependence, was turned to opposite, or at least less compromising, effect.

At the same time, people who have become dependents of an important person gain satisfaction of immediate needs and/or are assured long-term security. In this relationship there is something of the same tendency, as in vows, to obscure the exchange relations that underlie it. Mas Sulis, for all his efforts on behalf of Pak Lurah Karanganom, did not have "rights," nor did he receive any salary. Like many Javanese in subordinate positions, he could assume Pak Lurah's gifts of money when he applied for them, but he was wary of asking too often. To make his position more precise, to specify, say, his position's responsibilities and his pay, would have made of his relations with Pak Lurah a series of individual exchanges, each one complete (sah) and so without implication of further ties, rather than the relations "like those among kin" that Javanese prefer to see in patron-client relationships. In contrast, when Javanese villagers opt for short-term, wage-earning relations rather than long-term patron-client ones, they evince a concern to keep themselves free of obligations. They prefer not to have to take responsibility (tanggung jawab), retaining instead an autonomy that clientship, like vows, would compromise.

The political, status-diminishing side of vows receives vivid expression in a particular type of vow that I believe is pronounced only in efforts to cure a child's sickness. Called "to make a child beg" (ngemisaké anak, from ngemis, "to beg"; anak, "a child"), it consists of vowing to take one's child to the market and beg from strangers. A few informants said that one could tell a seller one knew at the market beforehand that one was coming to fulfill a vow. More of my informants insisted that one must play it straight: dress in rags and beg from strangers like any other beggar, revealing to them only afterwards what one was really about. India may have a tradition of ascetic beggars. Modern Java does not, and although a few young Westerners have seen in panhandling a form of political and social liberation, I know of no such sophistication or sophistry among Javanese, who, as one would expect in a society so concerned with status, see in it only extreme degradation. Vowing to dress in rags and beg means committing onself to an astonishingly humiliating act. It thereby dramatizes the subservience and dependence in which one places oneself in making any vow.

The obverse, that in fulfilling a vow a person regains autonomy, was made clear in a dhalang's wife's account of two different occasions on which she fulfilled vows. The first time, she sponsored a performance at a holy site in the hills, and it was a huge success. Another time, however, in fulfilling a similar vow to hold a performance, she let herself be persuaded to change the date from the one she had first intended to a later one. Everything went wrong: it poured rain, few people came, nevertheless there was barely enough food to feed them. In short, it was a disaster. This, the woman stressed, was all due to the fact that she had let herself be influenced by other people in her plans to carry out her vow.

Speech that is constraining over others channels potency, focuses it, and realizes it in the world. I believe it is this understanding of the relationship between speech and potency that underlies a crucial Javanese conception of signification, namely, that potency is manipulable—obtainable, and deployable—through one's relations with language. But a vow is a form of language that reinstates its maker's submission to authority. In making a vow, people throw themselves back into a position of dependence, one in which they hope to see immediate satisfaction, yet out of which they wish eventually to free themselves. Granted, the figure of authority in vows is vague, and the obligation is precisely limited. No one would willingly—though one fears one may unwittingly—put oneself into a bondage that admits of no release. Yet the phrase "you must fear/respect your own voice" (*kudu wedi karo swarané dhéwé*) points to the way that speech substitutes for an external authority, as it reestablishes an external authority over the self.

In this way, vows draw on attitudes toward language that are instilled in children as they grow up in a Javanese household. Because refined language is imposed quite arbitrarily on children at about the age of five or six, and because it stands as the clearest among several concurrent signs of the changed relations they must enter into with their fathers, language and the father must become for them two aspects of a single authority. Children must come to see language not as an instrument of their self-expression, but as an agent apart from them that they must use with care. The feeling that language, especially refined language, has a range and complexity far beyond their own competence persists for life. Most Javanese claim quite fervently that they cannot speak krama well, that there exist whole areas of it that are thoroughly obscure to them.[8] In part expressions of modesty, these protestations nevertheless point up a belief in language's independent authority, over which one can never be truly master.

In seeing their relative status defined by others' speech, people see themselves vulnerable to language. To free oneself from such authority, political or social, requires that one free oneself from such authority's coercive speech, this being the most vivid manifestation of its control. The ultimate escape is silence, though only the self-imposed silence of asceticism, not the timorous silence of a peasant in

---

[8] This view crops up in the oft-repeated remark that a wholly different language is spoken inside the palace. *Basa bagongan*, as this palace speech is called, while extremely interesting, differs lexically from contemporary Javanese in only a few items. (See J. Errington 1981.) As a result, although the rules of its use would be unclear to speakers from outside the palace walls, the sense of most utterances would actually be intelligible to most Javanese speakers, especially to anyone fond of wayang.

the presence of a prince. Short of that impassive silence stands a domestication of others' speech: by making of them wong tuwa, and of
their language a flow of beneficent influence (berkah). This escape
does not reverse or reject the pattern of superior-inferior relations. It
simply extends it, exaggerating it to the point that, in the family, the
father becomes so distant that as long as the son shows respect there
need be little more interaction between them. In a village, by the
same token, pressures upon a lurah to act the part of wong tuwa seek
to transform his speech from demands and commands to expressions
of his benevolent berkah. In either case, the subordinates' strategy
neutralizes the potential of the superiors' language to constrain their
own acts, even as it maximizes that language's capacity to assure their
prosperity and well-being.

   This program for resisting others' speech should complement a program for making one's own speech effective. Studying with a guru or
undertaking ascetic exercises in order to gain potency means *ipso facto*
gaining more potent language. Magical formulas (rapal) constitute a
form of language in which the world becomes susceptible to the
speaker's control, reversing the relationship of vulnerability to a superior's language by enabling people to master in their own right the
potency of language. A particular kind of rapal, *aji pembungkeman*,
illustrates the point well. *Mbungkem* means "to cover someone's
mouth" (in order to prevent him from speaking). Pak Cerma told me
that one *aji pembungkeman* he knew was effective in two ways: it prevented beasts from eating you, by keeping their jaws shut tight; and
it prevented adversaries from defeating you in a court case, by making
them unable to speak. Wild beasts and court cases seem to me almost
equally rare in contemporary Java. But the equation of words in court
with violent attack implies a violent potential in speech, and the existence of such a rapal suggests the ability of potent language to protect one from either. Rapal such as this one are not communicative.
They imply no listener. They are effective, which is what language at
its most important must be.

   Rapal may be obviously intelligible, but they are more likely to be
only partially so. This raises the issue of reference. Potency may be
seen as an arbitrary cut-off point in the continuous regress of referentiality. The relationship between potency and language grows particularly complicated, however, in light of Javanese conceptions of
signs. Language, first of all, may become more powerful as it becomes

more opaque, as it disengages itself from referentiality. Whereas educated Westerners will contemptuously dismiss vocabulary they don't
know as so much "jargon," Javanese often take difficult or obscure
language to be particularly awesome and significant. Words, as in rapal, that are learned and pronounced secretly, and that are (at the
surface level) meaningless, confusing, or pronounced in reverse order, convey less immediate sense but more immediate effect than
everyday language. During the "lottery madness" of the early seventies, the itinerant insane people who add a touch of color to Java's
commercial centers enjoyed a considerable vogue. Many people were
convinced that in the stream of their speech lay allusions to lucky
numbers, and at that time I occasionally saw one or another of Jogja's
rag-clad lunatics standing in a tree, holding forth in senseless ha-
rangues to people listening intently below.

In a very different context, the archaic vocabulary and conventionalized sentiments expressed in the florid style of ritual gatherings
are important in accomplishing a ceremony's purpose. The length of
the words and their marked status as formal and formalized expression
make them no more denotatively significant, but connotatively far
more important than their colloquial equivalents. One evening
shortly after a wedding at which Pak Lurah Karanganom had been invited to speak, old Pak Bayan Krama waxed highly indignant at Pak
Lurah's use of the opportunity to broach a number of topics concerning modernization. This was highly inappropriate and quite disgraceful, in Pak Bayan's view. Pak Lurah was justified to speak of family
planning, now among the standard topics addressed in a wedding
oration, usually as a way to get laughs. For the rest, what one says—
the sentiments expressed and the phrases with which one expresses
them—are *kata mati* (Indonesian for "dead words"). By this not at all
derogatory phrase, Pak Bayan meant that these words were not open
to variation at the speaker's whim. By introducing new subjects into
the ceremonial, Pak Lurah simply proved what Pak Bayan Krama,
who prided himself greatly on his grand oratorical flourishes, had already often assured me: that Pak Lurah lacked a talent for speaking
(*bakat omong*). He should have instead stuck to the elaborately flowery stock phrases that the occasion required.

In these conventional remarks, meaning is only slightly obscured,
since the deliberately uncolloquial style is more difficult to understand than normal speech, but rarely to the point of unintelligibility.

However, emphasis falls not on the informational value of such words, but rather on the way that words link this ceremony to other ceremonies, while distinguishing it from everyday interaction. As language shifts away from normal usage—whether toward unintelligibility or conventional stylization, or perhaps both at once—its referential function diminishes but its effectiveness grows.

I believe the potency of opaque language lies in its suggestion of reserved reference, of meaning held in readiness rather than released in intelligibility. Then effectiveness replaces intelligibility. Like potency itself, language that is formulaic but obscure can be registered only in its effects. One cannot understand rapal. It is telling that the nearest Javanese equivalent to the English verb, "to grasp," *nyekel* ("to hold" or "to grasp"), can be used in reference to rapal—not in the sense of understanding them, but rather in the impersonal passive (*kecekel*), meaning "to have committed to memory," and implying that one is ready to try them out. One cannot understand a rapal, but one can use it and see if it works. The promise of meaning, that is, effectiveness, is then not dispersed in mere sense but, like potency, unleashed.

It would clearly be false to claim that Javanese are oblivious to the effectiveness of direct reference. To address anyone except an intimate without using a title before their name, to refer too directly to any part of their body (especially the head), or to use a word from the crude (kasar) vocabulary set—each of these forms of directness is a serious social breach. That overt reference channels power just as non-referential rapal can is apparent in a prophylactic against being bothered by spirits when walking by a big, dark tree or other ominous spot at night. Although people must avoid naming what they fear (such as a wild beast or spirit) lest they attract its attention, they should joke with their companions and say things like, "Hey, that root looks just like So-and-so's cunt!" The crude language generates heat and will scare any spirit off. Here, it is the explicit reference that transmits power.

Nor are rapal and other forms of speech that are effective (mandi) necessarily unintelligible. A truly powerful person speaks in terse, clear phrases that effect themselves. One older dhalang stated that to need to use rapal indicated inferior potency. It is a stage one must surpass, as one's own speech grows more efficient. Yet here again, the relationship between sound and sense is special. Speech that mandi implies a correspondence so perfect between sign and effect that the latter follows necessarily upon—in fact, is in no way distinguishable from—the former. Rather than promising fulfillment in the displacement of sense, as opaque language does, the straightforward but potent speech of a king, say, makes sound and sense, intention and its accomplishment, intrinsic to sound. This relationship may bring to mind Austin's performatives (Austin 1962). The important difference is that the Western priest, for example, who pronounces and thereby causes a couple to be man and wife, can do so by virtue of his position in a particular hierarchy. In the Javanese view, it is not one's relation to hierarchy that grants one's words effectiveness. It is instead one's relationship to those signs themselves, the extent to which they are subject to one's own control, that matters. One's prestige and status then follow as a matter of course.

The affinities betweeen potency and language in Java stem from the fact that both exist in the world: neither is conceived as in any way original with self. One no more creates language than one creates potency. One seeks only to tap into each, or really, both at once, in order to shift one's relationship with them from vulnerability to resistance, and ultimately, to some degree of control. The potent self is an agent able to join the two together and so to realize them in the world. Language courses through people: one wants potency to do the same. Neither language nor potency finds a source in a person; individuals can only aspire to become conduits to them. People who cannot do this, however, either must turn to other figures, whose potency consists in their relations with language, or must turn to language itself, in a vow. And in submission to such forms of external authority as a dhukun or spirits or, as I will take up shortly, a dhalang, a person tries to gain some measure of control, or at least leverage, over events.

Ideas about self, potency, interpersonal relations, and speech, the subject of this and the preceding chapters, provide a basis for analyzing the particular workings, and the special allure, of wayang. The chapters that follow will treat the circumstances and content of a performance of wayang more specifically, but always with reference to these essential understandings about people's interactions with each other and the world.

5. RITUAL CELEBRATIONS

The dissimulation of exertion at the center, whether of kingdoms, of villages, or even of families, is necessary to maintain impressions of a respected figure's potency and prestige. It is in terms of this concepttion (of what might be called the dissembled center), that I wish to discuss the roles of the sponsors and the dhalang at a ritual celebration. The important and problematic fact about these events is that they are occasions in which "the center" is occupied by two such different kinds of central figures: the ritual's sponsors and the dhalang. Their simultaneous presence is made possible by their distinctly different comportment, the sponsors appearing reticent, the dhalang in contrast appearing commanding and even overbearing. This difference becomes particularly clear in the differing relations they enter into with speech: the sponsors say nothing, whereas the dhalang speaks all night. Yet the principles motivating their respective behaviors turn out to follow equally from Javanese ideas of power and its necessary dissemblance.

A ritual celebration enables householders, as sponsors, to assume a position of some importance and authority, though only temporarily and only within the limits of the ritual context itself. The notion of dissimulated power shapes the relations between the sponsors and their assistants and guests because it encourages the former to seek people's attendance while minimizing impressions of their overt control over them. Principles of reciprocity assure cooperation between sponsors and assistants, but with their guests, sponsors have other intermediaries substitute for them. In particular, these people take on the sponsors' voices. If the sponsors decide to hold a wayang, the dhalang performs this function especially grandly. But he, too, dissimulates his control over his troupe and the spectators, by means of the conventions of a wayang's performance.

In this chapter, I will describe at some length the net of relations that gathers sponsors, assistants, and guests together at a ritual celebration. I do this both because ritual celebrations are the context in which most performances of wayang take place and because they demonstrate especially clearly the importance of status considerations in Javanese interaction. In the following chapter, I will analyze the dhalang's role, and then, in Chapters 7 and 8, the conventions of performance that shape the interaction between spectators and the performance itself.

THE SOCIAL ORGANIZATION OF RITUAL CELEBRATIONS

Javanese speak of ritual celebrations as a realization of all they find distinctive and laudable in their own culture. The mutual assistance achieved among neighbors and kin, the dignity and refinement evinced by sponsors, guests, and speakers, and the pleasure of the bustling scene, are all highly esteemed. Yet there is a paradox at the heart of these grand events. Difficulties about status prevent cooperation among non-kin, and often among kin, in most contexts in Java. Village work projects fall into disarray because giving and following commands would arouse too many questions about relative status among potential participants. Status considerations certainly color every aspect of a ritual celebration, which is a unique dramatization of its sponsors' status. Yet ritual celebrations organize labor and resources on a scale otherwise impossible in Javanese society. They can do so, despite tension, because assertions of status are consistently diminished through the dissimulation of the sponsors' authority.

To hold a large-scale ritual celebration (*nduwé gawé*) is an enormous undertaking, requiring weeks or even months of planning, and the higher the family's status, the more elaborate and expensive the affair must be. Families demonstrate their status in the opulence of the decor, the food, and the entertainments. Above all, they prove their status in the number of people they manage to involve in the proceedings, whether as assistants in executing a great variety of tasks, or as guests who contribute money, foodstuffs, and their interested attendance to the affair. While great material resources must be available to the sponsors, more important still are the human resources a family relies upon to ensure a successful—busy, noisy, and at the same time uneventful—celebration.

The people who assist the sponsors are said to *ngréwang*, a verb de-

rived from a root, *réwang*, meaning both "servant" and "friend."[1]
The ranks of those who *ngréwang* are filled by relatives, neighbors,
and friends. They can be divided into three groups: 1) the women
who join in the cooking; 2) the men who participate in setting up for
a ritual (*tarupan*), a job that often involves removing sections of the
house, extending the roof, setting out mats or chairs, decorating entrances, and if there is to be a performance, setting up a stage, etc.;
and 3) the young people, of either sex, who perform the above functions and also serve guests tea, snacks, and food before and during the
celebration. Except for a few people who perform the most menial
functions (e.g., the man who boils water for tea, a grueling and endless chore), none of these people are remunerated for their labor. Instead, they work in fulfillment of the Javanese ideal of working together cooperatively (*gotong royong*, literally, "to bear together").
Their reward lies in the assurance that when they nduwé gawé, they
will be able to count on people whom they have helped to assist them
in turn. Javanese take great pride in this expression of solidarity
among neighbors and kin.

Despite normative pressures to dissemble disparities in status
among fellow villagers, almost all social relations in Java tend to demonstrate such disparities. So while informants usually choose to stress
the egalitarian side of mutual cooperation, saying that who does what
is a matter of chance, in fact the distribution of chores among réwang
reflects such status considerations. Among the many women who
gathered to cook in the home of Mas Tarno, the rice trader, at the
time of his daughter's wedding, his oldest female relative guarded the
supply of uncooked rice. This is thought a particularly important
task, one befitting the dignity of an older person, because there is
some fear that the guests will consume more rice than anticipated, or
that mystical action by one's enemies will cause the rice supply to diminish precipitously. Another high-status female relative coordi-
nated activities in the kitchen, distributing chores as she saw fit.
There seemed little differentiation by status among the many jobs of
preparing snacks and food. But another distinction by status was apparent in the amount of time a woman spent in the kitchen. Poorer
neighbor women spent many hours in Mas Tarno's kitchen. Bu

---

[1] *Réwang* means literally "friend," but it is normally applied, in contexts other than
a ritual celebration, to servants. (The unadorned word for "servant" is *batur*, whereas
the word actually used for "friend" is *kanca*.)

Cerma, in contrast, liked to comment on the fact that when she went to a neighbor's house to *ngréwang*, people would shoo her out of the kitchen, telling her instead to greet arriving guests, a much more prestigious responsibility. Bu Lurah Karanganom's job at a wedding was to make sure the bride was properly dressed and made up, that the bridal procession was properly arranged, and that the bridal couple were seated in a photogenic manner on their dais.

Status distinctions among males who participate in setting up for a ritual are less marked. All pitch in when walls of plaited bamboo get moved about, or when palm leaves need to be braided to decorate the scene. At the end of the setting up, which lasts a morning, all participants (at least one male from each household in the hamlet) are given a meal. Among the young people who *ngréwang*, older members of the young people's organization oversee the serving of tea, snacks, and food to guests, but all join in this work equally. Young men in their teens and early twenties actually do more work than anyone else, having to address and hand-deliver invitations, help set up, make decorations, serve guests, and afterward, restore the house to its normal condition. They receive several meals from the sponsors in recognition of their service.

The highest-status relatives and friends upon whom sponsors can call for service are asked to seat and receive visitors during the day or days prior to as well as during the ritual celebration itself. At a wedding or circumcision, a line of distinguished men, usually dressed in formal Javanese attire, greet each guest or couple as they approach the sponsors' house. One of them then ushers a male guest to his seat, while a female guest proceeds to the inner part of the house, where she is seated by a female representative of the sponsors. The people who seat guests must know a great many people at sight, since where guests should sit depends on their status. Notables, such as the lurah and any important male relatives or friends of the sponsors, are given places of honor. They are also invited to make speeches. Although such people are guests, not réwang, it reflects becomingly on the sponsors' status if they have been able to persuade an influential, wealthy, or distinguished man to address the assembled guests.

Guests make two visits to the sponsors' house. The first, as mentioned in the Introduction, occurs sometime during the day or days prior to the ceremony itself. A poor, low-status family receives guests coming to make contributions only on the day the ritual is to take place, or starting at most one day beforehand. A high-status family may receive guests starting three or more days in advance, in a constant traffic of arriving and departing guests. Ideally, a man escorts his wife on this visit, but often another male relative—brother, son, or nephew—escorts the woman instead. Occasionally, a woman must go alone, though a high-status woman is reluctant to do so, and nowadays one of fairly high status will balk at going at all unless taken there on a motorized vehicle. If her family has no such vehicle, then a relative who does must be prevailed upon to lend it long enough for the outing to be made.

There is, incidentally, an intricate gradation of prestige attached to modes of transport. Among motorbikes, in general, the more cc.'s, the better, although the dainty appearance and quiet engines of some smaller models lend them a certain refinement. Motor scooters, although acknowledged to be more dangerous than motorbikes because they are poorly balanced, confer much greater prestige upon their owners. This is because they are made in Europe, not Japan, and because they are so expensive. An automobile, of course, is the *ne plus ultra* in conspicuous consumption. It has much less value as an investment than a minibus (which can be used to collect fares on the highway), so it has much more value as a status symbol. The father of the lurah of Karanganom, Pak Karto, was the only person in the area who owned a car, and his arrival at any ritual celebration, headlights glaring, always caused a flurry of excitement. Many residents of Karanganom seemed innocent of the distinction between Pak Karto's Datsun 510 and his son's father-in-law's Mercedes Benz. Since Java is now securely locked into the international market, however, they seemed sure to learn the difference soon enough.

Making a contribution is the real purpose of a guest's first visit to a ritual celebration, and it is women's business. During this first visit, the male guest sits and chats with the male sponsor or his representative, and with any other male guests who happen to be present. He is offered cigarettes and tea, then a variety of snacks, eventually a plate of rice and certain side dishes, then more tea and cigarettes. If a performance is held during the day, he may watch for a while after he has finished eating. But it demeans a man to stay too long after he has been fed. Soon, the woman he has accompanied signals her readiness to go, and they take their leave.

The woman, meanwhile, has been served the same series of tea, snacks, and rice. Unlike her escort, she takes the opportunity of her hostess's greetings at the outset of her visit to give her money and, especially if they are relatives, foodstuffs. The quantity of money she contributes depends on two factors: her own status, and the history of exchanges between the two families. Most importantly, a woman recalls the size of the contribution the female sponsor made to her own most recent ritual celebration, and she factors in this sum, along with relative status and degree of intimacy, when calculating the present contribution. Women display a phenomenal memory for such figures. Bu Cerma could name people and sums for important ceremonies she had held dating back to the late forties. In lunar months such as *Besar*, when a great many people hold ritual celebrations, women complain ceaselessly about how much money they must hand out in this way.[2] Inflation affects contributions as it does all else, of course, and this fact further fuels women's ire.

In a sense, the network of loans a family makes to others who hold ritual celebrations constitutes a form of savings put away toward the time when they, the donors, need the considerable capital sums a ritual celebration requires. Yet the mechanism is hardly straightforward. For one thing, rich people must contribute larger sums, in view of their status, than poor people, so they cannot expect to recoup the sums they pay out. They will, on the other hand, obtain more free labor. Secondly, no one can presume that a recipient family will come through with a gift in return, especially if the family lives far away. Bu Cerma grew much exercised with her oldest son and his wife for making contributions to so many people. Here they were still young, with little income and many expenses. To contribute Rp. 500 or even more to people who were not relatives and whom they hardly even knew was to squander it. By the same token, who was to say whether such non-kin would reciprocate, years down the line, when

---

[2] I became aware of the distinction between auspicious and inauspicious months for rituals not just by variations in the number of wayang held. If I, like many Javanese guests, brought informants gifts of prepared foods (*olèh-olèh*) of good quality—more expensive and tastier than most, so more in keeping with my status, as well as my sybaritic appetites—in some months these snacks would reappear in the course of the visit, served up along with the tea. In other months, though, they would not, replaced instead by the dull, hard, tasteless Javanese version of Dutch cookies. At such times, it was easy to guess that my *olèh-olèh* were earmarked for someone else's ritual celebration. And I received a lesson in being *iklas*, without attachment to base pleasures of this world.

Mas Sarno and Mbak Tuti held their first large ritual celebration? After Mas Sarno's death, Bu Cerma felt vindicated. Now it would be easy for people to "forget" contributions Mbak Tuti had made to them, because when she remarried (as it was assumed she would do in a few years), people would consider the new household an altogether new unit, entering into a new network of exchange relations without reference to Mbak Tuti's earlier union with Mas Sarno.

The contributions that sponsors receive mark the difference between holding a celebration on a large scale (nduwé gawé) and marking a ritual occasion with a slametan but little other activity. (This smaller-scale observance is called "to be busy," éwuh.) In the first case, written invitations are sent out, and recipients who choose to attend the ritual itself make contributions beforehand. In the second case, invitations are made only orally, and no contributions are expected. A family decides which course to follow as each ritual need arises, paying careful attention to the delicate balance that must be maintained in exchange relations. A daughter's wedding is necessarily, and a son's circumcision is usually, celebrated with the fullest display a family can afford. Other ritual occasions, such as a son's wedding, the final funerary ritual, or a house-raising ceremony, may be marked more modestly. A family will be accused of milking people for money if they hold large-scale celebrations too often. Pak Cahya was deeply distressed when his oldest son got a young woman pregnant, necessitating a quick wedding and the eighth-month ritual of a woman's first pregnancy (mitoni) soon after. Each of these rituals would often entail a large-scale celebration. Yet it had not been long since Pak Cahya had nduwé gawé for the circumcision of his younger sons, and to solicit contributions again so soon would arouse much resentment. A carpenter in Karanganom was derided behind his back for deciding to nduwé gawé on the thirty-fifth-day ceremony following the birth of his fourth child. An important family might mark the event so grandly, particularly if they were to hold a major entertainment such as a wayang. Mas Dadi only rented a tape recorder and loudspeaker, however, prompting one neighbor to say that Mas Dadi's only aim was to broadcast to people far and wide: "Come here, come here and contribute money!"

A great assembly of guests occurs on the evening when the ceremony is to take place. Then each family that has made a contribution can send one male, accompanied by his wife or other female relative if one wishes to go. It is a man's attendance that matters at this time, however, because then status, prestige, and mystical influence come into play. Guests gather between eight and ten in the evening, high-status guests usually arriving stylishly late. Speeches follow any ritual procedures the occasion demands (e.g., the meeting of bride and groom at a wedding, bathing the pregnant woman at a first-pregnancy ritual). Entertainments such as music, dances, and/or comics follow the speeches. Tea, snacks, and eventually rice and side dishes, meanwhile, are served the guests by members of the young people's organization, both male and female. The quality of a performance, if held, and the sumptuousness of the food are important status markers, as are the form of illumination, the decor, etc. During my fieldwork (1978-1979), a very wealthy family might serve guests hors d'oeuvres of *lumpiah* (similar to egg rolls) and *lemper* (spiced meat and sticky rice wrapped in leaves), then soup, then rice and side dishes (including a small chunk of meat), and finally, a small cup of ice cream and a refill on tea. (Particularly chic was to serve a salad with mayonnaise. This is appropriately Dutch, but alarmingly ill-suited to a tropical climate. The newspaper carried stories from time to time of hundreds of people falling sick following some enormous ritual celebration.) The number of courses made the long parade of young people serving the food heighten the requisite "busy" atmosphere. Less-wealthy families provided fewer and less expensive dishes: no soup, no dessert, perhaps no meat, and only simple snacks rather than hors d'oeuvres.

Guests leave sometime after they have finished eating, the hour depending in part on whether there are any entertainments. It is thought improper to get up as soon as one puts one's plate down ("as though you had only come for the free meal"), but after a brief interval, guests get up en masse and take their leave, usually at about midnight.

Cooperation and Tension Among Sponsors, Réwang, and Guests

Réwang and guests—some neighbors and kin take both roles at a ritual celebration—are willing to pool their labor and resources in a ritual celebration, as I have said, to a degree otherwise without example in a Javanese village. Certain other projects, such as a roof-raising, or a hamlet-wide ritual celebration, elicit some degree of cooperation, but villagers are reluctant to engage in any village-organized projects. The reluctance cannot stem from laziness: the energy expended in aiding neighbors who hold large-scale ritual celebrations is enormous, and it demonstrates villagers' willingness to work hard for little immediate gain. Rather, cooperative labor is problematic in Java because it raises issues of status, self-interest, reciprocity, and etiquette.

An outsider might claim that if improvements need to be made in a road, all inhabitants of a village would benefit from such efforts and should do their bit. This fails to take account of the difficulties to which differences in status give rise. Who would issue orders and who would make decisions? And what sanctions could be imposed upon those people who failed to show? Can a high-status man with one educated son be expected to send him out to do menial labor? No one in Karanganom formulated such questions in response to my inquiries about cooperative projects: they simply said such things didn't work. But just such difficulties appeared to affect relations between people in the village in need of services and those people able to provide them. When several families had to build decorative walls in front of their yards, pursuant to Pak Lurah's village beautification program, they received some assistance from the youth organization in clearing away trees. They employed laborers from outside the hamlet to do the actual construction, however. When one man had a tree felled and cut up, he also employed laborers from outside the hamlet, even though three of his neighbors were carpenters. He explained that he would feel embarrassed or awkward (pakéwuh) about "giving orders" to fellow villagers, even though he would have paid them for their labor.

Indeed, Javanese villagers like to stress the egalitarian nature of social relations among neighbors. They point to the fact that at a slametan the distribution of food is rigorously equal among all participating households. Yet the way male guests take their places at such a gathering—higher-status guests sit furthest from the door, nearest the inner portion of the house—shows that distinctions in status are always present in people's minds.

Nevertheless, when people hold ritual celebrations, everyone rallies round. Organizations that cater to sponsors' needs also operate remarkably smoothly. An organization that made plates and silverware available for a small rental fee to families holding ritual celebrations, the kumpulan bola pecah, had lasted years when I lived in Ka-

ranganom, and occasional levies to buy new materials were collected
without a hitch. Of course, a major reason for the success of these
efforts is that in them each family's self-interest is clearly apparent.
No family could mount a ritual celebration without assistance, so all
see the need to assist others as a kind of insurance. But there is another point: the promise of an eventual reversal of roles cancels out
implications of disparate status. If Mas Tarno called the shots when
men did the setting up for his daughter's wedding, he would nevertheless be just another helping hand at the next such gathering. Any
suggestion of subordination to him was therefore dispelled.

Etiquette surrounding the initiation of cooperative efforts illustrates this need to dissimulate any suggestion of status differences.
The male sponsor must go to each neighbor's house a few days before
any ritual event is to take place and request assistance formally. If two
men have met at one's home when a neighbor comes to make such a
request, the neighbor first informs the host, in very formal Javanese,
of his plans. He then repeats it, just as formally and completely, to
the other guest. A person who knows about either a tarupan or a ritual gathering but has not been formally asked to come will sit self-
righteously at home, saying that the sponsors have said nothing to
him or her about it.

Although ritual celebrations are remarkably effective means of or-
ganizing people's efforts, some tension between sponsors and réwang
nevertheless lies implicit in them. One rather oblique indication of
such tension lay in a comment Pak Cerma made to me while speaking
of the time he and his wife held their daughter's wedding. He said
that during the days of preparation, he would often go about the
house and yard, joking and chatting with everyone at work at his or
her task. These little visits, he explained, cheered people on, making
them feel "cool" and renewing their energy. He said it would have
been different, however, had his wife gone about in this way. Then
people would have thought she was checking up on them, suspicious
that they were helping themselves to food or supplies. The story plays
on the conventional contrast between benevolent male figures of authority and chintzy women. But it also suggests that suspicion may
color feelings between sponsors, especially female ones, and réwang.

From their guests, sponsors hope for two things: handsome contributions that will raise the tally to a high sum when all have been
counted up; and their guests' attendance at the ceremony in great

numbers. It matters that many guests gather at the time of the ceremony for reasons both lair and batin. In manifest (lair) terms, the many guests and réwang support the family in times of life crises, which are seen as periods of some effort and strain. In terms of kebatinan, a wedding couple, a newly circumcised boy, or a newborn baby and its mother, all suffer particular vulnerability to spirits' attacks. In the bright lights, noise, crowds, and bustle of the ritual celebration, a family gains protection from spirits' interference. It is said, specifically, that among the many guests who gather, at least a few will be spiritually powerful, and their presence will generate the heat that spirits cannot tolerate, forcing them to be gone. In addition—though this receives less normative recognition—the number of guests that sponsors attract matters critically to perceptions of their status. To gather a huge crowd under one's roof indicates great "pull," a social power attributed ultimately to the sponsor's potency. Indeed, the house roof is actually extended to form something like the roofed structure without walls (pandhapa) in which the court assembles to make obeisance to the king.

The importance of attracting as many guests as possible gives rise to a subtle hostility in sponsors' relations with their guests. This hostility is apparent, first of all, in precautions sponsors take before and during a ritual. When Mas Tarno was arranging for the village youths to distribute the eight hundred invitations he extended for his daughter's wedding, all members of the organization gathered at his home to discuss who would travel to what areas to deliver the invitations. Each youth was given, in addition to piles of envelopes, a small amulet containing an itch-inducing leaf. This he was instructed to carry concealed on his person as he made his rounds, in order to make recipients of the invitations feel restless and uncomfortable if they stayed at home at the time of the wedding. In addition to the amulet, the youths were provided magic to protect them from attack when making these trips outside their own hamlet. The youths normally travelled to many of these areas without a thought. I infer that distributing invitations to a ritual is felt likely to arouse hostility and perhaps mystical repercussions. Furthermore, although sponsors wish a great many guests to come to the celebration, to the point of using magic on them to pressure them to do so, they also worry that guests will eat ravenously and exhaust the supplies of rice put aside for the ritual. This would bring terrible shame upon the sponsoring family, and special ritual measures are taken to prevent it.

There is also a curious *quid pro quo* about how late guests stay. Sponsors sometimes tell the young people charged with serving food at the time of the ritual to hold back in order to assure that the guests will remain at least until midnight. Mas Tarno's daughter's wedding ended at 11:15 P.M., when the hired musicians put away their instruments. The groom's relatives and friends, who had to travel about two hours to reach home, appeared happy to get away early. But many residents of Karanganom were scandalized by the early termination of what they had anticipated would be a big, lengthy affair. They expressed sympathy for Mas Tarno, whose dignity was thought somewhat affronted by his guests' early departure, but they also showed some impatience with him, since he had failed to manage musicians, guests, and the food service carefully enough to keep things going at least until twelve. I was told, however, that guests who are enjoying a night-long entertainment, such as a wayang or folk drama (*kethoprak*), feel embarrassed to remain late, "because then it looks like they're waiting to get fed again." Pak Cerma said that such guests often go outside and continue watching, but from some well-concealed spot among the crowd of uninvited spectators.

Rather than a question simply of food offered and accepted, I believe the issue of how long a guest stays gives rise to conflicting feelings because it implicates the sponsors' ability to influence their guests' actions. Visits in Java almost always suggest the superior status of the host. Classically, at the apex of power, the king's immobility was both evidence and guarantor of his own potency, and with it, the well-being of the kingdom. Only when the kingdom suffered under extraordinary attack, such as in times of plague or war, did the king disperse his energy in movement. For the rest, he summoned (*nimbali*) others to his presence. (The word *nimbali* is one of a very few krama inggil terms properly used only in reference to a king. Two others, *miyos* ["to come forth"] and *jengkar* ["to depart"], point to the special nature of a king's movement.) At lower levels in the hierarchy, the rules are not quite so inflexible. Yet although any of the four lesser village officials (*bayan*) in Karanganom might pay visits to villagers with whom they had business, they would usually prefer to summon someone to the kalurahan office for important business, and Pak Lurah Karanganom invariably did so. Among kinsmen, conflicts about seniority or cooperative action often take the form of members of different households sitting proudly in their respective homes, all saying that whenever the other party feels pleased to pay them a call, they will receive them happily. When sponsors, in contrast, gather a great many guests to their home and win their money and attention, they appear to garner something akin to tribute.

The question then arises of how attending a ritual reflects upon the status of guests. Do they simply bestow, like benevolent elders, their good wishes upon the sponsors? Or do they, in travelling to the sponsors' home, show some measure of submission? When important people arrive, in a great flourish, later than other guests, and take their leave as soon as or even before etiquette normally permits, people often joke that it is to make everyone think they have a great many important things to do. But I think it is as much to make plain their only cautious or provisional acceptance of a situation in which they risk appearing subordinate to the sponsors' authority. That is, aristocrats, bureaucrats, and military officials assert, in their grand entrances and early departures, that they have graciously condescended to attend the ceremony, but that in that gesture, as far as status is concerned, they have yielded nothing.

Ritual Celebrations as Status Displays

The ability to attract a great many réwang and guests to a ritual celebration indicates people's power, much as the ability to elicit respectful speech and behavior does in other interaction. Yet although style in personal encounter is dyadic and fairly private, a ritual celebration is an extravagantly public act. Nets of exchange relations, as well as estimations of relative status, become manifest in these brief but dramatic periods of ritual activity. And in contrast to the great normative stress on humility and a self-effacing manner in Java, and despite the constant talk of ritual celebrations as expressions of mutual help and respect, holding a ritual celebration invariably implies some attempt to maximize impressions of one's wealth, status, and above all, authority over other people. Suddenly, all of a family's efforts to assert their status, and all of the particular relations they enter into with others, come into sharp focus. The corporate vagueness that Clifford Geertz has remarked upon in Javanese villages (C. Geertz 1965) is counterbalanced, on the one hand, by the rigorously marked system of encounter in day-to-day life, and on the other, by these highly organized displays of status. Formal and resolutely conventionalized, such ceremonies can be distinguished from one another only by their magnitude, the quality of the food, and the type of entertainment, if any, provided. But in the context of Javanese social life, marked as it is by a kind of willed disconnectedness, these ritual celebrations are breathtaking in their complexity, discipline, and formalized assertiveness.

In view of the status implications intrinsic to visits, and in the exchange of labor, money, and food more generally, it is remarkable that the ritual cycle in Java operates at all. I have mentioned that such considerations make other kinds of cooperative effort close to impossible. That they do not obstruct the endless series of ritual celebrations depends, I think, on the fact that the gestures of respect, submission, and debt inherent in such celebrations, for guests as well as for réwang, are all so carefully insulated from other domains of social life. It is precisely because ritual celebrations gather réwang and guests together so briefly and then release them to go their own ways that they can operate effectively. The subordination implicit in working for or simply attending such a celebration can be tolerated because it is temporary and focused on a single event.[3] Furthermore, it is the non-compulsory nature of these obligations that makes sponsors' ability to attract a crowd an indicator of their potency, comparable, on a very modest scale, to a prince's ability to win the voluntary submission of great numbers of people. Sponsors speak proudly after a celebration is done of how many people came and from what great distances. Pak Cahya made much of the fact, after his son's precipitous wedding, that although he had sent out no invitations, a great number of guests had shown up. He was clearly gratified by this gesture of respect on the part of his kin and friends.

The stress laid on drawing a large crowd to a ritual celebration may suggest to an American an urban politician's need to muster a large number of people for a meeting. The politician, however, needs numbers to gain clout: control over votes, and eventually, labor and resources. Increasing clout means an increasing ability to attract (and deliver) votes, and so a steady rise in power. Attendance at a ritual celebration dramatizes status, but status is not clout. That is, sponsors

---

[3] I have argued much the same point about Balinese *sekaa* (Keeler 1975). In Bali, however, for reasons I outline in that article, such cooperative patterns apply to a great variety of activities, not just ritual ones.

demonstrate their capacity to command labor and resources in the ritual celebration—but only within that particular sphere. There is no necessary spillover into other domains. The ritual system does not make status a kind of capital that can be used to gain material or political ends. Instead, it realizes certain ties, ties that are otherwise obscured or that really exist only in the context of ritual celebrations. That realization can take place only, as I have said, because the obligations that it imposes upon people are so temporary and so univocal. In fact, many kinship ties beyond first cousins receive no attention except at times of ritual celebration. The net of relations drawn upon in ritual celebrations may reflect social organization—kinship groups, patron-client ties, and association through territory, work, etc.—and its history. Such events also affirm those bonds. But they do not necessarily forge, contest, or otherwise alter those relationships in other aspects of social life, except to the degree that a demonstration of potency is an assertion that some may find impressive.

Differences in status do often grow out of differences in material and political circumstances, and these then affect ritual celebrations. It is true that control over labor and resources enables people to stage great ritual celebrations. In fact, that is an important reason why people desire such control. Mas Haryono's status, and with it his ability to stage enormous ritual celebrations, increased upon his election to the office of village headman in Karanganom. And government and military officials will take advantage of people with political liabilities dating back to the early sixties to extort labor and money from them. But they do so most often for the purposes of their own ritual celebrations. Pak Cerma, for example, was obliged to perform for free when a local military authority held his son's circumcision ceremony, and many other artists find themselves pressured into making similar "contributions" to important people's celebrations.

It is possible to argue that the insulation of the ritual sphere from other types of social control represents a kind of degeneration. When land-use rights, birth, and proximity to the aristocracy and to the court as the center of potency all fit together, as they did to some degree until the 1920s at least, then control over people's labor in agriculture, general maintenance projects, and ritual celebrations all went hand in hand. An old servant of the court (abdi-dalem) in Jogja recounted how in the old days (I believe he was speaking of the reign of Sri Sultan VII), an aristocrat or abdi-dalem could go to a village where he held land-use rights and say he wished to hold a *tayuban* (dancing with hired dancing girls). Sharecroppers would not only provide all the labor to set up, they would also contribute livestock, rice, and other foodstuffs for the occasion. The aristocrat needed only to arrive at the appointed time, other high-status friends in tow, to enjoy the festivities.

My informant probably gave the memory an unrealistically idyllic cast, but the suggestion of a "feudal" concentration of control over land, labor, and resources in the hands of aristocrats, their associates, and their subordinates accords with the traditional relationship between rulers and ruled in Java. By this arrangement, bureaucratic rank was defined in terms of the number of people whose labor an official commanded (see Moertono 1968). Peasants won the right to work particular plots of land from low-ranking officials. A person who failed to cooperate in any village or corvée labor projects—and presumably, in preparations for a ritual celebration—ran the risk of losing land-use rights. A ritual celebration, therefore, simply made evident in another register certain relations of political and social dominance. The decreasing importance of patronage ties in Javanese society in recent times might be said to have detached the ritual sphere from other types of obligations.

It would be misleading, however, to take this model, in which ritual celebrations followed upon other, more materially based relations between aristocrats and their clients, as primary, one that commoners have imitated in the ritual sphere without getting at the real political control on which the ritual event was based. Commoners with few claims to any political authority or economic power still lay great store by their ritual celebrations. Dhalang and people reputed to have great esoteric knowledge (guru) are expected to have, and do their utmost to have, great, lively, and crowded ritual celebrations, even if they dispose of little wealth and no formal political power. For them, as I believe for aristocrats and bureaucrats, ritual celebrations are a means above all of demonstrating their potency, rather than of augmenting their command over others' labor and resources.

Clifford Geertz has argued much the same view of ritual celebrations at the level of the entire kingdom in the case of the nineteenth-century Balinese courts, stating that ". . . it was in the court rituals that the negara came alive" (C. Geertz 1980:116). Ritual celebrations in Java, at the much humbler level of villages, indicate how consistent understandings of power motivate peasant as well as courtly traditions. Whether at court or in a village, it is because ritual celebrations are conceived of as an expression of potency, rather than simply of worldly accomplishment, that they are more persuasive evidence of status than the mere possession of bureaucratic position or material wealth. It is possible, therefore, to see in ritual celebrations and the system of exchange relations they establish not the last tendons remaining in a society otherwise gone flabby, but rather the real crux of Javanese society insofar as it is an organizational structure— even though that ritual structure organizes little beyond itself.

THE SPONSORS' VOICE

There is one point about the sponsors' role that requires closer attention because it illuminates their relations both with their guests and, if they sponsor a wayang, the dhalang: their silence. Whether they hold large-scale ritual celebrations or a simple slametan, the sponsors never take overt charge of the proceedings.[4] They are replaced by at least one other person, usually by several others. The result at once diminishes the sponsors' apparent manipulation of the scene and augments the impression of their potency.

At the slametan, which forms the ritual crux of any observance (though, as C. Geertz points out [1960:14], it may be overshadowed in the bustle of a large celebration), the sponsors always entrust a male of at least rudimentary religious training with the tasks of greeting the guests, announcing the ritual purpose, dedicating the offerings, and leading the prayers. This training may consist only in an ability to chant, not understand, Arabic, or if he is Buddhist, Pali, prayers. Even if he knows the necessary prayers himself, the male sponsor must ask someone else to accomplish these tasks. (I will refer in the present discussion to the male sponsor alone, since it is he who appears in the front room of the house, where male neighbors gather for a slametan, while the female sponsor remains in the kitchen area,

---

[4] Clifford Geertz describes the sponsors of a slametan taking a more active role (C. Geertz 1960:12-15). I note, however, that another person still led the guests in chanting, and he was given the nominal payment, wajib, that I discuss below. It also strikes me, after too many years in Central Java, as typical of the East Javanese, among whom Geertz did his research and whom Javanese in the Principalities consider very little refined, that they should be so much less discreet in their mediation of the relations between sponsors and guests.

preparing the food.) Furthermore, although the sponsor greets guests individually as they enter his house, he often asks a high-status guest to greet all the guests as a group, inform them of the ritual purpose, and then invite the religious specialist to begin his remarks. When the chanting is completed, some of the lower-status guests begin dividing up the offerings, distributing equal portions for each household in the immediate area. The men (or boys) who have assembled for the slametan take only a few mouthfuls of food, then gather up the rest and go home. Certain variations in the offerings dedicated distinguish one slametan from another according to the particular ritual purpose. Otherwise, the pattern remains largely the same.[5]

A striking fact about these slametan is that the sponsors are so largely absent. Once the religious specialist starts to speak, or even sooner, the male sponsor is liable to slip quietly out of the room. He returns later, when the guests are ready to take their leave. No other member of the family is present. (On one occasion, the Cermas had to hold a funerary slametan on a night when Pak Cerma was engaged to perform. They left a neighbor in charge, and asked me to greet each guest as he arrived.) The sponsors' silence raises two questions: how can others' speech replace the sponsors' own? And why need this substitution take place?

There is one important responsibility the male sponsor must fulfill, and this sheds light on his role in the proceedings. In addition to providing offerings and greeting guests, he must give the religious specialist or specialists some token payment. (Funerary rituals often include chanting in unison by a group of men.) The precise name of this payment depends on the nature of the ritual need. The most common terms are *wajib* (meaning "requisite" or "obligatory") and *kancing donga* (*kancing* referring to anything that secures something else, such as a button or the wooden brace on a door, and *donga*, "prayer").[6] The sum is trifling, twenty-five or fifty rupiahs, and in Karanganom, the specialist always gave it immediately and rather ostentatiously to a member of the plate-and-silverware organization. He probably wanted to make it clear by this gesture that he did not

---

[5] Slametan held on certain holidays by each exchange group in a hamlet, rather than by a single sponsoring family, differ in that every family provides a tray filled with offerings. These are exchanged at a slametan held in some notable's house, and taken home.

[6] A few slametan seem to require no monetary payment, but my notes are unfortunately incomplete on this point.

fulfill the task out of greed. Nevertheless, the sponsor *must* present the wajib, I was told, to make the ritual sah. Sah, as mentioned in Chapter 4, means "complete" in reference to a transaction, eliminating debt and any grounds for complaint.

One informant explained that by giving the specialist money, the sponsor is telling him, "Your speech is my speech" (*Unimu uniku*). The gloss suggests that the specialist speaks for the sponsor, drawing on his superior religious knowledge to intervene between the sponsor on the one hand, and God and spirits on the other. In order to transfer the benefit of those words to the sponsor, something must be exchanged for them, namely, the wajib. By the same token, what the *kancing donga* given the men who chant at a funerary ritual secures is that the benefit of those prayers fall to the sponsors and their deceased kinsman, even though the male sponsor does not join in the chanting.

The transfer of speech or its effects from one person to another may seem unexceptional in the case of ritual action. Rituals in many cultures are carried out by officiants whose labor must be in some way compensated if the sponsors wish to enjoy their fruits. Yet it is not only God and spirits that are addressed by an intermediary. The male sponsor asks the religious specialist, and often another guest in addition, as I have mentioned, to address the assembled guests as a group, rather than address them directly himself. This suggests the need to have someone intercede not only between sponsors and spirits but also between sponsors and guests.

The pattern is repeated in more elaborate form when a family holds a ritual celebration on a large scale (nduwé gawé). Then a moderator and a series of high-status speakers address the guests and speak for the sponsors, the sponsors again remaining silent. These speeches begin with the moderator standing before the guests, flanked by the male and female sponsors. The moderator's first words consist of an elaborate and conventional welcome to the guests, the moderator noting that he has been asked by the sponsors to extend these greetings because their *bombonging manah* prevents them from speaking. *Bombonging manah* refers to a feeling of great pride and satisfaction, and the moderator explains that the sponsors are deeply honored by the presence of so many distinguished people at their ritual celebration. He goes to on to express their profuse thanks and their deepest apologies for any insufficiencies or errors that have been or will be committed in the course of the event, and their sincere wish that the guests feel satisfied and pleased by what transpires. He states the nature of the ritual ceremony, then again expresses the sponsors' thanks, and again their apologies. Other speakers who follow may choose to touch on other topics, perhaps including advice appropriate to the ritual occasion. But they, too, often speak on behalf of the sponsors in thanking the guests for their attendance and apologizing for any shortcomings. The moderator thanks each speaker on behalf of the sponsors, and later, again in the sponsors' name, he invites the guests to eat their fill without feelings of shame or reticence. He voices the sponsors' thanks and apologies yet again before the guests leave. If a performance is included in the agenda, he urges the guests to stay until its completion. All these remarks, those of the moderator and those of other speakers, while they may be embroidered, nevertheless fall into what Pak Bayan Krama referred to as "dead words." A speaker should never stray beyond the range of topics and sentiments appropriate to the occasion.

Sponsors do often feel themselves inadequate to the task of addressing their guests. Many Javanese lack the ability to speak in the well-turned, flowery phrases thought suitable to public speaking. Yet the rhetorical ability of sponsors is actually irrelevant, as is their emotional state at the time of the ritual celebration. Never do sponsors address the guests as a group.

I believe it is because speech is of note in its effects rather than in its origin that it is transferable. Such transfers are explicitly acknowledged in the case of ascetic rigors. By coordinating the day on which they do ascetic rigors with a formula from numerological calculations (pétungan), people can direct the rewards of their action to themselves, their elders, their children, or their grandchildren. Such transfer of merit can even occur beyond the conscious control of the ascetic. If at the time of his death an old person who has done many ascetic exercises has not enjoyed the good fortune he would appear to deserve, then his offspring or other relatives will be seen eventually to reap the benefit of his rigors. Bu Cerma noted sadly that her father, a dhalang, had done ascetic exercises assiduously, yet never enjoyed popularity as a performer. Since neither she nor her sister had really prospered, she assumed that her children would come in for the benefits her father had earned but not enjoyed.[7]

[7] The enjoyment of good fortune, in contrast, diminishes the fruits of hardship. The

A person can also do ascetic rigors on behalf of a non-kinsman. A young man, Mas Sulis, did ascetic exercises on behalf of his patron, Pak Lurah Karanganom, in order to help him find his lost brooch. And anyone's great success is liable to be attributed by the envious to his having engaged a powerful dhukun to do such exercises in his place.

Speech appears to be thought susceptible of transfer in the same way that the fruits of ascetic practice are. Certainly Javanese admit a curious dissociation of speech and speaker. If vows can turn back upon a speaker, they are a kind of semi-autonomous language. Other instances imply still greater alienation of person and speech. A dhalang in Jogja explained that when he wished to repair an old puppet, one made well before his own birth, he first said aloud to his ancestors, in madya, "I'm just going to fix this puppet's hair a bit, Mbah [mbah: 'grandparent,' 'ancestor']." Then he answered for them, in low Javanese (ngoko), "Yes, okay, go ahead, may things go all right for you." He did this, he noted, to make everything "feeling-less" or "neutral" (tawar), that is, to keep his ancestral spirits from becoming startled or upset on seeing him take tools to a venerable puppet, and to relieve any anxiety he felt in doing so. That he could speak for both himself and his interlocutors in order to attain these ends follows, I think, from an impression that words matter as much if not more for how they fit a situation, rather than simply for how well they express the views of the people who speak them. The dhalang did not put words in his ancestors' mouths, he simply played their hand for them, getting the requisite words into the arena at the proper moment.

Another instance of this assumption of different voices took place shortly after Mas Tarno held the wedding for his daughter. The hamlet youths gathered at his house to receive a meal and Mas Tarno's thanks for their efforts. Mas Tarno said a few words of appreciation, but he then deferred to Pak Bayan Krama, who spoke at considerable length in formal phrases to express Mas Tarno's gratitude. Pak Bayan then switched roles and gave a long speech in acceptance of Mas Tar-

---

sons of Java's most famous dhalang of the fifties have failed to achieve popularity in their own right. People attribute this failure to their father's success. Never having known hardship, the sons lack the potency to become successful, while their father exhausted the rewards of his own ascetic efforts, presumed to have been great, in his considerable good fortune and wealth.

no's thanks, on behalf of the youths. In each case, Pak Bayan of course made fulsome apologies for any slights or indiscretions unintentionally committed, and he assured the opposite party that no grudges were held. Finally, he made a number of cautionary remarks, addressed to the young men from the perspective of an older man concerned for their dignity and good name, about how to behave at a ritual gathering. Most people present paid little or no attention to this Javanese Nestor's copious and conventional remarks. As at a ritual, there was little compulsion to attend to anything in particular; one simply had to be there while the "exchange" of remarks took place in fulfillment of the occasion. Had Pak Bayan not been so fond of speaking, the head of the village youth organization might well have responded for the youths. Yet it struck no one as odd that Pak Bayan should respond to his own remarks, probably because the words concerned not him personally but the circumstances. Even his final remarks, spoken more specifically from his own vantage point, were wholly conventional and so expressive of a social place, that of village elder, rather more than of a particular person.

Funerals provide an even more startling example of this assumption of voices. It is customary for a high-status speaker (often the lurah) to make an oration just before the body is borne to the cemetery. Frequently, he speaks on behalf of the deceased, who takes his leave and begs forgiveness from his relatives, and then on behalf of the relatives, who ask forgiveness on their side. The speaker may also speak in turn for the bereaved family, and then for their guests, at the time of their leave-taking. The speaker speaks for all these different parties in order to make sure that the appropriate words are "exchanged."

I do not mean to say that who speaks in Java is irrelevant to the import of spoken words. Often, it is the status of speakers that makes their words important, more than the words' sense. The grander the status of any speaker at a ritual, the more glory redounds to the sponsors. Yet clearly, spoken words can be thought effective beyond the identity of their immediate source. If a dhalang about to repair a puppet can take heart in words he has spoken in the place of his ancestors, it must be because those words fulfill the necessity of an exchange regardless of who actually speaks them. Speakers, as I have mentioned before, do not express their "selves." Their words are not thought necessarily to represent them as particular individuals: their unique pasts, their original opinions, or their hidden desires. Instead, situations elicit words that are appropriate, and these words should order any individuals in attendance according to established patterns. They should also effect the business at hand. In doing so, individual voices matter inasmuch as the status of the speakers affects the efficacy of their speech: their greater status implies the greater power communicated through their words. But the content of their words need not refer to the speakers personally, as unique or original individuals, particularly not in formal speech. In fact, people's words should not reveal anything idiosyncratic or unusual. The conventional nature of their words should instead enable everyone to make their way through events without worry of surprise, upset, or any affront to their dignity. As a result, less intimately tied to speakers than we are wont to assume, words in Java are attributable to sources—sponsors, guests, ancestors, the dead—who do not actually speak them.

Yet the fact that words can be pronounced by one speaker on behalf of another does not explain the need for such substitution at a ritual celebration. In this context, I believe the dispersion of responsibilities to speak works in two ways at once. When the sponsors do not speak, they dissemble their own control of the proceedings. They diffuse the impression of superior authority that gathering so many people to their home implies. To play up that image of their own authority by speaking for themselves would be unbecoming in sponsors. In fact, they would appear to exert the control over the operation and everyone associated with it that their identity as sponsors suggests but much of the ritual tends to obscure. In confronting their guests, they would be seen to have taken charge of them. Yet for all the baroque expression of deference and humility that inheres in remarks made to the guests, the meaning of the entire event, as an assertion of the sponsors' superior authority, is clear. The meaning of the speeches—hospitable, deferential, but at the same time status-asserting—remains undiminished, no matter who actually speaks them. They remain words addressed to a large crowd of people who have come to attend upon the sponsors at the time of their ritual need, and glory.

The sponsors' withdrawal from the limelight probably represents more than mere hesitation before making too-bold claims to power, however. In their silence, the sponsors maintain the authority of power never overtly deployed. They assume the role of an authoritative figure whose potency is only subtly manifest, in its myriad effects.

So they protect themselves from the vulnerability necessarily implicit in interaction, and from the diminution of that authority implicit in obvious acts. They enjoy some of the powerful aura of the almost immobile and invisible prince. They need never confront their guests directly, yet in their capacity as cause of all the activity the ritual occasions, and as providers of food and entertainment for the people who have come to their home, the sponsors take on the unassailably superior position of the potent, though largely absent, center.

6. THE STATUS OF DHALANG AND RITUAL SPONSORS

When sponsors invite a dhalang and his troupe to perform at a ritual celebration, the guests' attention is further distracted away from the sponsors. The performance once again dissembles and enhances the sponsors' aura of authority, as the sponsors seek to make the dhalang's voice an extension of their own. In particular, they hope his voice will win the guests' voluntary, yet total, submission. Relations between the sponsors of a wayang and the dhalang who performs it, however, are complicated. Is their authority shared, or are they instead locked in competition? The status of dhalang in Javanese society has long been mooted, and the problem reflects ambiguity about the status of a dhalang, relative particularly to his sponsors. Not surprisingly, estimations of his status vary according to the status of the informant. Above all, it is because the nature of a dhalang's authority is so equivocal that such estimations of his status vary from something quite exalted to something close to that of the much-scorned musician.

At the same time, the dhalang himself plays on contrasts between his total control and the dissimulation of his voice and person in his performance. The constraints he must observe and the criteria by which he is judged press him to exert his authority by dissembling himself, and in this way, the dhalang repeats the pattern of exerting power while dissimulating his authority. The diverse and even contradictory images of authority I have discussed in the previous chapters coalesce, in fact, in the particularly ambiguous and imposing figure of the dhalang.

THE DHALANG'S STATUS

Dhalang were often likened in the past to birds on the wing because of the way they moved about the countryside following the harvest. Annual village cleaning (*bersih désa*) rituals have traditionally been thought necessary to assure the safety and prosperity of every village. Often a village's territorial spirit (dhanyang) is said to demand that a wayang be performed in the village for its enjoyment at least once a year. Failure to do so would provoke its wrath and lead to great misfortune. (Some village dhanyang, in contrast, are known to despise wayang and forbid its performance. Such dhanyang often turn out to inhabit *santri* [orthodox or strict] Muslim villages.) Whereas the new rice strains now make it possible for farmers to keep rice fields within a small area at very different points in the growing cycle, the older strains were planted and harvested in a single area at the same time. Differences in altitude and climate did stagger harvests, however, from one area to another, and by moving about a dhalang could hope to be engaged for harvest celebrations in many hamlets. Many dhalang worked the same villages year after year, and their sons after them, the villagers believing it more important to stick with dhalang familiar and acceptable to the village's dhanyang than to seek out novelty by engaging new ones.

Any performer in Java who travels about the countryside is said to *mbebarang*. This is considered a very humble way to earn one's living, only slightly less demeaning than begging.[1] The ritual importance of a dhalang in accomplishing the village rites saved his prestige from the lowly regard in which itinerant dancers were held. But he was by no means guaranteed respect. Frequently, a dhalang and his family took up residence in lodgings provided them by a lurah, district officer (*camat*), or other influential figure. An older dhalang I spoke with reminisced about travelling about the area of Klaten with his parents as the rice came ripe. In one village, the lurah owned a second house right next to his own, and he invited the dhalang and his family to stay there as long as they liked without paying any rent. He even gave them rice to cook for themselves. Such support was of course a great boon to the dhalang. It meant, however, that he became attached to the lurah as a subordinate who, like the many artists and other ser-

---

[1] In the early seventies, a group of five dance-drama (wayang wong) performers arrived in Purwasari. After they performed in the yard in front of the hamlet headman's house, putting out a hat for contributions, they were permitted to lay their mats out and stay the night in the hamlet's meeting room. The next morning they performed again, briefly, once more taking up a collection. By noon, they were on their way. People showed a little suspicion, but also some compassion, for these gypsy performers, and much pleasure was taken in the unexpected diversion they provided. They appeared to represent the last vestiges of a fading tradition, and people treated them with the gentle curiosity Westerners show old photographs.

vants at the royal courts, added luster through loyal service to a patron's name.

Even dhalang who *mbebarang* stayed within fairly localized areas, which they considered their own turf. Whereas now a popular dhalang will be invited to perform in villages and towns throughout Java, in the old days he rarely performed beyond a radius of a few miles from his natal village. Dhalang have always been jealous of their territory. Many stories relate a dhalang's use of black magic to make an interloper fall sick in performance. To this day, a dhalang who is asked to perform in an area far from his usual domain will ask a particularly high fee. He thereby quiets the suspicions of local dhalang, if not their resentment, since he makes it clear that he did not win the engagement by undercutting their fee. On the other hand, dhalang have long had to seek out new areas. Younger dhalang who saw their native locales growing crowded with competitors often moved to other areas where they were more likely to obtain engagements. At present, many young dhalang are advised to move to Javanese settlements in Sumatra, where dhalang are much in demand but in short supply.

Today, the status of dhalang is much higher than it once was, though like the tradition itself, it is in some flux. In the future, much will hang on how well wayang weathers competition from other, increasingly popular entertainments, such as movies and television, and even from commercially released tapes of wayang performances. The introduction of tape recorders, loudspeakers, and tapes of complete performances has enabled peasants to create the requisite amount of noise for a ritual celebration at about a quarter the cost of sponsoring the humblest dhalang and troupe. Since many peasants can afford the tapes who could never afford to sponsor a live performance, not every tape recording blaring over the fields represents a dhalang's loss of income. Still, younger dhalang and less popular ones are certainly suffering a loss of opportunities to perform.

Though rival forms of entertainment and commercial recordings pose some threat to wayang's viability, what will probably prove much more deleterious to the tradition in the long run is the shift to luxury goods as signs of high status. A family that might in the past have put much of its wealth into great ritual celebrations held at frequent intervals is now likely to save its money to buy a television set, motorbikes, minibusses, a car, a Western-style house, and college educations and jobs for its younger members as they mature. This greatly reduces the likelihood of their sponsoring many performances of wayang.[2] Perhaps the most dramatic example of this change is the reduction in royal patronage of wayang in Jogja. There three command performances (*bedhol songsong*) were held annually until 1978. (*Bedhol* means "to pull up," like a stake out of the ground; *songsong* means "the royal parasol." The phrase refers to the movements, signalled with great fanfare, of the king.) Since then, the number has been reduced to only one, held at the end of the fasting month, the Sultanate having found, like so many contemporary Javanese, other ways to spend its money.

Several older dhalang nevertheless assured me, after recalling the old days, that the lot of dhalang had greatly improved. Each year, fewer villages hold wayang at the time of the harvest, it is true. But more families sponsor wayang at ritual celebrations than was the case, they said, before Independence. This means that dhalang can expect to be engaged in a greater number of months out of the year, and on more frequent occasions. Pak Cerma often described the dire straits in which his parents, his siblings and he found themselves during the the time of great shortages (*paceklik*) just before the rice harvest. As they ran out of rice, they would be forced instead to eat cassava root, flavored with only a thin vegetable broth. Often they could eat only once a day. Improvements in rice yield and distribution in Java have reduced the incidence of such hardship for all peasants in the lowlands, not just for dhalang. But to the extent that Java has enjoyed some prosperity, however tenuous, since Independence, it has bettered the lot and standing of dhalang.

Still, aristocrats and many other high-status people have often treated dhalang with some contempt. That they required a dhalang's services on occasion meant only that they employed him as they employed other servants. The specialized nature of a dhalang's knowledge did little to distinguish him from other performers, regarded on the whole as a dissolute and lowly group. This attitude still shows through at times. In 1978, I visited one of Jogja's foremost dhalang, a man whom I had met very briefly at a performance he gave in a village in 1972. Recalling that performance, now six years past, he

---

[2] For a very interesting discussion of changing patterns in ritual celebrations, focusing on the non-Muslim Tengger Javanese but pertinent to lowland Javanese as well, see Hefner 1983.

spoke indignantly of the way the sponsor, a military man from Jakarta visiting his natal village, had failed to greet him on his arrival and paid no attention to him whatever in the two hours or so before the performance started. Any high-status guest in Java must be *ditunggu*: a host must sit with him, ready to do his bidding, for as long as he chooses to stay. Having failed to do anything of the kind, the military man had shown his arrogant estimation of his own status relative to the dhalang's, earning the latter's still vehement censure.

Very different is a dhalang's view of a dhalang's status. In conversation, dhalang dwell at length on the special status of the dhalang once the performance has begun. No one has the authority to interrupt his performance at any time. Even a king, I was often told, must defer to the dhalang during the performance: it is the dhalang who is in charge (*kuwasa*) until the performance ends. To tell the dhalang to stop lays a person—whether one of the sponsors, an important political figure, or a policeman—open to misfortune, a divine punishment for this usurpation of the dhalang's authority. (It has recently become common practice for the moderator to interrupt a performance in order to invite the guests to eat the food served them, but most dhalang deplore this practice.) By the same token, it is the dhalang who must take responsibility (*tanggung jawab*) for the proceedings. If spectators get into a fight, if thieves take advantage of the hubbub to burglarize a neighbor's house, if any type of misfortune occurs, it will be seen as a failure of the dhalang's potency to maintain the security of the ritual scene and surrounding area. So closely is the dhalang's influence tied to events that take place in the hamlet during his performance that if a baby is born nearby, the dhalang is said to have received a boon of mystical energy (*wahyu*). The newborn is taken to the dhalang, who cradles the baby in his arms and gives it a name. The child is then called the dhalang's *anak sampiran* (*anak*, "child"; *sampir*, "to carry something slung over one's shoulder"), establishing a bond that should be maintained throughout their respective lifetimes. If, on the other hand, anyone in the hamlet dies, the dhalang will be thought to exert an inauspicious aura.

Given the grand claims dhalang make for themselves—and many commoners follow them in this high opinion of their powers—it is interesting to note the nature of the relations between dhalang and kings. Abdi-dalem dhalang figure among the ranks of servants at each of Java's courts. At present, their responsibilities include periodically airing the royal wayang sets, which number among the great and potent heirlooms (*pusaka*) of the king, repairing them when necessary, and performing in public on certain days in the year. In the past, wayang performances at the palace were deemed essential to the well-being of the court and the country. During the reign of Sri Sultan VII, a wayang called "after jousting practice" (*bar watangan*) was held every Saturday night, and another was held once every thirty-five days, on the eve of the Sultan's *tingalan* (the conjunction of seven- and five-day cycles on which the Sultan was born, that is, what for commoners is called one's *weton*). Bapak Sastrapustaka, archivist of the palace gamelan in Jogja, lived in the palace compound as a boy, and he recalls that no one actually watched the *bar watangan* performances. They were held as part of the ceremonial of the court, not as entertainments, and when he asked, late at night, if he could take over for one of the gamelan players, he was told he could—provided he played softly. In Solo, I was told, a wayang was held once a week when the Sunan was present but every night in his absence. This was because the dangerous powers of dhanyang and other spirits were much harder to control when the king was not in residence. In either case, whether in the king's presence or absence, the dhalang functioned to maintain and demonstrate the king's power.

All the activities of dhalang in the past are sometimes represented as such extensions of the king's power. Many people, including many dhalang, explain that in the old days dhalang were sent out to travel through the countryside in order to instruct villagers how to show deference to the king. In performance, a dhalang described the appearance of the palace, the hierarchy of titles, and the etiquette that that hierarchy entailed. Most importantly, he taught people how to bow and how to speak to and about the king. In a word, he taught them *basa*, the etiquette of respectful language and gesture, and this assured the king of the commoners' deference. Such a portrayal of the dhalang sees him as an agent of the king, able to spread the effectiveness of the king's presence without the latter's recourse to coercion or even movement. In a sense—though no informant would be likely to agree with this formulation—the dhalang is represented as having augmented the king's power by imposing its demonstration upon people previously insensitive to it. The dhalang, in such a rendering, is an active aspect of the royal power, of which the king, in his stasis, is the quiet and perfect one.

There is a rather popular but quite different reading of the same relationship, however. In this view, the king is suspicious of the dhalang because the latter "lays bare the king's secrets" (*miyakaké wadiné ratu*). That is, people can observe in wayang the machinations and even evil-doing intrinsic to politics, including the politics of the court. A verb often used by informants making this point is *molitiek*, the active form of the root *politiek*. It means "to manipulate people to one's own purposes," and it often implies doing so to attain corrupt or selfish ends. In depicting the weakness and pettiness of such high-status characters as Kurupati or Bathara Guru, a dhalang reveals the scheming that may go on in high places. This makes the dhalang, and the whole tradition of wayang, inimical to the king's prestige. Many dhalang explain that in writing the *Pustaka Raja*, a literary rendering of wayang stories, the Solonese court poet Ranggawarsita doctored them so as to make them more flattering to the dignity of kings. However, dhalang are believed by many to teach ngèlmu to all those discerning enough to understand. In this way, they reduce people's dependence on any figure of authority, including kings and dhukun, by enabling them to attain their ends without having to rely so heavily on others' potency.

This view of the dhalang as something of a free spirit helps to explain the gain in status dhalang have enjoyed over the past forty or so years, at a time when other figures have seen their former glory diminish. Though the Javanese aristocracy lost its political autonomy to the Dutch long ago, the Javanese populace believes their princes still to have been extremely powerful, both practically and spiritually, until the Second World War. Since then, however, the nobility has suffered a steady erosion of its power and prestige. That the court in Solo has now been quite thoroughly eclipsed in villagers' minds was made clear to me in Karanganom. People with any knowledge of the present, twelfth, Sunan spoke of him with little respect, noting that he was merely an army official, and not even a top-ranking one. Many were unaware that he was the twelfth king, having lost track of the succession in the forties. Some were even unaware that there was any Sunan now, sure that the institution had collapsed at Independence. (The Sunan's court sided with the Dutch during the independence movement, causing the Sunan to be stripped of his powers by the Indonesian government after Independence.) These people were residents of an area traditionally subject to Solo. Most were more impressed with the Sultan of Jogja, who has remained influential in the national government. But some said his, too, was only a vestigial authority.

The decline in prestige of king and aristocracy, and their inability to cope with the shifting conditions of state, economy, and society since the war, have caused Javanese to look elsewhere for images of potency. I have suggested that the pressure upon Javanese lurah to display kakuwatan batin may be greater now than it was in the past, as may be, too, many people's preoccupation with asceticism. In any event, it seems to me likely that as belief in the authority of the nobility has declined, in particular the belief that in aristocrats' great kakuwatan batin there lay some measure of protection from natural disaster and civil disorder, so belief in, or really, the need to believe in the dhalang's ability to grant such mystical assistance has grown. Precisely because a dhalang's power is not linked to overt political control, dhalang have been able to maintain and foster the image of an authority apart. They are ready to intercede on behalf of those in need of their services, but they cannot be held accountable for the vagaries of mundane affairs.

Dhalang indeed like to emphasize to one and all that they stand as something of a breed apart. At ritual gatherings, they do this both by keeping to themselves and by flouting some conventional rules of etiquette. Pak Cerma mentioned that when he converted his house from plaited bamboo to brick and plaster construction, he was careful to add a room to one side. This was in order to have a place for dhalang to gather when they came as guests to a ritual celebration. "Dhalang don't like to sit with other guests," Pak Cerma explained. "They like to be able to lie about, stretching their legs out and joking, rather than sitting politely cross-legged on mats or sitting on chairs, and having to watch their tongues like other people do." The Cermas held no ritual celebrations while I was living with them, but at ritual celebrations held by other dhalang there was often a screened-off area where dhalang sat together, apart from other guests. And at the venerable Ki Poedjosoemarto's funeral, a group of dhalang sat in the back rows of chairs set out in the yard for male guests, joking and cutting-up outrageously.

SPONSORS AND DHALANG

Understandings of a dhalang's capacities impinge on sponsors' selection of a dhalang when they decide to hold a wayang, and these understandings, as well as estimations of his status, generally color the relations between sponsor and dhalang. Sponsors choose a dhalang according to two principal sorts of criteria, those that are lair and those that are batin. One of the former is cost. To hold any performance increases expenditures considerably, because in addition to the cash payment, sponsors must provide all members of the troupe at least one, more often two, preferably three meals. As mentioned in the Introduction, the sponsors can take responsibility for renting a gamelan, finding players and singers, and renting the necessary equipment for a performance if they like. They keep costs lower in this way, though everyone agrees that a performance goes more smoothly and the dhalang is happier if the sponsors entrust all these arrangements to him. Then the dhalang, who very likely owns a gamelan, puppets, screen, and lamp, and has a troupe of musicians who perform with him often, can charge a much higher fee, more than offsetting the wages he gives his troupe. The greater expense entailed in inviting a dhalang to bring his own troupe reflects well on the resources and munificence of the sponsors.

During my fieldwork in 1978-1979, when a kilo of rice cost between Rp. 100 and Rp. 130, and a laborer received between Rp. 350 and Rp. 500 per day, a young and inexperienced dhalang might receive only five to ten thousand rupiahs for a performance. A dhalang of moderate reputation might receive anywhere from fifteen to twenty thousand rupiahs for his services alone for a night's performance, thirty to a hundred thousand rupiahs if he was asked to bring his own troupe and to perform during the day as well as at night. It is my impression that the number of sponsors who wish to hold a daytime performance in addition to one at night is diminishing, except when a *ruwatan* performance is held. This ritual defense against Bathara Kala necessarily takes place during the day.

Java's most famous dhalang can command fees ranging from Rp. 150,000 to Rp. 500,000, while Ki Nartosabdho, the most popular though also the most controversial dhalang in Java, was rumored to charge as much as Rp. 800,000 for one performance. No one is ever charged admission to a performance sponsored privately. An admission charge would contravene impressions of the sponsors' munificence. The spectacular expense of engaging a famous dhalang of course figures prominently in the prestige it brings sponsors. Including such a famous name on the printed invitations assures a large crowd of guests, and, since the news will sweep through the countryside, an immense mob of spectators outside the sponsors' house. It occasionally happens that one goes to a performance expecting to see one of Java's top dhalang, only to find, on arriving, that one is watching an obscure dhalang who happens to have the same name as a very famous one. Two young dhalang in Jogja who shared their respective names with two of the city's most popular dhalang seemed to me to perform far more often than their modest talents warranted. I presume that their popularity stems from the opportunity their names provide sponsors to spread word that "Ki So-and-so" is going to perform. I also suspected, when rumors flew that some famous dhalang was going to perform in a village and those rumors proved unfounded, that the sponsors had started, or at least done nothing to squelch, such reports.

Another mundane (lair) consideration in engaging a dhalang is the sponsors' own taste. Such factors as the dhalang's voice, his manipulation of the puppets (sabetan), style of performance, etc., all influence a person's appreciation of his talents. But more important, according to ideology if perhaps not in practice, are issues concerning kebatinan. A dhalang is believed to exert great energy (daya), the energy that radiates from potent persons or objects. Such energy can work to either good or evil effect. To possess great energy gives someone an impressive presence, called prabawa. Sponsors hope that the dhalang's prabawa will be such as to keep spirits at bay,[3] and the guests, réwang, and other spectators happy and quiet at the time of the ritual celebration, thereby assuring that the whole affair will take place without mishap. Ultimately more important still is the effect the dhalang will have over the sponsors' fortunes in the months and even years following the ritual. That is, the sponsors hope that the dhalang's daya will cause their family to be healthy and prosperous, and their income to increase. But daya is equivocal. It is possible that, even though the performance satisfies everyone at the time, there will follow in its wake misfortune, sickness, and the dissipation of the sponsors' property. There are many stories abroad of sponsors

[3] The importance of staving off danger supports Becker's point that wayang addresses an "unseen, essential" audience of spirits (1979:234). However, I don't think these spirits can be identified specifically as ancestral spirits, and I find the use of the word "essential" exaggerated. Although sponsors are concerned with the mystical ramifications of a performance, the impact of the performance upon the audience is very much on everyone's mind.

who saw their finances wrecked and their families visited by tragedy in the year or so after they sponsored a wayang.

The eventual effects of the sponsors' association with the dhalang depend on whether they are a good match (jodho), and as with prospective spouses, little can be done to determine that compatibility beforehand. Evil intentions are not ascribed to a dhalang following whose performance, perhaps months later, sponsors suffer some hardship. Intentions are irrelevant to the mysterious effects of the dhalang's daya upon the sponsors, and a very popular dhalang might turn out to bring suffering down on the head of sponsors through no intent of his own. However, it is true, I was told, that if a particular dhalang is seen to have performed in the homes of several people who experienced setbacks soon after, he may be thought to exert an inauspicious aura—and he may soon find himself out of work. In contrast, older dhalang whose voices have grown weak and whose performances arouse little interest are often still engaged because their daya is known to be great and compatible with that of many families, for whom they have performed for years.

The ambiguous potential of a dhalang's performance in its longterm effects upon the sponsors suggests some distrust of his power. Efforts to keep the dhalang bribed into good behavior during the performance also suggest tension between dhalang and sponsors, or at least its possibility. Most sponsors are usually careful to ask of a dhalang whether he has any particular wants. Unlike the musicians, no dhalang should eat during a performance. To do so would compromise his prestige considerably. A dhalang drinks and smokes throughout the night, however, and he does usually eat at least a little rice before and after performing. Sponsors try to learn whether the dhalang has any favorite foods or snacks, and what brand of cigarettes he prefers. By keeping the dhalang well supplied with these, sponsors hope to prevent the dhalang from making derogatory, thinly veiled allusions to them and their efforts.

Dhalang often laugh, in conversation, at the way sponsors overinterpret remarks made in the course of a performance. Stories are told of the elaborate lengths to which some sponsors have gone in the middle of the night in search, say, of a particular kind of fish just because a character in a play in progress has expressed a desire for it. In their nervousness, sponsors think a dhalang is making demands when he is actually just following the plot. Dhalang do, however, voice dissatisfactions and demands in just this way, occasionally for themselves, more often on behalf of their troupe. If, for example, a performance is well under way but the musicians have not yet received tea and snacks, a dhalang may have a character in the departure of the troops scene remark on how thirsty the soldiers are getting. No high-status wayang figure would normally allude to such a common need, and the break in tone makes the dhalang's meaning clear. Other shortcomings, such as faulty lighting or a bad sound system, may also provoke these oblique references. The audience roars at such times, and their laughter is very much at the sponsors' expense. It is considered deeply embarrassing to sponsors to be exposed to laughter in this way, and sponsors do all they can to prevent it.

I believe the tension between sponsors and dhalang, apparent in the equivocal impact a dhalang is thought to have on sponsors' present dignity and long-term fortunes, stems from the unresolved issue of their respective roles. Sponsors invite a dhalang to perform in order to benefit by his potency. Does this suggest their dependence upon the dhalang, who deigns to exert his superior kakuwatan batin on the sponsors' behalf? Or is the dhalang, who accepts the sponsors' invitation to perform at the latter's home and in return for payment, really just another person put in service to the sponsors, who remain masters of it all? Dhalang believe the former, aristocrats in most cases the latter, but other Javanese seem unsure. The lack of any clear resolution makes the collaboration of sponsors and dhalang subject to some stress.

When asked if he has a favorite story (lakon), wayang figure, or gendhing, a dhalang invariably replies that a dhalang must have no *kareman* ("preferences," but the word suggests weakness, as in "an Irishman's weakness for drink"). I was told that if he did and the sponsors requested, for example, a lakon other than his favorite one, then the dhalang would feel disappointed and not perform well. Nor should a dhalang have any particular likes in food, since he would again be liable to suffer disappointment. This conventional position suggests that, like any person with claims to potency, a dhalang must protect himself from dispersion in desire and from the vulnerability implicit in any personal investment. By extension, I believe, if the dhalang did express a liking among foods to the sponsors, then he would be more easily neutralized by them—won over by the blandishments of the sponsors' attentions—and thereby lose the edge in their disguised but nevertheless real competition.

The relations between dhalang and sponsors, that is, suggest both alliance and hostility: cooperation in achieving the ritual purpose and competition in the assumption of authority. But I believe that the logic of their interaction only repeats in a more complicated manner that between sponsors and the religious expert at a slametan, as discussed in the previous chapter.

Except in the rather specialized instance of the ruwatan, the dhalang does not usually accomplish a specific ritual purpose (though he can help sponsors free themselves from vows). Putting aside speculation, which must remain speculation, about the dhalang's "shamanistic" origins,[4] I think it possible to see in his speech a substitute for the sponsors' own voices. Once again, the substitution depends on relations of exchange. The money sponsors pay a dhalang is the most obvious element in this exchange, but it is not the only one. Sponsors must also provide a dhalang certain ritual offerings (*sajèn*), which are dedicated to God, Muhammad, the dhanyang, and other spirits, and placed near the screen during the performance. The dhalang takes these offerings home in the morning. One dhalang, while speaking of the most elaborate and valuable sajèn for a wayang performance, those assembled for a ruwatan, explained that these belong by rights to the dhalang, but the benefit—really, God's favor—granted to the giver of these offerings actually goes to whoever gives them up. That is, a dhalang lets the merit go to the sponsors when he takes the sajèn home, but he is happy to let the sponsors keep them if they wish to, knowing that the gesture will win him, the dhalang, divine favor.[5] The underlying assumption, I believe, is that the payment, in the form of both money and offerings, enables the sponsors to assume the benefit of the dhalang's actions.

---

[4] See Ulbricht 1970 for a recent formulation of this position.

[5] Not all dhalang are so uninvested in worldly things (*iklas*) as this informant claimed to be. When an older relative of Bu Cerma performed a ruwatan in a village one day, his wife gathered up all the sajèn well before the performance ended. She loaded them onto a buggy, and she, her daughter, and her husband could be seen making good their escape within minutes after the final gong. "She was afraid somebody might ask them for something," Bu Cerma said contemptuously. The ruwatan performance depicts villagers and spirits requesting sajèn of the dhalang as powerful boons, and spectators reputedly often do just this at a ruwatan's end. This woman, known for her shrewish and selfish ways, was taking no chances.

That the dhalang receives payment, particularly cash payment, for his services suggests some denigration of his status. Some sponsors, as mentioned above, adopt just such a demeaning view of the dhalang. It is probably in order to stave off such unflattering reflections that dhalang often stress in conversation their total indifference not just to the sajèn, but also to the sum they are paid, or even whether they are paid at all. They insist that they will perform for indigent sponsors for little or nothing—even a ruwatan, the most important and ritually elaborate performance in the repertoire. Anyone who asks their assistance (and here dhalang attribute self-humbling krama, or krama andhap, to the prospective sponsors, underlining their status as suppliants) will gain a dhalang's gracious charity.

However, these conflicting attitudes about payment and status strike me as something of an overlay. They obscure but do not contradict the fundamental understanding of exchange relations between sponsors and dhalang as a way of effecting the substitution of the dhalang's voice for the sponsors' own. Actually, the dhalang's voice becomes only the most prominent one among several, including that of the moderator and each of the speakers, all motivated by the single, silent authority of the sponsors. The dhalang is responsible for protecting the sponsors' family, their guests, and their neighbors, from spirits' attacks, from thieves, and from internal dissension. Sponsors entrust, that is, the entire scene to the dhalang, confident or at least hopeful that the latter's prabawa will stave off danger. But in addition to this release from responsibility for the safety of all those assembled, the sponsors also gain the privilege of remaining silent. As when the sponsors let the moderator speak for them, this obscures somewhat the assertion of superior status that gathering so many people under their roof implies. It also means, however, that the sponsors can absent themselves from the scene, becoming the mysterious and apparently immobile power behind all the activity. Ideally—though the tension between dhalang and sponsors shows that the ideal falls prey to its own contradictions—the dhalang enables the sponsors to become a dissembled center.

The triad of sponsors, dhalang, and spectators resembles that of king, dhalang, and villagers implicit in the popular view that dhalang first taught villagers basa. The dhalang who performs at a ritual celebration distracts attention away from the sponsors, and he displaces the sponsors' voice. But in so doing, he exercises great power over the spectators, and this in the sponsors' name. It is this image of a great crowd gathered to pay silent and orderly attention to the dhalang, but under the auspices of the sponsors, at the sponsors' home, and in observance of the sponsors' ritual need, that redounds to the glory of the sponsors, and should make their authority a brief but effective repetition of the king's.

7. THE DHALANG, THE TROUPE, AND THE TRADITION

The dhalang becomes the central figure at a ritual celebration from the time he starts performing until he stops eight or nine hours later. During this time, the sponsors recede discreetly into the background as an unseen though crucial force. Yet if the dhalang appears in some respects obvious, even flamboyant, in his performance, the active agent of an evasive authority, much about the dhalang himself repeats the play of power both constraining and restrained, pervasive yet dissembled. Actually, more diversely and dynamically than in relations between dhalang and sponsors, the links between the dhalang and his troupe, the dhalang and the wayang tradition, and the dhalang and the audience play on degrees and kinds of authority. I will discuss each of these relations in turn, reserving the last-mentioned—the relations between the dhalang and the audience—for the next chapter.

THE DHALANG AND THE TROUPE

Before World War II, at least outside town, a wayang was a much less elaborate affair than it is today. The gamelan consisted of only a few instruments, and there was no female vocalist (*pesindhèn*). Classically, wayang was performed exclusively in *sléndro*, but recently it has become fashionable for a sponsor to rent a gamelan with both *sléndro* and *pélog* components.[1] In that case, dhalang then play a few scenes in *pélog*, though most of a performance continues to be performed in *sléndro*. If the sponsors do not rent a *pélog* set, a fairly complete *sléndro* set, at least, is thought essential, and the absence of a *pesindhèn* would strike everyone as aberrant.

---

[1] There are three basic scales in gamelan music: *sléndro*, *pélog barang*, and *pélog bem*. The *sléndro* scale is played on one set of instruments; the two *pélog* scales must be played on another. In the case of the various *gendèr* (metalophones consisting of bronze keys suspended over individual resonating chambers), it is preferable to have three different instruments, one tuned in *sléndro*, another in *pélog barang*, and a third in *pélog bem*, though one occasionally finds a *gendèr* that can play either *pélog* scale by the substitu-

A successful dhalang has a fairly stable group of players who accompany him whenever he performs. A less active one knows where to find musicians to call upon when needed. These usually include brothers, uncles, cousins, sons, and/or nephews. Traditionally, a dhalang's musicians were members of his immediate family, both male and female, and his wife played the *gendèr*. (One reason a dhalang's son was pressured to marry a dhalang's daughter rather than a peasant's was in order to avoid having to hire a *gendèr* player.) More recently, though, the ponderous Victorianism that the Javanese think modern has led people to find mixed sexes among musicians inappropriate. The lamentable results are the elimination of all female players from village performances of wayang, and the proliferation of gamelan groups for bourgeois ladies, "*ibu-ibu*," in town. (I say lamentable because village women do not deserve to see yet another traditional source of income, however minor, closed to them, while city ladies do not deserve the astonishing amounts of radio time given over to their embarrassing attempts to pick out simple tunes on the most basic instruments of the gamelan.) In any case, a wayang usually requires at least seven or eight musicians, and a very fancy performance would draw on the talents of twenty or more.

The dhalang's control of his troupe is at once total and covert. The musicians must be responsive to a variety of subtle cues the dhalang gives them. The number and rhythm of raps he gives with a wooden mallet (*cempala*) at the outset indicate which of certain long musical compositions (*gendhing*) will accompany the opening scene. At other points in the performance, the musicians must discern in some phrase the dhalang utters reference to the title of a gendhing he wishes them to play. These allusions are sometimes obvious, at other times quite subtle, though most are fairly conventionalized.[2] Other signals, some of which the dhalang gives with the heavy metal plates (*keprak*) that he bangs with the mallet held between his toes, some with the mallet held in his hand, still others by singing a particular note, induce the musicians to play sections of certain set pieces (e.g., battle music), or to stop playing, on very short notice. The drummer must pay very

tion of one key in each octave. The two stringed instruments, the *rebab* and the *clempung*, in contrast, since they can be returned easily, need not be duplicated.

    [2] For a thorough account of these allusions, plus a list of many of them, see Heins 1970.

close attention to the puppets, because he must time his playing to highlight the puppets' moves, especially in battle. The *gendèr* player plays a soft but almost constant accompaniment to the dhalang as he sings and speaks, providing him with a guide to pitch. (One of the many marvels at a performance of wayang is the way that a *gendèr* player, at three or four in the morning, can continue to run velvet-tipped mallets over the *gendèr*'s bronze keys even though he is clearly fast asleep.) All the musicians' finely disciplined moves must be accomplished without overt communication between dhalang and players. The group should work precisely and smoothly without the dhalang needing to voice explicit commands. It is considered rather amateurish for a dhalang to inform his players before the performance begins what gendhing they are to play for the court scenes, and I have occasionally seen dhalang wait in contemptuous silence while confused and usually sleepy players argue among themselves about what gendhing it is they have just been signalled to play.

Thus the relations a dhalang enters into with his players musically are predicated on subtle allusion. Precisely the same play on reference and its dissimulation characterizes another side of their interaction: the many inside jokes a dhalang makes, through the puppets, that are directed at the musicians. Javanese delight in remarks that purport to speak of one subject but really address another. (The practice is called "to throw north and hit south" [*nggutuk lor, kena kidul*].) Some of a dhalang's jokes about his players are accessible to the audience, such as those about the gong player flirting or napping hidden in there among the gongs. Most are more esoteric, referring to some recent incident known only to the players. So the players guffaw while everyone else present sits looking on blankly. Dhalang justify these jokes on the grounds that they help keep the musicians awake. (Doing so can pose real problems, especially if musicians follow a dhalang who performs, as some popular ones do, twenty to thirty times in an auspicious month.) Aside from this function, though, the practice enhances the image of the dhalang and his troupe as a privileged group, even a secret society of sorts. It also shows the dhalang's words to have hidden meanings, evidenced though not explained in the musicians' raucous reactions. As a result, the dhalang's words, and his image, gain an aura of secret but effective power.

The dhalang's dissembled control over his players at once obscures and makes more mysterious his place at the center of the performance, as the single authority in control of its execution. Just as unanticipated laughter from the musicians reveals unsuspected jokes, the subtlety of the dhalang's commands makes their effectiveness all the more arresting. His relations with the tradition of wayang play more complicated variations on these themes of autonomy, variation, and control, suggesting both the dhalang's freedom from the constraints of any text and his dissimulation in the many constraints or conventions of the tradition as a whole.

THE DHALANG AND THE TRADITION

Three general criteria applied when evaluating a dhalang are his genealogy, his training, and his sensitivity to his audiences' tastes. A dhalang should be able, in the opinion of many, to trace his genealogy back through several generations of dhalang, and I was struck by the ability of some dhalang to recount their genealogies back several generations further than other commoners. Only dhalang in such long lines of descent are thought to be in possession of a great store of esoteric knowledge (ngèlmu padhalangan) necessary to make their performance truly effective. However, belief in the need for a long genealogy is certainly declining. The Javanese conviction that genealogy distinguishes people in important ways, while still strong, nevertheless lacks all ideological support today, supplanted by the stress on ascetic endeavors. Several of Java's most famous contemporary dhalang have little or no genealogical connection to the major dhalang lines of Central Java.

Schooling distinguishes dhalang in a way similar to genealogy. Public schools, and more importantly the schools for dhalang at royal courts in Jogja and Solo, give dhalang a level of general learning thought important to their performance. The dhalang schools in Solo especially are considered the ideal places in which to study the classical Kawi vocabulary necessary for performance, and to learn the precise links among all the different wayang characters. Furthermore, these schools have permitted something of a canon to be established, particularly in Solo, about the "correct" versions of many aspects of a performance, such as the long lines (suluk) the dhalang sings, the stories (lakon) he relates, and the gendhing the orchestra plays. (The prestige of Abirandho, the palace school for dhalang in Jogja, has never equalled that of the older Radya Pustaka school, and now the national Akademi Seni Karawitan Indonesia, in Solo. As a result, Jogja has seen less standardization of performance styles.) The conviction that there is and should be a correct version of any aspect of performance suits a court-biased view of wayang, one that makes wayang beholden to the court's efforts to establish norms in Javanese culture, particularly in the arts.[3] A dhalang who displays his diploma from Radya Pustaka, or now ASKI, lays claim to a kind of neo-aristocratic title.

Even dhalang who hold degrees in awe, however, share the general view that a dhalang can and should introduce his own variations in performance. Otherwise he is scornfully labelled a student dhalang (*dhalang pelajar*), presumably not descended from dhalang and still dependent on book learning when he performs. The different lines of dhalang families in Java are expected to inherit variants in the tradition, and any member of such families retains at least a little of his father's style, as well as eventually adding his own variations. Furthermore, dhalang are known to be a stubborn lot, unlikely to agree among themselves or with any external authority about the best way to do anything.

Another counterweight to the authority of the courtly wayang tradition, particularly in respect to the length and number of narrative descriptions and the number and type of gendhing included in a performance, is the requirement that a dhalang perform in a way that will please his audience. Dhalang lay much emphasis on this point in conversation, saying that a dhalang should pay careful attention during the opening portion of a performance to his audience's reactions. If they make no response to his jokes, he realizes that they prefer a serious performance to a comic one. If the audience thins in the court scenes but swells when a battle starts, he understands that they most appreciate the martial side of a performance. Aristocrats in town are assumed to prefer quiet, serious, and classical performances, but audiences' tastes are otherwise believed to vary geographically, not sociologically. In East Java—this example is conventional—where people are known for their hot-headedness, a dhalang must be sure to bring on Baladewa, the valiant though gruff and excitable king of Madura.

It is remarkable that dhalang lay so much stress on the need to perceive and respond to an audience's wishes when another, equally

---

[3] For a very interesting discussion of the politics of Solonese and Jogjanese musical styles, see Sutton 1984.

conventional and pervasive opinion holds that a dhalang must be impervious to all influence. Ki Poedjosoemarto was the most famous and distinguished puppeteer in Java in the 1950s. He is universally praised to this day for his straightforward, unadorned manner of performing, true to classical form and with few jokes or references made to the sponsors or context. "If he made a joke and heard people laugh, he didn't make another joke all night," one dhalang told me approvingly. A dhalang, this received doctrine has it, never turns his head during performance. For a dhalang to make jokes at the expense of anyone present is also called "to look aside, to turn one's head" (*nylèwèng*), a verb that implies wandering from the path of righteousness (and in other contexts means "to commit adultery"). However, despite all this praise for Ki Poedjosoemarto's unimpeachably correct manner of performance, I was told—when it eventually occurred to me to ask—that there were never any spectators left much past midnight when he performed. What dhalang and many older Javanese praise in a performance is not necessarily what they actually like to see. Their praise describes an ideal, one that they might not much enjoy seeing realized in practice.

Paradoxically, dhalang are enjoined to adhere to the standards established in the court and/or state-supported schools, yet they are expected to maintain distinctive family and personal styles. They should be sensitive to the likes and dislikes of their audiences, yet they win praise if they appear impervious to those audience's reactions. These contradictory attitudes, all expressed with equal frequency and conviction by dhalang and wayang afficionados alike, stem once again from the ambiguous status of the dhalang relative to that of his sponsors and that of his audiences. Is he in charge or is he their subordinate? There is a further ambiguity in the dhalang's status, in this case relative to the wayang tradition itself: is the dhalang its authoritative interpreter and so free to shape it as he thinks appropriate, or is he simply another in a long line of servants to that tradition, and so obliged to follow its norms and conventions with conservative deference? This issue implicates the dhalang's relationship with the body of materials upon which he draws in performance, and it requires extended discussion.

Sung Verse and Its Readers
    The relationship between the wayang tradition and the dhalang's rendering of it is best grasped in the parallel but simpler relations be-

tween classical verse and its readers. Traditionally, all Javanese literature was written in sung verse, called *tembang*. There exist several
different tembang forms, each with a distinct name and each distinguished from the others by the number of lines to a verse, the number
of syllables to a line, and the final vowel sound in each line. A Javanese reader traditionally read, that is to say, sang, aloud. Only very
rarely did anyone read literature in a speaking voice, and Javanese do
not, as a rule, read silently. But readers choose to sing the tembang
following whatever vocal line they wish. Several well-known vocal
lines exist for each type of tembang, and some among these are
thought suitable for particular moods. But those decisions are left to
the reader. A text indicates at most, at the beginning of a series of
verses in a particular form, the name of the verse form that follows.
Often it is instead left to the reader to discern the meter without benefit of such overt references. Having elected to sing a verse with a particular vocal line, readers also embellish each phrase with variations
or decorations (*céngkok*). Their use, again, is a matter of personal
taste and skill. In public performance, singers will extend their rendering of a single verse with elaborate displays of their vocal tech-
nique. Simpler, less highly worked versions of each tembang are
thought more suitable to the reading of longer sections of classical
texts. In either case, however, readers must be able to vary their reading of verses with these graceful and well-executed additions.[4]

[4] The art of reading in Java is in terrible decline today, and with it goes popular
knowledge of Javanese literature. A few city people still cultivate the performance of
tembang. In villages, traditionally, tembang and the related *kidung* were sung by individual guests at a gathering of males (jagongan) held for several nights after a woman
gave birth, in order to protect mother and child from harm. Two developments have
virtually erased this practice. The failure of the public schools to teach children Javanese script means that many copies of the texts currently available to villagers are now
illegible to most people under age forty. Further, radios are now numerous in villages,
and at a jagongan held following a child's birth, a radio blares while the men play
cards.
    Young people may know a few tembang. But they don't read. In fact, there is a pe-
culiar version of illiteracy in Indonesia today, concentrated among relatively highly
educated young people. Unless they have taken a special interest in the performing
arts, especially wayang, young Javanese (also Balinese, and I assume Sundanese) are
ignorant of the classical vocabulary that their fathers, even if illiterate, can often understand. At school, these younger people have learned Indonesian, and they can read
the modern amalgam of Malay, Arabic, Dutch, and English that that language, especially when written, comprehends. Yet they read no literature in any language, except
for a few city people who read short stories published in the weekly or daily press in
Indonesian. Classical Malay literature is as alien to them as their own cultures' literary

This distribution of responsibilities between author (usually anonymous) and reader means that the distinction between them is obscured. The Javanese tradition of tembang makes an author conform to highly formalized meters. In fact, Javanese literary genres are extremely conventionalized, so that language and manner of narration as well as meter are limited to a particular, quite restricted range. The author must conform to this tradition closely in composing a "new" text. A reader must then conform to that finished text. But the reader adds so much to the text, and that addition is so essential a part of the transmission of the text, that the reader in a sense participates in creating the text—more so, or at least more obviously, I would claim, than silent readers of a Western text do in their reading. A Javanese text, that is, is never more than half-finished as long as it remains in its written form. Only as realized in a sung and embellished version does the text become fulfilled, and there are definite limits on how far the text can control the reader's reading.

However, each completion of the text is also purely ephemeral: the reader completes the text without in any way affecting it beyond the moment of that reading. The text, on the one hand, exerts only partial control over the reader. The reader, on the other, for all the authority he or she enjoys over the text's realization, leaves no trace.

Author and reader are therefore co-participants in the text's generation, while both are subject to quite strict, given form. The relative importance of author and reader in any particular reading depends on whether a highly embellished "concert" version of a tembang or a simpler reading takes place, the latter laying more emphasis on the sense of the words. The considerable constraints the tradition exerts upon both author and reader, however, means that any text and any performance represent variations within an all-embracing and deeply conservative tradition. These constraints stress both the authority of the tradition as a whole, in its permanent exigencies, and the transient play of vocal line and embellishment at the

---

heritage. As a result, many young Indonesians, including the younger members of the elite, not only lose touch with the written sources of the oral traditions, they also lack appreciation for the "literary" side—flowery, often recherché, but also at times indefinably elegant and graceful—of the languages of the traditional performing arts. They are perhaps awaiting, if they are not themselves trying their hands at creating, an Indonesian literature. But it seems possible that they have simply moved out of a rich, if conservative, oral tradition into a much impoverished visual one, typified by the old American programs broadcast on Indonesian television.

surface, which is where readers show their own skills. The double emphasis on tradition and variation deflects attention away from any particular center or meaning in an individual text. There is an assimilation of text and tradition that tends to undercut the supremacy and uniqueness of the author and particular text alike.

A dhalang stands in a similar relation to the corpus of the wayang tradition (*ngèlmu padhalangan*) as a Javanese reader to a text. His text is the story (lakon) that he performs. It leaves him free to improvise dialogue, perform routines, sing, and perhaps to rearrange the order of scenes. Were he to follow a written text slavishly (a few published texts of performances provide complete dialogues, not just plot outlines), he would be dismissed contemptuously as a neophyte and a dhalang with notes (*dhalang cathetan*), a phrase that implies all the mastery of a person who paints by number. He must be able to make his performance distinctive in its céngkok: the particular variations he makes in dialogue and in his manipulation of the puppets, and the minor shifts he introduces in the presentation of the lakon. Yet all of these are constrained by the tradition as a whole, which defines the characters, motivations, and situations, as well as the musical and structural limits within which he works.

THE DHALANG'S SKILLS

Both general expectations of a dhalang and certain more technical constraints set up conflicting demands, as I have said, that a dhalang be both conservative and flexible, impervious to influence and sensitive to his audience's wishes, "original" in performance and yet "respectful" of the tradition. Pressured to perform inventively and entertainingly, he must nonetheless do so in such a way that he will leave no mark upon the tradition he transmits. The result makes him an active agent of the tradition, yet one who is, in theory at least, wholly transparent to it. In his relations to the constraints of the tradition, in fact, as well as in the circumstances of the performance as a whole, the dhalang demonstrates especially vividly the paradox of effective but dissimulated authority.

The specific points on which a dhalang's performance is judged can be reduced to four essentials: his dexterity and style in manipulating puppets, his musicianship and the beauty of his singing voice, his ability to arrange scenes and make up dialogue in a pleasing way, and his ability to differentiate voices.

Sabetan

The manipulation of the puppets is called *sabetan*. Anyone new to wayang can only marvel at the variety and subtlety of effects a good dhalang can achieve in the manipulation of the leather puppets, which are jointed only at the shoulder and elbow.[5] Ingenuity and dexterity abound in the routines dhalang devise, especially in battle sequences, and audiences watch these moves with avid interest. The battle between a knight and a monster (usually the fanged monster, Buta Cakil), which takes place in virtually every performance sometime between two and three in the morning, provides a dhalang a special opportunity to display his sabetan. In this battle, the monster threatens the knight with his sword (*kris*) until, after increasingly frenetic efforts to win out over the knight's perfect self-control, the monster loses his *kris* to his opponent. The knight delivers the ultimate humiliation, stabbing the monster with the latter's own *kris*, and the monster dies. A less spectacular but still critical aspect of a dhalang's sabetan is his ability to make each wayang move in a manner appropriate to its temperament, illustrating its refinement, modesty, conceit, impetuousness, or whatever. A fundamental rule of sabetan is that the dhalang must try never to let his hand cast a shadow upon the screen. Another way in which he must maintain the illusion of the puppets' independent motion is to hold them well away from the screen when picking them up or putting them down.

While good sabetan is much appreciated by an audience, it is considered secondary among a dhalang's skills. The most popular dhalang in Java today, Ki Nartosabdho, had only rudimentary sabetan for many years. His skill has improved in recent years, but even when it was judged inadequate by most aficionados, it did not prevent his attaining great popularity, thanks to his other talents.

Musicianship

A dhalang's musicianship determines the range of gendhing he uses in the course of a performance and the skill with which he integrates his own singing and sabetan with those gendhing. Many spec-

---

[5] See Long 1982 for a thorough discussion of sabetan.

tators lack the musical sophistication to pass judgment on this aspect of a dhalang's performance. The beauty of his voice, however, figures prominently in public appreciation of a dhalang. A powerful voice, capable of holding the sustained notes of the suluk and covering an extended range from high to low registers, wins a dhalang great fame. One of Jogja's top dhalang is notoriously lacking in dramatic skills— his stories rarely make any sense whatsoever—but the sumptuous beauty of his voice, plus the musical skill he demonstrates, put him much in demand. Sheer beauty of tone seems to matter less than the technical virtuosity with which a dhalang sings the ornamented lines of the suluk, although it's true that a very nasal tone can seriously diminish a dhalang's success. Ki Nartosabdho's voice is not the purest in tone, but is probably the most flexible among those of current dhalang, and it is one reason for his great popularity.

Sanggit

The third major aspect of a dhalang's skill, his *sanggit*, could be translated roughly as dramatic skill. It concerns, essentially, the way a dhalang mediates two constraints upon his performance: the required scenes (*pathokan*) that structure every performance, and the story (lakon), which is the outline of the story he presents.[6] The lakon may be traditional or it may be a dhalang's own invention. Sponsors may request a particular lakon at the time they engage a dhalang to perform, they may wait until the dhalang is about to perform before making the request, or they may defer to the dhalang's own judgment. It is a point of pride among dhalang to be able to perform any lakon requested without reference to any notes or aids, though dhalang do often keep brief written synopses of dozens or even hundreds of lakon at home. I was frequently astonished by the ability of some dhalang to recall on a moment's notice the complicated, interwoven lines of a great number of lakon, including the order of court scenes in which the performance would be organized. But no matter what the lakon, the pathokan can be altered only by the omission or inclusion of certain scenes, never by the wholesale revision of the performance's shape.

The pathokan determine the progression of every performance,

[6] A. L. Becker discusses the relations between pathokan, which he calls "plot," and lakon, which he calls "story," in somewhat greater detail (A. L. Becker 1979). Brandon 1970 also dicusses the order of scenes in a performance.

from the long opening gendhing at about nine in the evening to the final battle and brief courtly audience and celebration that end it between five and six the next morning. A performance is divided into three sections—theoretically equal in length, though in practice rarely so—that are distinguished by the musical *pathet* used in each. *Pathet* denotes emphasis in range, somewhat similar to modes in Western music.[7] The first section of a performance, lasting until around midnight or one in the morning, is in the scale *sléndro* and the pathet *nem*. The middle section of the performance, from the scene in which the servant-clowns (*punakawan*) first appear until about three or four in the morning, is in the pathet *sanga*, while the final section is in the pathet *manyura*. Each of these pathet is slightly higher in the scale of *sléndro* than the preceding one.

Within these large divisions, the pathokan establish sequences of scenes, and the general content of many of these scenes. The description of the lakon *Senawangi* provided in the Introduction indicates how closely the dhalang followed the pathokan on that occasion. A performance necessarily opens with a long, conventionalized description of a kingdom in prosperity and peace, narrated by the dhalang against the soft accompaniment of the gamelan. (The kingdom may turn out to be under attack and in disarray, but that fact comes out only later, after this opening description.) Only after a long series of greetings among characters assembled at court is the business of the particular lakon broached. In Jogja, a guest then enters the audience hall and his mission provokes battle. In Solo, the first scene, which takes place at court but does not necessarily include the arrival of a guest, is followed by the king's withdrawal to his private quarters, the external prime minister's report to the royal troops, and their departure to battle. The next scene introduces a second court, often one of people from across the sea (*wong sabrang*), and their entry into the action either elaborates on whatever issue was discussed at the outset or introduces another subplot, usually another source of conflict with which the first set of characters will have to contend. The meeting of troops from the first and second courts usually leads to battle by about midnight. This battle ends inconclusively. In *Senawangi*, there was no shift to a second court, but the arrival of Kresna and Baladewa ac-

---

[7] See Hood 1954 for a complete discussion of pathet.

complished the same purpose of introducing another set of characters, and for the rest, the pathokan were observed.

In Jogja, the second section of the performance opens with the *gara-gara* (a cosmic upheaval). A knight is experiencing some distress, and this, in view of his great potency, generates such heat and disorder that the whole world registers its effects. Narrated by the dhalang, this account leads to the first appearance of the four *punakawan* (servant-clowns), Pétruk, Nala Garèng, Bagong, and their "father" (actually only their adoptive father), Semar. Each sings and dances, and they joke and spar with each other for a while. In Solo, their first appearance occurs instead in the context of a monk's hermitage to which a hero has repaired for guidance. In *Senawangi*, as in most performances, the monk was Abiyasa and the knight was Abimanyu. In both Jogjanese and Solonese performances, the routines of the punakawan are followed by their progress through the forest in attendance upon their master. En route, they encounter hostile monsters, and the battle with the Buta Cakil or other monster then takes place. Another court or hermitage scene follows this battle: in *Senawangi*, it was Senawangi's place of retreat. Following it, the pathokan become more flexible, allowing greater leeway in the arrangement of scenes, and the plot advances much more quickly as the various subplots join and are resolved in the concluding battles.

Up until the last two hours of a performance, while a dhalang exercises some freedom over the inclusion or exclusion of certain scenes, he devotes more time to set-pieces than to the particular issues of the lakon. For example, he may choose to reduce the king's return to his chambers to a brief narrative, rather than going through the elaborate descriptions of the gate that leads to those chambers, of the king's apparel, of the queen's beauty, etc. This account, totally stereotypical, displays the dhalang's classical Javanese vocabulary (Kawi) to its fullest advantage, but it makes many spectators grow restive. The departure of the troops, however, while also conventional and in no way instrumental in advancing the plot, is never omitted, and a dhalang often lavishes much time upon it. The entrance of the punakawan, and the battle with monsters that ensues, are equally extraneous to the plot and equally essential to the performance. A dhalang includes further meetings of characters according to the nature of the lakon. Nevertheless, as one dhalang said airily but in no way critically, "Every performance of wayang is the same until three in the morning."

Below the level of the order of scenes, pathokan determine the way that a single scene progresses from greetings to discussion and often to battle. They further shape the course of a single battle, since a set pattern pits opponents of progressively higher status against each other.

The power of the pathokan is extraordinary. Only ruwatan and *Bratayuda* lakon (the first is a ritual exorcism, the latter any of a series of lakon depicting the final cataclysmic war in the *Mahabharata*) are said to escape the invariable order of scenes. But of the performances I saw of *Bratayuda* lakon, all adhered to the pathokan quite strictly. Even Nartosabdho's new, unprecedented performances, in which he follows one character from birth to death, observe the set divisions. So neither the chaos of civil war nor what many see as the chaos of Nartosabdho's innovations is strong enough to subvert the given structure.

A dhalang's dramaturgy (sanggit) consists in the way he fits the particular lakon he performs to the constraints of this fairly inflexible shape. This means first of all the order in which he chooses to present the different sets of characters: whether the long opening scene, for example, will take place in the palace of one kingdom or in another. Though many classical lakon are traditionally played in a particular order, a dhalang may vary that sequence. One dhalang explained that he may shift the order in which characters appear in order to permit a figure to do battle against a particular figure from another camp, that pairing being unusual and suggestive of novel jokes. However, tampering with the usual arrangement of a classical lakon does expose a dhalang to the criticism of many wayang devotees, who rarely find the taking of such liberties warranted.

Aside from the overall arrangement of the lakon, sanggit concerns as well the skill with which a dhalang creates dialogue. Each figure must speak in a manner suitable to his or her character. A dhalang's language must also conform to certain standards. He must not introduce modern words, particularly borrowings from Indonesian or other foreign languages, except when a punakawan is speaking. Furthermore, the progression of the dialogue, particularly in the longer court scenes, from polite greetings to mounting tension and eventually battle, must appear artless. There should be no sudden or unmotivated jumps in excitement. Finally, the story lines initiated early in the performance should be adequately drawn together and resolved by the end. Dhalang enjoy making fun of colleagues who introduce a character in the evening and then forget to reintroduce him or her in the final section of a performance. The proliferating number of subplots and the great number of issues that must be settled in the closing sections of a performance make the danger of such oversights real.

The term *sanggit* may also be applied to a dhalang's ability to make up new lakon. J. Kats lists 140 classical lakon in the collection of the palace in Jogja (Kats 1923). Of these, he estimates that forty or fifty were in common use in the 1920s. Today, certain classical lakon still receive fairly frequent performance. Some of these are what I will call principal lakon (*lakon pokok*, *pokok* meaning "principal" or "essential"), that is, lakon that relate critical events in the two epics, the *Ramayana* and the *Mahabharata*, on which wayang stories are based. Others are *lakon carangan* (from *carang*, "branch"), and still others *carangan ginancar*. The distinction between the last two categories is moot: I will refer to both as secondary lakon. The important contrast is between those lakon that actually advance the action of the epic cycles, and those that depart from them without actually developing or contravening them. For example, a dhalang may make up a lakon in which a threat is posed to the security of the five Pandhawa (the righteous cousins), a marriage pact is proposed, etc. He can indulge his fantasy in working out the implications of these standard situations provided that at the end of the performance no basic element in the epics—how two familiar characters are related to each other in the kinship relations of the two factions, or how each camp is situated politically—has been affected. *Senawangi* is just such a lakon, in which common themes are rewoven without making any advance in the epic cycle. Many older secondary lakon are now established and considered "classical." Recently, however, a great many new lakon have been created. Some of these, particularly those created and recorded by Java's most famous dhalang, have become very well known and may enter the permanent repertoire. The vast majority, however, are ephemeral.

Paradoxically, newly created lakon tend to be more thoroughly conventional in story line than the classical lakon, particularly more than principal ones. This follows in part from the contrast between lakon that recount the major events of the epics and lakon that are cast in such a way as to avoid contradicting those events. But there is another reason. In creating "new" lakon, or simply choosing to perform such recent creations, a dhalang purports to be original, inventive, distinctive. That is, he frees himself somewhat from the constraints of the epic cycle. Yet these lakon, since they are completely conventionalized, are also safe. A dhalang who performs a lakon in which a priest from across the sea arrives in Ngastina (the kingdom contested by the two sets of cousins) and tries to impose a peaceful settlement upon the disputing parties, as occurs in a plethora of new lakon, can change the name of the priest and a few of the incidents that take place along the way. But a debate with Kresna, who insists that the decisive war, the *Bratayuda*, must take place, follows almost inevitably, as does the eventual unmasking of the "priest" to reveal one of two or three characters who invariably side with the covetous Kurawa cousins. *Senawangi* moves the action from Ngastina to Pringgadani, but otherwise follows this formula very closely. The novelty of the names and a few of the incidents that transpire in such lakon give an impression of "creativity," but the fundamentally stereotypical shape of the lakon makes it in no way tendentious or startling.

I have used the word "creativity" here, and "original," "inventive," and "distinctive" above. The Javanese word for "original," *asli*, is a borrowing from Indonesian. It could not be used in the sense I mean here, since it connotes "place of origin or source," not "imaginativeness," as it may in English. (A *dhalang asli*, incidentally, refers to a dhalang descended from many dhalang.) "Creative" is sometimes rendered *kreatip* in Indonesian now, and educated Javanese sometimes avail themselves of the term. What they mean by it, I think, is the Javanese term with which most people would praise a dhalang, namely *pinter*, which means "clever," "skillful," or "shrewd." The term would not be applied to a dhalang who came up with entirely unprecedented lakon. Nartosabdho's experiments with biographical lakon, really just a selection of key moments from principal ones, were considered outrageous by a great many people. Nartosabdho himself told me that he created such lakon only at the urging of some very influential friends, and that he himself preferred to stick to the classical repertoire.

Good sanggit means above all sanggit that does not counter any of the pathokan. By conforming to the essential structure of the pathokan, and further, by conforming to the usual overall order of scenes, a dhalang protects himself from charges of incompetence or irresponsibility. He can distinguish himself, he can be thought *pinter*, for the way in which he makes variations in the surface of a performance: for the comedy, verbal and visual, of the routines; for the mounting tension in debates and battle; for the unusual juxtaposition of particular characters. But this makes his role a deeply conservative one. He does not alter the tradition in any way: his performance leaves no trace. The fulsome praise bestowed on Ki Poedjosoemarto, as I have said, always dwells on the classical purity of his performance and his devotion to the full range of the pathokan, down to their finest details. Only a few of the most famous dhalang in Java now make any modifications in the pathokan. These changes consist primarily in introducing divertissements—light gendhing and dancing and/or clowning routines—in places in which they did not figure in the past. An abomination in the eyes of many conservative wayang fans, these win popular approval. But they really only exaggerate a tendency to make the dhalang's relation to his material that of propagator and embellisher of a set form.

Antawacana

It is telling in this regard that, according to Javanese, the most important skill that a dhalang must possess is not good sanggit but good *antawacana*. This refers to the ability to distinguish the timbre of each character's voice and his or her manner of speaking. The interplay of convention and variation is particularly interesting here. The voices of perhaps ten or even twenty of the most popular characters in wayang are so well individuated that an experienced listener can pick them out almost without reference to the content of their words. Of course, each dhalang reproduces these voices slightly differently. Yet adherence to the general pattern is so close that it is often possible to tune into a broadcast of wayang and know within seconds which main characters are speaking. Even when lesser characters play a scene, a good dhalang can have the different figures identify themselves at the outset and then differentiate their voices sufficiently to keep the identity of each speaker clear without any further cues.[8] Of

---

[8] During a long court scene, a dhalang usually props several wayang up against the screen, the central support of each one stuck into the banana trunks along the base of the screen. He then moves one hand of each character slightly as it speaks. Some dhalang get lazy and neglect to do even this. Pak Cerma loved to tell about an older dha-

course, a dhalang must distinguish not only the vocal color and intonation of each character, but also the speed and fluency of his speech, and its volume. Titles, terms of direct address, and speech levels are particularly intricate in the language of wayang: a dhalang must know precisely how each character addresses any other character in view of their respective statuses, genealogical connections, etc. (He must also attribute to them sentiments, ideas, and turns of phrase appropriate to their temperaments and to the moment. This is an aspect of his sanggit.) In scenes in which arguments break out between characters, a dhalang must be able to distinguish all these points—vocal quality, style of speech, and character—for each figure at great speed. Skilled dhalang can make parties to a fight interrupt each other with only split-second intervals between "speakers."

Ki Nartosabdho's reputation depends beyond all else on his antawacana, which is unequalled for its dazzling skill and accuracy. As many Javanese repeat, it becomes impossible to believe, on listening to him perform, that only one man is speaking. In a very famous routine Nartosabdho often did in the early seventies, the three punakawan brothers tried to sing a light gendhing, Lembung Desa, composed by Nartosabdho himself and something of a hit tune in Java at the time. The song includes several lines of lyrics followed by nonsense syllables. Pétruk assigned sections of the song that each one of the brothers was to sing. Chaos of course ensued, as each of them anticipated his part, confused words, sang flat, or otherwise gummed up the works. The punakawan exchanged insults, then exchanged parts, and things only got worse. A howlingly funny routine, its effectiveness depended on the listener's instantaneous recognition of each voice as one brother interrupted another. This was possible because the voices of the punakawan, especially, are as readily identified by the Javanese as the voices of their closest kin. People will exclaim about a dhalang's rendering of a character's voice, "That's *exactly* Bagong's voice!" Bagong and his voice being as real and familiar to them as the child they nickname affectionately after him.

When he is speaking not in a character's voice but as narrator, a dhalang uses a highly stylized manner of speaking that exploits the

---

lang who used to bow his head while he spoke for the characters and moved their hands, without checking to make sure he had the right one. The incongruous impression obtained by listening, say, to the refined Arjuna's voice and seeing the brawny Bima's hand move struck audiences as wonderfully hilarious.

full range of his voice, from deep and resonant to high and slightly shrill. He listens to the gamelan to guide the pitch of his speaking voice and also to differentiate the voices of the different figures, tying characters' voices to particular notes and in some cases shifting to higher notes in the course of the performance. The pitch of each voice also varies slightly according to what figures are present in a scene: in order to maintain sufficient contrast, voices may have to be "pushed apart" temporarily. All of these considerations and modifications are set by tradition, although different dhalang observe them more or less scrupulously.

THE DHALANG'S PRESENCE

In contrast to an actor in the modern Western theatre, whose every line of dialogue is set, a Javanese dhalang enjoys considerable freedom. He is playwright and director, as well as actor, in each performance. Yet his "contribution" to the tradition, that is, his realization of it in performance, is always only momentary. Even if a lakon a dhalang creates should become a standard one in the repertoire, his name becomes detached from it within a generation. Although certain dhalang, especially since the spread of radios and cassette tape recorders throughout Java, have become extremely famous and their voices are easily recognized by many people, it remains true that under the constraints of the tradition, the figure of the dhalang as a particular artist tends always to disappear.

The importance of antawacana in evaluating a dhalang epitomizes this effacement of the dhalang's presence. Antawacana, like sanggit, challenges a dhalang to conform in as accurate and entertaining a manner possible to preestablished norms. A dhalang must splinter his voice into a great array of distinctive voices, those of all the characters plus the narrator. The latter, as I have mentioned, is particularly stylized, as is the language, highly Sanskritized and often obscure, that he uses in narration. The narrator's voice is not the dhalang's "own" voice. In Jogja, the punakawan Pétruk should speak in the natural speaking voice of the dhalang outside performance. Particularly since Pétruk speaks in a direct but right-thinking and at times sententious manner, as dhalang tend to do on formal occasions in "life," I long assumed that Pétruk was to be understood as the dhalang speaking for himself. No dhalang would agree to that formulation,

however, insisting that Pétruk is just another character. So the dhalang's "own" voice loses its special status by being put on an equal
footing with all the other voices. It becomes just one more among a
great many voices, none of which can be identified with the dhalang
personally. The result further dissembles the existence of a dhalang
"behind" all the puppets. If the sponsors dissemble their presence by
giving up their voice, letting the moderator, speech-makers, and
dhalang all speak in their place, the dhalang, in turn, dissembles his
presence by speaking in a great many voices, but never his own.

The dhalang, in a word, disappears: into the refractions of his
voice in antawacana, into the constraints of the tradition as a whole,
and into the white ground of the screen on which the shadow of his
hands should never fall. For all that, of course, the impression of his
potency is enormous. In fact, I believe it is precisely the impression
the dhalang makes of a hidden, unlocatable, but all-encompassing
authority that is so compelling to Javanese.

A counter-example helps to illustrate the importance of the dhalang's self-dissimulation. I have made reference several times in this
account to the special skills and reputation of Ki Nartosabdho. There
is one aspect of his performance that I always found disturbing and
that I believe helps to explain the vehement denunciations that he
earns from conservative wayang enthusiasts. Nartosabdho is, as almost everyone in Java seems to know, far and away the most expensive dhalang now performing, as well as the most famous and popular
one. He is also particularly concerned with his personal prestige. Unlike other dhalang, he is very willing to make allusion to himself—
his fame, his fee, and his home address—in the course of his performances, usually in the routines of the punakawan. Occasional allusions
on the part of any dhalang to the particular context are startling, and
the sudden contrast in reference makes such asides especially pi-
quant. Nartosabdho's self-indulgent references to himself trade on his
own personal situation and reputation, however, dispelling the image
of the dhalang's impersonal authority. The result is grating, even if it
further magnifies the name of Nartosabdho and the glory of the sponsors who have paid his extravagant fee. Wayang has long operated by
a version of the star system. But when the star shows himself too
clearly, the impression of his power palls, and I believe this fact explains much of the censure heaped upon Nartosabdho.

Incidentally, Ki Nartosabdho's appreciation of his own unusual place in the contemporary Javanese arts has set him to writing his autobiography. This is an extraordinary thing to do in Java, suggesting a conception of the self quite out of keeping with traditional (and still current) ideas about surpassing the self in pursuit of potency. Yet the fruits of Nartosabdho's efforts, when he was gracious enough to read parts of the text to me, turned out to be less startling than I had anticipated. First, he sang the text, since he has composed it in classical tembang. Second, he ascribed his unusual gifts (which are, at times, very impressive) to a mystical encounter with a traditional figure of great potency, a meeting that he experienced following rigorous ascetic action when he was nineteen. (His mentor was Sunan Kalijaga, about whom Clifford Geertz has written [C. Geertz 1968:25-29].) He traced thereby his many innovative moves—some highly controversial—as well as his uniquely skillful and faithful renderings of the classical repertoire, to a thoroughly conventional account of how a person attains any goal. I came away feeling that Ki Nartosabdho's acquaintance with Western literary traditions, coupled with his not inconsiderable vanity, made him receptive to the form of the autobiography, but without really undermining a deeper Javanese understanding of how to justify claims to status and power.

Javanese speak of political figures always with a curious skepticism. They tend to see in an obvious leader the puppet of a more powerful but self-effacing agent. For years, Indonesians in the know spoke of President Suharto as too weak, passive, or unlettered to exercise real control over the national government. Events seem to have proved these accounts wrong. Yet it is remarkable how long many people remained convinced that Suharto was a puppet manipulated by an unseen dhalang. The formulation is not mine but theirs. I think it reflects not a world-view forever colored by wayang, as some romantic Westerners tend to read into many Indonesian political events, but rather a succinct summation of ideas about the relative power of obvious versus dissembled authority. When a dhalang speaks in a multiplicity of voices, when he exercises his wit within the boundaries of the tradition, and when he makes the wayang appear to move entirely on their own, he diminishes the impression of his person—as a particular speaker, as a recipient and transmitter of ngèlmu padhalangan, and as a single human manipulating several three-pronged leather puppets. He gains in return the mystique of a centerless, per-

vasive, yet invisible presence, as ostensibly oblivious to history as the
tradition itself. In fact, his authority becomes indistinguishable from
that of wayang, a word that refers at once to each puppet, the performance, and a tradition that can be traced in Java at least as far
back as the tenth century.[9] But he is at the same time, of course, em-
phatically present, as evidenced in the movement of the puppets, in
the rapping of the wooden mallet and the clatter of the metal sheets,
and above all in the sound of his voice. It is particularly that voice
that the sponsors seek to put in service to their own purposes. They
hope it will assure both the safety and entertainment of all people
present at the ritual celebration itself, and also their own prestige and
long-term prosperity. Yet just as the sponsors withdraw from the act
of speaking even as they rely on the medium of speech to attain their
ends, so, too, does the dhalang dissemble the fact that he is the
source of all the voices he takes on. Sponsors and dhalang alike engage in the assertion of authority through the dissimulation of
speech, and beyond speech, of action and even presence. They make
of themselves, that is, further exemplars of the dissembled center.

[9] Zoetmulder signals a reference to a performance of wayang in a royal charter issued
in A.D. 907, though he cautions that there is no way to tell what kind of performance
the word designated (Zoetmulder 1974:208-209).

8. THE PLEASURES OF THE PERFORMANCE

Javanese accounts of submission to a king exaggerate the notion of his beneficent berkah to the point of seeing in it a deeply satisfying influence. It is still threatening, however, in fact all the more so, and both the pleasure and the threat can be described as a kind of forgetfulness. Pak Cerma related that his father, Mbah Mardi, was offered the opportunity to become a dhalang at the court (abdi-dalem dhalang) at the Susuhunan in Solo.

> The pay was poor, but it's easy for a servant of the court [abdi-dalem] to make money on the side because of the prestige of his position. And anyway, Javanese say that working in the king's service makes one *ayem tentrem* ["serene," "satisfied," "contented"] because of the beneficent influence [berkah] and *sawab* [similar to berkah] of the king. But while a man stays at court, his family may be in bad straits. Maybe they have no money to make contributions to other people's ritual celebrations—and here the man's contented [*tentrem*] at court, completely unaware of their hardship. It's like the guys [arrested in the late '60s] who are still in prison. They no longer have to worry about getting killed, since there are laws against that now. And they know nothing of any difficulties their families may be going through. So they're very comfortable.

In accepting a dependent role at court, a man enjoys the security and serenity assured by the king's powerful aura. This induces a pleasant but irresponsible forgetfulness: the man forgets that others are dependent upon him. Meanwhile, his wife is out there trying to maintain the family's position in ritual exchange relations. The association Pak Cerma made between servants of the court and prisoners is particularly telling in that their similarity is seen to lie not in their common submission to authority, but in the comfort and forgetfulness that that submission wins them. In each case, in place of the authoritative role he plays in the family, a man enjoys a passive, protected contentment, trusting in a superior authority's care.

This account of a pleasurable but seductive forgetfulness illumi-
nates, as I will try to show, much about Javanese reactions to wayang
in performance: what it is people savor, and what it is they fear. Comments about wayang's value stress the normative, didactic function of
the art form, but reactions to performance indicate a more enticing,
yet potentially disorienting, effectiveness. The unresolved nature of
these reactions gives rise to the simultaneous resistance to and fascination with wayang that Javanese evince, reactions that call to mind
the seductive appeal of service at the royal court that Pak Cerma described.

WAYANG AND MEANING

Before broaching the topic of how wayang pleases, or tempts, I
must consider the topic of what wayang means. The content of a performance of wayang is obviously not conceived of as a representation
of life. Though the vagaries of its plots and the motivations of many
of its characters may be familiar, it does not attempt, as most Western
drama has attempted, to mirror and comment upon a reality outside
itself. No doubt realism in Western drama is as much a convention as
any other style. Yet wayang's disregard for realism, in contrast to the
West's embrace of it, marks a critical difference between the two traditions.

If drama in the West is thought ideally to focus on a particular
problem or set of problems, and to make its own form and content
conform to the nature of some message, wayang engages in a much
more fluid and analytically less focused relationship with the "real"
world. It is a commentary on that world inasmuch as certain essential
Javanese concerns—with kinds of power, roles, and styles—motivate
much of its content. But it exaggerates, distorts, or even contradicts
much ideology without ever really confronting those inconsistencies.
Issues tend to arise and disperse in the course of a performance, often
resolved only temporarily, or by some fortuitous shift in the plot. For-
tuitousness is not insignificance, as A. L. Becker has made clear. Coincidence, he argues, has a power in Java that it lacks in Western aesthetics and thought (A. L. Becker 1979). Although coincidence may
suggest imperceptible forces operative in the world, however, it does
not suggest any resolution of the conflicts that inevitably arise within
an inconsistent, though normatively binding, ideology. Wayang

does not proffer solutions to such problems. If conflicts between, say, loyalty to one's kin and the pursuit of kakuwatan batin in asceticism arise in the course of some lakon, such conflicts never become central problems around which a performance is organized. When, for example, a relative of the Pandhawa disappears mysteriously, as Wrekudara did in *Senawangi,* and it turns out on his return that he was attaining great powers through asceticism, his new powers enable him to defeat the enemy that has put his relatives in jeopardy. The crisis is resolved, but not the intrinsic tension between kinship solidarity, which is much stressed in Java, and responsibilities to one's batin, which are also found compelling.

Actually, whatever issue motivated the first part of a performance—usually the topic under discussion in the long opening scene—is often left unresolved or obscured later in the performance, receiving only cursory attention again before the performance ends. What was critical from nine to midnight may well be unimportant by three, when a whole new series of events is initiated. Form is inflexible, but content often constitutes a running series of events, rather than a cumulative one.

Instead of searching for a core of meaning in a particular lakon, therefore, or in a particular rendering of it in performance, I think it more fruitful to examine certain repeating patterns in plot and character, and, too, in the reception of performances. I take this approach because to seek unique or specific messages in a single performance of wayang, as we demand of great drama in the West, imposes demands upon it that are at best irrelevant, at worst fundamentally misleading. A few classical lakon (e.g., lakon about the origin of rice and the *Murwakala* lakon used in the ruwatan ritual) seem to me susceptible of closer analysis because they originate in Javanese myths. Such an analysis is not to the point here, however.[1] Particular turns in plot must be considered, not in terms of a single lakon, but rather in the repertoire of conventions that crop up in wayang repeatedly. I will first discuss a few such conventions for the ways in which they reflect critical concerns of Javanese culture on which I have already commented: the self and status, encounter, and power. In these areas, wayang suggests alternatives to the way things are in life, as it is experienced and/or as it is conceived. But it does not do

[1] I have suggested some readings of these lakon elsewhere (Keeler 1983).

so critically or satirically, only contrastively. By following out the implications of Javanese social norms, wayang surpasses without really undercutting the tenets of Javanese culture.

Aside from the issues these recurrent conventions of character and plot pose, however, I wish to recast the question of what wayang means more radically. The evocativeness of a performance should be sought, not in what a particular lakon means, but rather in the range of issues, such as authority, consciousness, and submission, that every performance of wayang plays upon by virtue of the medium itself. By considering the "meaning" of the medium, not the message of a particular lakon, I will treat all performances as equivalent. Javanese commentators do the same, but to make a very different point, and I should state at the outset that my interpretations diverge greatly from Javanese views of wayang. I hope I have not distorted any facts, but I have certainly fitted those facts, plus informants' comments, into arguments many Javanese would reject.[2]

STATUS, POTENCY, AND WAYANG

Issues of style, status, and potency underlie the relations between characters and many turns of plot in wayang. Time-honored oppositions in style and status distinguish the characters in wayang with even greater clarity than in social life. All characters are marked by distinct types of eyes and noses, degrees of distance between the feet, kinds of dress, and qualities of voice, all of which establish both the status and general temperament of any character.[3] It is a system of pertinent oppositions: each trait means something only by virtue of the fact that it differs from other possibilities within a delimited range. And one trait tends to imply others. The pitch of a character's voice, for example, depends on the angle of the tilt of his or her face, and the higher the puppet's gaze, the higher is its voice. In this as in other respects, the primary distinction is in degrees of refinement, and Javanese culture is weighted normatively toward what is refined (alus) over what is crude (kasar).

Status, regardless of style, is also critical to interaction in wayang,

[2] I have not attempted, in the following remarks, to present a general description of wayang, because many such accounts have already been published. Van Ness and Prawirohardjo 1981 is a recent presentation of the essential information.

[3] For a recent discussion of types of wayang figures, see Solomonik 1980.

and its signs are another essential aspect of the differentiation of characters. No matter what the lakon, the status and style of a character should be respected at all times. The structure of authority is apparently quite straightforward. The gods have superior position and power to those of the knights (satriya) and servant-clowns (punakawan), and within each of these sets there are further gradations according to rank and age. In support of the official hierarchy stands the official, if unstated, conviction that superior status depends on superior accumulations of potency. As Anderson has pointed out, the loci classici for this notion of potency are, in stasis, the description of the perfect kingdom with which every performance begins, and in action, the satriya's fight against monsters at around 2:30 in the morning (Anderson 1972b:39). In the first case it is the noble qualities and mystical power of the king that cause all to submit voluntarily to his suzerainty. In the second, it is the same store of kakuwatan batin that makes the knight invulnerable to attack and fearsome in the efficacy of his counterblows.

The hierarchical distinction of types of characters does not apply so clearly, however, to the two sets of cousins, the five Pandhawa and the hundred Kurawa, whose struggle for the kingdom of Ngastina forms the basis of most wayang performances. The tension that motivates the Mahabharata stems from the intricate and intertwining claims of the opposing cousins, each party having at least some justice on its side. The Javanese response to this complexity, however, at least the current one, is to simplify the issues and to distinguish the sides as far as possible. Differences in status among the cousins are fine, but contrasts in appearance and character receive great emphasis. No Kurawa has the form of a truly refined knight. All are large, or misshapen, or at the least look straight ahead unashamedly. One has a speech defect, another a loud laugh, another an East Javanese accent. Their characters are unattractive: they are unscrupulous, selfish, often cowardly, stupid, and/or rude. By depicting the Kurawa in these unflattering ways, dhalang magnify the contrasts and minimize the connections between the Pandhawa and the Kurawa.

The division into good—righteous, attractive, admirable—and bad—devious, unattractive, unworthy—is so thorough in wayang as to rule out the analysis of character, motivation, and ethics on which much Western drama is based. In fact, the aggregate of known traits that constitutes a puppet's appearance and manner permits no char-

acter development. Each character has a voice and style that a dhalang must recreate in every performance. This maintains the careful
and comprehensive separation of characters into contrasting sets.
Action follows upon the movement of one or more sets of characters
out of their proper domain. But they cannot move outside of their
established type.

Wayang does posit one means of escape from the constraints of status and type, however, in the common plot device of *alihan*. *Alihan*
refers to the capacity of one character to take on the appearance,
manner, and voice of another, often entirely different sort of figure.[4]
In *Senawangi*, Bathari Pramuni changes form (*malih*) to become Begawan Durawicara. In many lakon, Bathara Kala uses the same ploy,
and in many others, it is Bathara Guru who does so. Since appearance and status *are* identity in wayang, when characters malih they
overcome the constraints of their own identities. They impinge on
others' behavior without revealing anything about themselves. In
this way, they minimize their implication in their own and others' action. When, for example, Bathara Guru takes on the appearance of a
priest in order to negotiate a settlement between the Kurawa and the
Pandhawa, his disguise is double. He pretends to be a priest, rather
than a god, and he pretends to work for the good of all when he really
seeks the Kurawas' gain. His pretense is often explained as the means
by which he hopes to further the interests of the Kurawa—one of
whose daughters he lusts after—without sullying the image of a god.
Gods, after all, should not be given to such base self-interest, and
they should not support injustice. His inevitable defeat at the hands
of a powerful knight or one of the few gods who outrank him lays bare
the deception. Then he must return to his proper place (heaven) and
form. Only the most powerful characters in wayang are capable of this
dissimulation of identity through alihan: the gods, the Pandhawa,
and one or two of the most powerful characters on the Kurawa side.
And only an extremely powerful opponent can dispel the disguise
through battle.

As long as a disguise has not been penetrated, a figure who malih
escapes, without in any way subverting, a critical element in Javanese

---

[4] To *malih* (this is the active verbal form of the root *alih*) should not be confused with
the phenomenon of incarnation, such as when Wisnu is incarnated as Rama or Kresna.
To be incarnated in this way is to *manjing* (literally, "to enter"), or to *nitis*. See Parnickel 1980 on this point.

interaction: the constraints of etiquette, status, and style. Note, however, that these constraints are never contradicted, despite all the dissemblance of identity. On the contrary, they are exploited. It is precisely because a priest (*pandhita*) deserves great respect that Bathara Guru can take advantage of the situation in Ngastina by pretending to be such a priest in order to further his own aims. Wayang does not undercut the binding authority of etiquette, it only imagines a kind of escape from an individual's particular place in the social hierarchy.[5] To malih constitutes in this regard a logical extreme of the impulse underlying asceticism. In "life," that is, in understandings of daily life, people achieve the power of a wong tuwa through ascetic rigors. They may thereby attain titles and high office, or they may gain great capacity as curers or advisors, for example. In any case, as I have argued in Chapter 1, it is through their withdrawal from interaction and the minimization of their susceptibility to others' speech that they manage to gather potency and increase their status. To malih exaggerates the pattern to the point of a total dissimulation of identity. The result assures a character's invulnerability, even if only provisional, to others' behavior.

The convention of alihan suggests that potency can be used in such a way as to play the rules of status and etiquette to one's own advantage. People whose concentration of potency is sufficient can escape social definition while availing themselves of etiquette's control over others' actions. There is another kind of escape as well: in subservience. The punakawan who serve the Pandhawa, their ancestors, and their descendants contrast with all the heroes, gods, kings, and priests in wayang by their immediate accessibility.[6] It is difficult to find any parallel in the West for these figures, who are as well-loved and intimately known as brothers to Javanese. (Buster Keaton's or the Marx Brothers' consistent personae, sustained in all of their films, probably resemble the punakawan most closely.) They first appear at about one in the morning, and their arrival always signals an interlude of jokes, light popular gendhing, and dancing. In the rest of the performance, they contrast with their high-status masters in the directness of their speech, in their practical concern with food and money, in their willingness to use any means, no matter how un-

[5] Benedict Anderson pointed out to me this iconic regularity that alihan cannot contravene (Anderson, personal communication, May 1979).
[6] J. J. Ras has recently published an article on the punakawan (Ras 1978).

heroic, to defeat their opponents, and in their complete lack of fortitude, self-restraint, or resistance to their own emotions. Nothing could be further from the heroic ethic of the epics, or from the normative stress of Javanese culture on self-control and discipline, than the punakawans' forthright expression of gut feelings. Yet they enjoy, precisely because of their humble status, a freedom of action unique among all wayang figures. They escape social constraints not by concentrating potency, as characters do when they malih, but rather by abjuring all claims to status.

The punakawan are all that is not caught up in status and language. They can mock each other, argue, and have fist-fights. They can fight against their enemies, using trickery, farming tools, and even excrement. Semar often uses his great flatulence to lay an opponent low. They can sing and dance, weep, beg for money, and express their fears. They can do all these things because they need not protect their status. They have no status. They are dependents.

The punakawan are also exempt from time and history. They are servants to all the heroes from the *Ramayana* through the *Mahabharata*. Whereas their masters are linked in long genealogies, the punakawan are virtually without genealogy. And very little ever happens to them. They are married, it is true, and a few lakon revolve about their own adventures. But one never sees their wives or children. They have no social context aside from each other and their masters. They are both thoroughly constrained, because they are servants, and virtually without constraint, because they have no status to protect. Perhaps the clearest indication of their lack of status is that they, alone among the figures in wayang, can be made to use any words at all, from Indonesian, or even Dutch or English (fractured), whereas at all other times a dhalang must be careful to avoid obviously anachronistic and foreign usages.

Representations of the punakawan evoke the casual, humorous interaction of Javanese youths, who need concern themselves with their dignity and obligations far less than their elders. Such scenes, however, do not simply reflect a stage in a Javanese male's social career. The complete dependence of the punakawan on their masters means that they enjoy a security Javanese society does not afford commoners today. They are as certain of the satisfaction of their basic needs, and as unfettered by responsibilities to their own status, as the servant at the court who has "forgotten" his family. So they represent an ideal, even though the ideal is located not at the apex but rather at the base of social hierarchy. That ideal is perhaps best summarized by saying that they, in their complete dependence, need be mindful of nothing except their loyalty to their masters. Aside from that, and the respect they must show their superiors, they need be careful about very little else.

Of low status, deformed, and dependent, the punakawan might seem to be perfect representatives of what Victor Turner calls marginality—anti-heroic, anti-structural, the domain of those who criticize and reject the distinctions on which a society's power structure is based (Turner 1969). But unlike the role of marginal figures in many cultures, the punakawan are neither satirical nor critical. They are non-structural in that they wield no official power, but they are not anti-structural. They do not affirm pan-human or pan-social values in conflict with heroic ideals and strictures. They simply present a contrast with them, an alternative rendering that does not put the normatively dominant one into question. The punakawan "know their place." They speak respectfully to their masters (although some jokes hinge on their forgetting themselves and responding too casually to a superior's remark). Among themselves, they engage in a relaxed, unself-conscious, and spontaneous mode of interaction that Javanese society only occasionally permits an adult, particularly an adult male. The price the punakawan pay is their autonomy, in that they are servants, but what they gain is freedom from responsibility. That such a position of subordination and ease must be attractive to many Javanese, who show such fondness for the four figures, does not mean that Javanese need see in the punakawan a critique of social reality. Rather, this idealized version of low status rounds out the base, as asceticism and alihan round out the top, of wayang's social hierarchy.

While wayang suggests, therefore, two types of release from the binding considerations of a person's own status in interaction, one in a superior concentration of potency, the other in a complete disclaimer of status, neither alternative, I must stress, in any way subverts the values of the system. The punakawan, once again, do not satirize the ethic that they appear to flout. They are outside its constraints inasmuch as their own status is minimal. But they are not against the system.

If alihan and the punakawan suggest opposite extremes, but never contradictions, of social hierarchy, two figures, Bathara Guru and Se-mar, provide further examples of how wayang points to inconsisten-cies without confronting them: in this case, in conflicting impres-sions of the father. Guru is a god and the king of heaven. In those lakon hinging on alihan, he and his monstrous wife, Bathari Pramuni (actually the monstrous aspect of his queen, Dewi Uma), are the two characters most likely to be revealed in the dénouement to have ma-lih and caused havoc among the cousins. Whereas Guru is powerful in hierarchical terms, Semar is at the bottom of the hierarchy but very potent. Semar is something of a permanent alihan. He, Guru, and another punakawan, Togog, also misshapen and a servant to whichever foreign adversary figures in a lakon, all arose out of an orig-inal egg. Semar and Togog were forced to become servants on earth, while Guru became the king of heaven. Semar, nevertheless, is im-mensely potent, and he is considered the dhanyang of Java. That his familiar, ugly form is really just an alihan is demonstrated in certain lakon in which he regains his original, elegant appearance. (He is never thought of in this form, however. One somewhat daffy dha-lang-cum-dhukun showed me Semar's "photograph," which he had taken during a meeting with Semar. It showed, in a very vague im-age, Semar's usual, obese figure dressed in the checkered cloth char-acteristic of the punakawan.) Claims are made that he still resides in certain caves in Java, and he crosses the boundary between the world of wayang and the everyday world more than any other character.

Both figures, Guru and Semar, are important images of paternal power. Guru's children, especially Wisnu, Bayu, and Mahadewa, are among the most important gods in the wayang repertoire. His mon-strous son, Bathara Kala (born of Guru's seed when it falls in the sea), and the relations between Guru and Kala, form the frame of the ru-watan ritual, the most important ritual use of wayang. Semar is thought of as the father of the three other punakawan who join him in serving the righteous party (although according to certain rela-tively obscure stories, they are actually only his adopted sons). What is striking about both Guru and Semar, however, is that they fulfill the image of the strong and effective father so imperfectly. Guru is a conniving and lustful figure who is impelled by his own selfishness to side with the Kurawa. He is ostensibly both structurally powerful and spiritually potent, yet his machinations lead over and over to his dis-grace and rout. Semar, for all his great potency, not only must play

servant to high-status figures, he must put up with the constant insults, teasing, and tricks to which his sons subject him. While the
punakawan evince respect in their obeisance to their masters, to their
own father they are rude and hostile in a manner both scandalous
and, to spectators, vastly entertaining. Pétruk, Nala Garèng, and Bagong treat Semar with a kind of jocular scorn out of kilter with all the
notions of respect for one's elders that Javanese normally espouse.

In Guru and Semar, paternal power is undercut, distorted, occasionally mocked. It is never contradicted for long, however. Guru
may depart in disgrace at the end of a performance, but he remains
the king of heaven. And Semar usually proves in the end that his own
power is superior to that of his sons. Like other contraventions of ideology in wayang, these examples of aberrant paternal figures are never
pushed to their critical limits or resolved. Instead, in exaggerating
contradictory versions of the figure of authority, suggesting alternatively extraordinary powers, great selfishness, foolishness, and at
times, in Semar, heroism, Semar and Guru remain ongoing sources
of tension. In fact, they motivate much of what happens in wayang.
When I asked one dhalang why Guru often behaved so outrageously,
he said, "I don't know. But if he didn't, there wouldn't be any lakon."

Much of an audience's interest in a performance, I believe, depends on the resonance wayang suggests with their lives. But that resonance is by no means univocal or even deliberately cultivated by
dhalang. I have tried to show that certain conventions in wayang
play upon important aspects of Javanese ideology and interaction
without really resolving or even confronting the contradictions and
inconsistencies that inhere in them. Perhaps the relationship is most
succinctly typified in the many battles that take place in every performance. Popular dhalang often win an audience's attention in the
long opening scene by staging a debate among several characters. As
tension mounts, the debate grows increasingly hostile, turning into
first a verbal battle (prang omong), and finally, after epithets fly, a
physical one. These contests, verbal and physical, arouse avid interest. They contravene, however, the resolutely pacific bias in Javanese interaction. This discourages all but the most veiled expression
of displeasure in most situations. (The exception is when a person of
much higher status chastises a low-status person. Open expression is
then permissible because the disparity in status should prevent any
retort or argument.) To enter into sustained argument, let alone a

fist-fight, is disgraceful no matter what justification either party may have for anger. Hostility and bitterness are always thought best dissembled until they recede from consciousness, or at least from view. The relentless pressure for smooth, polite interaction usually suffices to prevent their overt expression. If it does not, people often simply break off all relations.

When restraint gives way to insults and then violence in wayang, etiquette's compelling force is abrogated. Spectators' insatiable taste for battles, both verbal and physical, must stem from this exciting contrast with their own experience. Nevertheless, even in battle, the strictures of status must be maintained: characters should do battle in a series of single encounters with adversaries of equivalent rank, and a king must never be struck above his shoulders. The world of wayang suggests, therefore, departure from the principles of interaction that are binding in the world of humans. Yet at the same time it asserts the capacity of status to determine relations more surely than it can in real experience. When violence does break out in Java, as it only very rarely does but then with astonishing vehemence, issues of status and honor may well underlie people's acts, but etiquette falls by the wayside.

RESISTING THE PERFORMANCE

A performance of wayang may suggest tensions within the basic assumptions of Javanese culture, but it is unlikely to draw out the implications of those conflicts. This lack of interest in developing a specific problematic contravenes Western criteria for great drama—but that is beside the point. I remark upon the contrasts between Javanese performances and Western aesthetics not to criticize the former, but rather to raise questions about the nature of Javanese aesthetics. The lack of a sustained problematic is interesting because it can be linked to a broader issue: the ways in which Javanese deliberately insulate themselves from the impact of wayang, both in their reactions to a performance and in their commentary upon the tradition.

Audience's tastes in lakon already point to a curiously defensive or resistant attitude toward wayang. I have mentioned that the ethical nuances intrinsic to the *Mahabharata* are little developed in wayang. The inclination to reduce the complexity and dimensions of lakon is particularly clear in the proliferation of those new lakon mentioned earlier, in the discussion of the dhalang's dramaturgy (sanggit). The vast majority of performances given today are set in the time just prior to the *Bratayuda*, the climactic war. They pit Pandhawa against Kurawa, therefore, plus other ephemeral characters "from across the sea," rather than depict the ancestors of the warring cousins. The great prestige of principal lakon (lakon pokok) depends on the fact that they *urut-urut*: they follow one another in an inevitable series. So-called "old" lakon (*lakon tuwa*), which recount events prior to the cousins' birth, present incidents great and small that eventually redound on the struggle for Ngastina. Each lakon in the series adds one or two strands to the story, and these strands pull taut in the twelve lakon that depict the events just before, during, and after the *Bratayuda*. Such old lakon are little performed, however. People say that they do not recognize "older" characters and so cannot enjoy performances in which the familiar Kurawa and Pandhawa do not appear. Yet of course the inability to recognize such older characters is due to the older lakons' disappearance from the active repertoire. Ignorance of these earlier events in the epic cycles necessarily diminishes the resonance and historical motivation of events that take place, as most popular lakon take place, on the eve of the *Bratayuda*.

The fate of certain classical lakon that are "modernized" epitomizes the effects of this chronological bias. They are "Pandhawaized" (*diPandhawakaké*): the action is transferred to the era of the Pandhawa. In the case of such an important lakon as *Sri mulih*, which recounts the abduction of the rice goddess, Sri, and her eventual return to Java, the temporal shift cancels the whole etiological significance of the story. No matter: the Pandhawa have appeared, replacing other, less familiar characters, and the audience is satisfied.

It is also claimed that people are tired of the classical lakon and wish to see new ones in their stead. Yet the majority of classical lakon are not known to the contemporary Javanese populace. And as mentioned above, new lakon, although they introduce new names and an occasional novelty in plot, are far more formulaic than classical ones. It is much easier to guess the outline of yet another lakon about the obtaining of a mystical boon (wahyu), or yet another lakon that begins with the presence of a "priest" in Ngastina who claims he can make peace among the cousins, than to anticipate the surprising connections among characters and events that come to light in "old" lakon.

Another stated reason for the frequent performance of new lakon is that lakon are believed to exercise a certain power over events. A lakon that recounts a hero's wedding is thought suitable to the ritual celebration of a wedding because the lakon will exert its influence to the benefit of the newlyweds. If a wayang is held for a final funerary ritual (one thousand days after death), a lakon describing a character's admission to heaven is appropriate, since it will facilitate the similar passage of the soul of the deceased. More importantly, many lakon are considered dangerous. *Bratayuda* lakon and other lakon that depict the violent deaths of heroes are thought highly volatile, likely to bring misfortune to sponsors who request their performance. Better always to stick with tried-and-true, formulaic lakon that depict no such dramatic events. Then the sponsors can rest assured that no one present will suffer any ill effects. New secondary lakon fit these requirements better than principal lakon that relate important and often disturbing events in the epic cycle. Dhalang, too, tend to avoid lakon that they fear might unleash destructive powers. If sponsors request such a lakon, a dhalang is careful to explain the danger and to stress that it is the sponsors who must take responsibility (tanggung jawab) for any mishap that follows.

It is not only sponsors and dhalang who express a preference for new, rather bland lakon. Huge crowds will assemble to see dangerous *Bratayuda* performances held by villages, organizations, or other assemblies, and excitement runs particularly high on such occasions. *Bratayuda* performances can be performed under such circumstances because large numbers of people—the village as a whole, or an organization's entire membership—take responsibility for any consequences that may ensue, rather than just a single sponsoring family. However, some dhalang mentioned that many *Bratayuda* performances were sponsored by committees in the early sixties. People saw what happened next, the "Bratayuda" of 1965-1966, and now they are leery of repeating the pattern. On the other hand, a person with claims to potency can put his kakuwatan batin to the test by sponsoring a *Bratayuda* performance at his home. If no disaster follows, his strength is proved great.

In the absence of such special events or purposes, when the choice is between principal lakon and new ones, most people express a preference for the latter. They believe that new lakon afford a dhalang more opportunities for jokes, battles, and other entertaining routines. To an extent, the opinion is justified, since if there is very little plot to get through, a dhalang can devote more time to such incidentals. Still, many principal lakon provide ample opportunity for very amusing scenes, as older dhalang often recount in conversation.

It is difficult to establish to what extent the proliferation of new lakon is a recent phenomenon, as some older Javanese claim. Many dhalang say that "in the old days" there were only three *lakon wahyu*. These are lakon that depict several characters' efforts to obtain a mystical boon, a wahyu, that is eventually obtained by a Pandhawa, usually Arjuna's son, Angkawijaya. At present these are the most common type of new lakon, suitable for performance at virtually any ritual celebration. People who cite the great frequency with which such lakon are now performed as evidence that wayang is in a state of decline, however, as some people I spoke with did, may exaggerate the contrast, failing to recall the prevalence of equally insubstantial lakon in the past. Wedding lakon were apparently very common in former times. To make up yet another wife or wives for Arjuna to add to his collection has long been thought acceptable invention, and it is possible such conventional performances were as common in the thirties or fifties as *lakon wahyu* are now.

The important point, I think, about new, lightweight lakon is that they reduce particularly easily to a number of enjoyable parts, with no compelling plot and little suspense about their resolution. They are isolated units that make no advance toward the epic cycle's cataclysmic dénouement. Though they take place in the time shortly before the *Bratayuda*, the references to the coming war are so stereotypical as to be thoroughly tame. These new lakon efface themselves immediately, and in fact, they exert little emotional or intellectual hold upon their audience even while they are in progress. They can therefore be easily enjoyed but also easily resisted.

The consistent diminution of the epic cycle's tragic dimensions provides further evidence of a resistance to wayang's hold upon its audience. In the character of Karna, for example, there inheres a potentially tragic character. Born to the Pandhawas' mother before her marriage to Pandhu, and set adrift by her in a basket in order to conceal her shame, he was found and raised by the Kurawa. He is aware that the Kurawas' cause is unjust, but he feels bound by loyalty to support them. So he must do battle against his own half-brothers, in the *Bratayuda*, and he dies at their hands. Certainly the ethics of his situation are complex, and the figure of Karna affords the opportunity for highly dramatic encounters. He is instead usually represented as faintly ridiculous: hot-headed, impetuous, liable to get into scrapes he should have been able to avoid. Exegetical comment about him is rarely any more generous. In performance and in commentary, the shading to his character implicit in the epic is cast aside in favor of straightforward contrasts, releasing people from the need to consider his character and situation at all deeply. The pathos implicit in Karno's predicament is thereby resisted.

I will return to the subject of Javanese interpretation in the next chapter. In the remainder of this one, I wish to point to other manifestations of what I have termed resistance to the art form in performance.

Popular appraisal of great dhalang would seem to contradict any notion of resistance on the part of wayang's audiences. When people praise an especially fine dhalang, they invariably say, "When the scene he played was joyful, everyone in the audience felt happy, and when it was sad, members of the audience wept." Such praise is usually reserved for dhalang who are now dead. It proves that Javanese fans of wayang are concerned with a performance's emotional impact, that is, with its ability to exert an effect upon a spectator's mood. But the remark always surprised me, since I have never seen a dhalang play a scene in such a way as to create and sustain a tragic mood.[7]

Tragedy seems not alien to the tradition, but rather suppressed. The reason for that suppression, I believe, is that to become too engrossed in a performance would threaten a spectator's awareness and equanimity. Even in performances of *Bratayuda* lakon, in which the heroes beloved to the Javanese are killed, dhalang persistently undercut the aura of sadness with comedy.

Certain village performances of *Bratayuda* lakon illustrate especially clearly this need to avoid tragedy. In many villages, there is a tradition that a *Bratayuda* lakon must be given each year. To perform other lakon, it is feared, would disappoint the territorial spirit (dhanyang) and incite his reprisals. Yet to perform the violent and distress-

---

[7] Peacock mentions a similar absence of tragedy in ludrug (Peacock 1968).

ing events that occur in any of the eight or twelve-night-long lakon that make up the full cycle is also thought very risky. To stave off such dangers, the whole series is compressed into a single performance. As a result, the critical events pass so quickly that their power, both in the world and over the audience, is neutralized. The impression of danger does not stem exclusively from the tragedy of the heroes' deaths. To represent the violent death of kings, even of the unjust Duryudana, is thought dangerous, and even *Bratayuda Rampasan* performances, as these synoptic performances are called, often stop short of that climactic moment. The collapse of hierarchy among kin and in the kingdom, and the demise of the Pandhawas' sons, are too mystically powerful as well as too upsetting, to receive extended dramatic treatment. Similarly, when I asked a dhalang about a performance he had given in which Baladewa is taken into heaven, he said he could relate in conversation what he could not perform before the screen: that the much-loved Baladewa is actually defeated in battle, not simply invited to enter heaven. But to portray that incident would have been "ill-advised."

Javanese speak of this dramatic discretion as a way of avoiding mystical ill effects, rather than of limiting the effects of the illusion upon a spectator's feelings. But as an outsider, I believe it fits with a general effort on the part of most spectators to maintain some emotional disengagement. The same tendency to resist the art form's hold upon oneself comes out in the course of a performance. Bright kerosene lamps are kept burning throughout the performance, greatly reducing the clarity of the shadows, and, by illuminating the entire performance area, making one's attention more easily distracted from the puppets. When a dhalang makes a joke, it usually evokes an instant of spontaneous laughter, then a stylized hoot. The stylization puts a stop to the humor's effects: the spectator regains self-control.

Which side of the screen a spectator observes depends on whether he numbers among the invited guests, who watch the shadow side, or the uninvited spectators, who watch the puppet side.[8] But most peo-

---

[8] The literature on wayang is remarkably inconsistent on the matter of who sits on which side of the screen, but at all non-commercial performances I have seen since 1968, guests have sat on the shadow side and uninvited spectators on the puppet side. Virtually all of these spectators are males, only a few women sitting far behind the screen, inside the house. I find Rassers's comment that women watch the shadow side, whereas men watch the puppets, particularly puzzling (Rassers 1959).

ple I asked said they preferred to watch the puppet side, so that they could see the dhalang. Play on the size and clarity of the image that occurs on the shadow side is then lost, and seeing the dhalang manipulate the puppets detracts from the illusion of their life and movement. That seems to be just the point. On two occasions dhalang told me they preferred to watch the dhalang in order not to be deceived. Watching the shadows, they said, one might think him better than he really was. I find the remark paradoxical, since the effectiveness of the images should be the measure of the dhalang's skill. But the attitude shows a desire to isolate the dhalang as the source of all the voices and gestures, and in this way to limit his power. Older people also say that in the old days people who started to talk at a performance were hushed by other members of the audience who were intent upon hearing the dhalang's voice. Now that the sound of his voice, though distorted by poor equipment turned to full volume, floods the scene, everyone talks, often making the dhalang's words unintelligible inside the performance area.

By speaking of patterns of resistance in people's reactions to wayang, I do not mean to suggest their lack of interest. Just the opposite; resistance is aroused because of the art form's effectiveness. The dramatic illusion, particularly any sad or disturbing feelings it might arouse, threaten a spectator's capacity to éling: to remain in conscious control of oneself, and to resist the control implicit in a dhalang's hold upon one's interest and feelings. To support this contention, I must open an excursus on Javanese understandings of consciousness.

CONSCIOUSNESS, FORGETFULNESS, AND PLEASURE

Éling means "to remember" and "to be conscious."[9] It can take no direct object. (To specify an object the root must be given the affixes ke- and -an, forming kélingan, a passive form.) When informants said the phrase, which is common, "You must éling" (kudu éling), I often tried to ask what it was one needed to be mindful of. The most common response was "God." Further commentary suggested an ascetic's withdrawal from mundane affairs, his attention focused on God in

---

[9] I was prompted to examine Javanese ideas of consciousness by James Siegel's analysis of the Acehnese term akal (Siegel 1969). Siegel's illuminating work on Acehnese literature has also stimulated my thoughts on the links between ideas of consciousness, aesthetics, and resistance (Siegel 1979).

meditation. In fact, some informants declared both the ultimate example of éling and the most advanced form of ascetic exercise to consist in an ability to do meditation (*semèdi*) while engaged in everyday interaction. No crowd, however noisy, no shock or disappointment, can distract a person whose asceticism has advanced to this sublime degree.[10] Discrete ascetic rigors such as fasts or ngebleng then appear as so many neophytes' devices, steps toward a truly ascetic state of mind, one that should suffer no interruption under the impact of mere events.

Éling suggests remaining calm, untroubled, unmoved. A person, I was often told, should become neither very sad nor very happy. Either extreme implies an unwarranted lack of control, the opposite of the even, flat awareness of éling. To éling, then, grants a person an emotional invulnerability which Javanese greatly value. Yet it does not mean passivity or the ability to turn the other cheek. On the contrary, speaking of it often evokes another common Javanese remark, that "you have to be careful," "you have to be on guard" (*kudu sing ati-ati*). This means that people have to beware of all the hostile influences and feelings that others bear against them and their kin. They have to set their own steadiness of gaze and their impeturbable awareness against others' attempts to manipulate, shame, or take advantage of them. Often this requires assuring themselves—and perhaps others—of their own superior status. Then they recall, not God, but their own birth or station. One venerable dhalang explained that after he had absented himself from his family for two or three years in his early adulthood, he and his wife of course had some suspicions about each other's fidelity. He told her, however, that they must both recall that they were descended from long lines of illustrious dhalang, and all suspicions immediately disappeared.

Remembering one's genealogy and "who one is" is never an introspective act in Java, but rather a recollection of one's ties to other people. This understanding links éling to the understanding of memory in many cultures of Indonesia.[11] Yet the diminishing value placed on genealogical claims to status in Java, particularly among the new bourgeoisie, makes this genealogical side of éling less important now

[10] S. Errington notes the same notion among aristocrats in Luwu (S. Errington 1983).

[11] See for example Siegel 1969 on the Acehnese and S. Errington Forthcoming on the Bugis.

than it probably used to be. For that matter, for the mass of commoners who not only lack high status but also lack firm connections of any
sort to high-status figures, yet who share the view that to éling is essential to their well-being, the term clearly means something more
diffuse than genealogical memory. That is, while mindfulness of
one's obligations and solidarity with one's kin is a key aspect of éling,
above all éling is an attitude of rigorous self-control. And in the
power such self-control demonstrates, it also implies control of one's
environment. People who éling are never overwhelmed by their reactions to events, but neither are they unaware of attempts to deceive
them, say, or of slights to their prestige. They are able to detect all
such maneuvers because they are so perfectly attentive, and they are
able to respond effectively to all events because they never let any
passion make them forget themselves.

Lali ("to forget") contrasts with several meanings of éling. The terror of 1965-1966 is recalled now as the time when "children forgot
their parents and parents forgot their children," that is, when people
let no loyalites stay their tongues or hands in the condemnation, ar-
rest, and/or murder of so many people. The many relatives who move
to Jakarta or Sumatra and never send news or money back to their kin
are said simply "to forget." The same is said of those people who fail
to repay loans. When people forget something of great importance to
their own interest, then some external agent, often God, is said to
have caused them to forget (nglalèkaké). Bu Cerma was told by a respected elder that her husband should change his name. She failed to
mention this to Pak Cerma, however, and when their son, Sarna,
died soon after, she was sure that she had been "made to forget" the
elder's advice. A thief who uses magic to fool people into letting
down their guard and permitting themselves to be conned also causes
his victim to forget. When a singer gave up her diamond jewelry to a
man who was ostensibly taking her to a performance and the man
made off with it, people commented that the thief must have gotten
a rapal from some dhukun with which to cause the unfortunate
woman to forget.

Another term that contrasts with éling is ngalamun: to be blank,
mindless, or distracted, letting one's thoughts wander off, often after
some object of one's desire. A person who is distracted (ngalamun) is
highly susceptible to attack from spirits and to the machinations of
black magic. Mbak Painah, whose possession by spirits was men-

tioned in Chapter 4, was said to be distracted following the death of her child, causing her to become "empty" and so easily entered by spirits. It is not just powerful negative emotions that cause a person to ngalamun, however. To let one's mind drift about, in whatever mood, is ill-advised. It may cause people to laugh by themselves, or get angry by themselves, both signs of incipient madness. Desire for anything suggests becoming preoccupied with it, so laying a person open to disappointment and distraction. In such cases, people may remember (*kélingan*) that one thing that they want, and as a result, fail to éling.

To forget is usually negative in connotation, and ngalamun is invariably so. In more equivocal relation to éling is sleep, which arouses feelings both negative and positive in Java. Distrust of sleep is great. As a form of ascetic exercise, to go without sleep is considered more effective even than fasting. Many men told me that they never retired until after midnight, or got up most nights at two A.M., that they slept outside in the yard with only a palm leaf for a mat, and/or that they did frequent all-night vigils at holy places. (These were of course claims to potency and not necessarily to be taken at face value.) To sleep makes one susceptible to mystical attack, as ngalamun does, whereas waking people have their defenses in better order. Sleep, it is often said, makes people's bodies strong but their batin weak. Nevertheless, or really, by extension, sleep represents an escape. Javanese react to many sorts of distress by falling asleep. Everything from disappointment to real trauma induces sleep. When I went to find a friend who planned to go with me to a wayang one evening, he told me he had learned he had to work that night. "I was so disappointed I slept all day," he told me. When Pak Cerma's son, Parto, went to visit his sister and her family in Semarang, he saw his brother-in-law slap their four-year-old boy. Parto reported the incident to his parents on returning home, saying that it had upset him so much it had made him feel *lemes* ("weak," "flaccid"), and he had had to go lie down.[12] Parto reacted to his older brother's death by sleeping through much of the funeral.

[12] His father's reaction was interesting. Pak Cerma told Parto that he should have *ngandhani* his brother-in-law: advised, or remonstrated him, as an older person does a younger one. After all, Parto was Suprih's "older brother," and so Suprih would have listened to and even appreciated Parto's remarks. Parto was Suprih's classificatory older brother because Parto was older than the sister Suprih had married. In view of the two

If sleep is a way of avoiding consciousness in the face of trauma, that loss of consciousness is also threatening. In fact, consciousness itself requires a careful grip. Often when I returned home after sunrise from a performance, I would bathe before going to bed, feeling that I could sleep longer and more soundly as a result. I asked Sigit, my usual companion, why he didn't do the same. He agreed that to bathe made you feel more comfortable, but he was afraid that he would "go too far" (*kebablasen*), that is, not just lose consciousness in sleep but die. I think Sigit's anxiety depended as much on the attraction sleep exerts as in its similarity to death. The attraction consists precisely in letting one's guard down, giving up control in a comfortable loss of consciousness. The concern Javanese feel for their dignity, status, and vulnerability means that many situations call for studied moves and reactions. Sleep compromises such self-consciousness, so it is at once suspect and enticing.

Pleasures of many sorts, in fact, are described in terms of a loss of "memory" and self-control. The crude (kasar) word for penis, *peli*, has a popular gloss: *yèn wis ngethapel, lali* ("with legs hooked round, you forget").[13] *Ngethapel* describes the way a child puts his legs around someone who picks him up or a man uses his legs to hug a coconut palm he is climbing. Here its intent is clearly sexual, and physical pleasure is described as obliviousness to all else. A particularly delicious variety of mango is called *pelem lali jiwa* (a mango [to make you] forget your soul).

Pak Cerma's description of an abdi-dalem at court who "forgets" his family is another rendering of the pleasures implicit in forgetfulness. To éling means, among other things, to be cognizant of responsibilities to one's kin. To forget one's kin is both risky and somewhat alluring. It can remove a considerable burden from people's shoulders, though it also leaves them defenseless in times of need. Mbok Paira had "forgotten" when she fought with her kin, and none of them "remembered"—recognized their responsibility for her wel-

young men's respective places in the family's status hierarchy, Pak Cerma was confident that Suprih, a somewhat cocky civil servant, would have heeded Parto's advice, this despite the fact that Parto was chronologically younger, unemployed, unmarried, and generally thought far from wise.

[13] I owe this and several other wonderful examples of the genre of *kérata basa* to Robert Klotz, whose work on Javanese theories of language I have found very stimulating (Klotz, personal communication, October 1981). I will discuss *kérata basa* in the following chapter.

fare—when a snake bit her hand, as recounted in Chapter 3. To entrust oneself wholly to the care of a powerful authority, however, as a servant at court submits to the king, presents an escape from these two extremes: from the obligations of kinship, on the one hand, and from the defenselessness that results from disregarding those obligations, on the other. In complete submission people must "remember," too: they must observe the constraints of status difference. But they need be mindful, as the punakawan are mindful, of little else.

The abdi-dalem's contentment is an idealized extreme, the patronage system as it exists today only in some people's imaginings of the royal court and prison. Wayang provides another image of this contented submission, in a conventionalized exchange between king and prime minister or other courtier that takes place in court scenes. The king summons one of his courtiers before him. The courtier states that on receiving the order to appear before the king, he felt stunned, as though struck by lightning, terrified that he had committed some error for which he would now be punished. However, on entering the audience hall and the presence of the king, he felt deliciously cool, "as though bathed in a thousand waters" (*lir siniram ing tirta sèwu*). In place of fear, he felt perfectly calm. Now he offers himself to his lord's bidding, accepting and indifferent should the king wish to sever his head from his body. The exchange ends as the king accepts the courtier's obeisance but explains that he desires only some news, such as word of the condition of the kingdom. As in Pak Cerma's description of the abdi-dalem at court, the coolness that the king's presence induces in the courtier makes him perfectly indifferent to all else. He loses all investment, not only in his kin but also in his own life: the king's potency is sufficient to drive all else out of mind.

In detailing these Javanese attitudes toward consciousness and its opposite, I wish to point to affinities between two conceptions of pleasurable experience that Javanese informants would keep rigorously distinct. One is sensual pleasure as a release from normal consciousness. The other might be called "political" pleasure, a pleasant release from concern for one's kin and even oneself, specifically, one's own status, in submission to a superior authority. The repeated image of an escape from the need for attentiveness, guardedness, and "consciousness" conceived of as readiness and control, complements a similar understanding of escape as surrender, whether to sensory impressions or to a prince. That such submission counters all the emphasis on clarity and autonomy in Javanese ideology is precisely what constitutes its enticement, and its danger.

PLEASURE AND FOCUS IN JAVANESE MUSIC

To attend a performance of wayang combines what I have called sensual and political understandings of pleasure. Both are translated into a constant play on degrees of focus. The gamelan accompaniment to a performance illustrates this changing focus especially clearly, and since it plays such an important role in the varying impressions a performance of wayang makes upon its spectators, I will begin this discussion of wayang's aesthetics by reference to its music.

Gamelan integrates a great variety of musical lines in shifting degrees of aural clarity. Judith Becker points out that melodic line was not originally essential to the formulation of Javanese musical pieces (gendhing) (J. Becker 1979). Instead, principles of gong structure, in which the coincidence of gong strokes marks off sections of repeating cycles, underlie each gendhing's organization. Sumarsam, it is true, speaks of an "inner melody" in Solonese gendhing (Sumarsam 1984). But although this musical line is present to the mind of the players, no single instrument plays it. Judith Becker contrasts this Solonese tradition to the Jogjanese one, in which the formal gong structure is more clearly evident. But in either tradition, as one goes through the series of different rhythms, and from one gendhing to the next, the *balungan* or skeletal line (also referred to in English, somewhat misleadingly, as "nuclear melody") becomes first increasingly obscure, then increasingly clear. This is because of changes in "rhythm" (*wirama*), each one of which indicates a different ratio of strokes on the instruments that play the skeletal line to strokes on instruments that play embellishments. As one passes from *wirama* one to two to three to four, which is like shifting gears, the strokes on the *saron* and *slenthem*, which play the skeletal line, become rarer. This permits the other "inner" or embellishing instruments—the *gendèr*, *gambang*, *clempung*, and *rebab*, each of which has a highly distinctive tonal quality—plus the female singer (*pesindhèn*), to superimpose increasingly long and complex variations. The result is greater aural richness and less aural clarity. A wealth of embellishment takes precedence over any clear line. In Solo, especially, the embellishing instruments simply take over, playing such a variety of almost autonomous variations as to create a sea of sound. In Jogjanese *soran*, martial gendhing that are Jogja's pride, the *saron* and *bonang* take on the equivalent function of playing variations, but in a great clangor of heavy mallets striking bronze. One finds in either case a similar impulse to obscure what there is of a single musical focus in favor of embellishment.

Connoisseurs of gamelan insist that it is the long, slow "great gendhing" (*gendhing ageng*) that are most enjoyable to hear. When gendhing are played in a series, one always proceeds from longer to shorter pieces. As the progression continues, the gong periods become shorter, and as a result, all musical lines clearer. The dispersion or diffusion of focus characteristic of the first gendhing in a series gives way eventually to the speedy, clear, heavily accented *gendhing dolanan* ("play" gendhing, short and catchy) or battle music. These display much clearer musical lines and provide the listener with a much better sense of direction and a clearer focus of attention. So they establish much more straightforward relations between listener and music—at the expense of aural richness and subtlety.

The use of microphones and the method of taping gamelan now current in Java greatly overemphasize the *pesindhèn*'s line. When gamelan is played without sound amplification, the expanse of sound it generates, with no single line highlighted to the detriment of the others, is much fuller. Even with an overemphasis on the vocalist's part, however, the vocal line cannot assume the dominance it does in Western music, because the singer chooses variations as she goes. So in listening to a *pesindhèn*'s singing, one never listens to a vocal line one knows by heart.

Pak Cerma said of the great gong (*gong gedhé*) that its stroke is "startling but uniquely satisfying." *Ngegèti* (startling) is usually negative in connotation, since to be startled (*kagèt*) is dangerous to a person's well-being. It is liable to make one not *éling*, whether in emotional disarray or in actual loss of consciousness. Here, however, the word's connotation was clearly positive. I believe Pak Cerma described the gong this way both because of its singularly deep and resonant sound, and because it sounds so rarely. The overall effect of longer gendhing, as I have said, is to create a great flood of sound with a range of contrasting textures but no clear focus. Their form is discernible only to people with a fair familiarity with the art of gamelan. Even an experienced listener often loses track of the gong period. (So may some of the players. This is why the gong is often said to be the most difficult instrument to play in the ensemble, since the gong player may himself lose track of where they are, as well as the most important instrument, since other players orient themselves by reference to the gong.) The orchestra slows briefly in anticipation of the gong stroke, however, interrupting the otherwise steady rhythm, and the uncanny quality of the gong's sound, felt more than just heard, makes its effect particularly mysterious. A listener is deliciously surprised by this interruption in the steady but diffuse sound characteristic of longer gendhing. The gong, that is, fits into a gendhing's diffuse context as a massive, form-determining stroke, contrasting with other instruments by the enormous range of its overtones. It thereby drives all the other instruments momentarily out of hearing. As its sound diminishes, the sense of diffuseness and equilibrium returns. The pleasure of a gong stroke, therefore, its capacity to make one feel satisfied or contented (*marem*), as Pak Cerma suggested, depends on the play on focus and diffuseness that is essential to gamelan's beauty.

Javanese who find gamelan music boring often say that it puts them to sleep. Gamelan enthusiasts in Java often say that one reason they enjoy listening to it is that it puts them to sleep. Pak Cerma said that the word that best describes the pleasurable feeling caused by listening to gamelan is *nganyut*, and he defined it with the phrase, "It's enjoyable such that it makes your feelings billow" (*muluk-muluk rasané saking kapénaké*). Poerwadarminta glosses *nganyut* with words meaning "to send downstream," and *nganyut-anyut* as "to be attractive" (literally, "to draw the heart"). The displacement in space implicit in both *nganyut* and *muluk-muluk* ("to billow") suggests being pulled along or upward, and so being "caught up," as we might say, in the music's effect.[14] To describe the sound of gamelan, Pak Cerma went on, there is the word *ngrangin*. Poerwadarminta defines this as "soft and slow, enjoyable to hear, in reference to the sound of gamelan." He links it to *karangin*, a literary form of *kanginan*, "blown by the wind." As a poetic word, *karangin* evokes the pleasurable sensation of being cooled by the breeze. But *kanginan* is also the term used about clothes blown off the line, and worse, to describe the ill effects on one's health caused by wind. (*Kanginan* in this sense is equivalent to

[14] The American phrase "to go with the flow" comes even closer to the overtones of the Javanese term *nganyut*. That a phrase so Californian could be applied to anything Javanese is telling comment on the special status of gamelan's pleasures, which lie in large measure outside Javanese normative stress on clarity and self-control.

the Indonesian *masuk angin*, which refers to all symptoms we describe as a cold or the flu in English.) *Nganyut* also has a negative side. It is used in the phrase *nganyut jiwa* (*jiwa*, "soul") as a euphemism for *nglalu*, "to commit suicide."

The words that describe aural pleasure, therefore, also suggest passivity, vulnerability, and death. In ancient Javanese literature, this association is made explicitly, as Zoetmulder's discussion of the Old Javanese antecedents of the word *nganyut* shows.

> The words *ahañutan* and *anghañut*, which mean literally: to seek death by letting oneself be carried away by a stream, are also used of someone who gives himself up entirely to aesthetic pleasure.
>
> The two meanings become blended in one passage of the *Sumanasantaka*, in which the waves of the sea are described as resembling "a light of crystal stairs down which the poet descends when, in old age, he ends his life by plunging into the raptures of beauty." (Zoetmulder 1974:171)

Rapturous suicide suggests a kind of aesthetic intoxication. But modern attitudes toward alcoholic intoxication point up the contrast between such classical notions and current inclinations in Java. Contemporary Javanese show a general antipathy to both opiates and alcohol, and I believe this aversion stems from a distrust of the disorientation they cause. In light of gamelan's play on focus and the pleasure implicit in its loss, it is fitting, therefore, that musicians are the exception to this rule of Javanese abstemiousness. They often pass around a bottle of gin or the alcoholic version of *beras kencur* (an herbal stimulant) during a performance. In the past, dhalang were frequently opium addicts, and one of my oldest informants, a very distinguished dhalang, never performed without taking some opium just before moving to his place before the screen.

Both opium and alcohol consumption were apparently much greater in the past, and though Javanese attribute the change to progress (in Indonesian, *kemajuan*) and greater consciousness or awareness (in Indonesian, *kesadaran*), I would instead link it to an increasingly defensive attitude toward the world. Economic and political upheaval cause some people to react with cynical or despairing abandon. But in Java, all cultural sanctions make the proper response to trauma a concerted calm. It follows that disorder in their environment makes many Javanese cling all the more tenaciously to the order within their grasp, that is, in physical orientation, hierarchy, and linguistic and social etiquette. All of these risk dissolution when under the influence of opium or alcohol, and only a few younger Javanese— aside from musicians, and a few beer-drinking members of the urban elite—enjoy taking such risks.

PLEASURE AND FOCUS IN WAYANG

Wayang plays on degrees of focus and attention in much the same way gamelan does. In fact, shifts in the degree of musical focus in a series of gendhing parallel the dramatic progression within each of the three sections of a performance of wayang. As mentioned above, a different musical mode (pathet) is used in each section of a night-long wayang. Every section begins with a formal discussion and ends in battle.[15] The structure of each of these parts could be seen as a play on the sort of attention a spectator gives. The initial scene opens in each case with a long, conventionalized description of the place, with a musical accompaniment that exploits the full range and subtlety of the gamelan orchestra. Conventionalized greetings among all characters follow. At this point, spectators either listen in diffuse enjoyment to the music and the dhalang's torrent of words, or they pay no attention whatever, chatting instead with friends or, later in the evening, falling asleep. As the discussion among the characters becomes more specific, there is greater focus, and the spectators' attention is captured. Yet the kind of interest aroused by whatever problem gives the lakon its impetus is soon dispersed by the set pieces, such as the departure of the troops and the battles that conclude each section. These battles, while watched avidly, are curiously uninvolving. They are often funny and are accompanied by a poundingly repetitive musical piece played by only the loudest of the gamelan instruments. But they draw attention to the excitement of the moment and to the dhalang's skill at manipulating the puppets, not to any overarching dramatic conflict. The outcome of the battle is in each case foregone: the first ends in a draw; the second in the death of monsters; and the

[15] In Jogja, the second section of a performance, that in *pathet sanga*, begins with the dhalang's narration of cosmic disorder (*gara-gara*) and then the appearance of the servant-clowns (punakawan). A formal discussion usually follows their antics, however, when a hero meets with a sage, and the progression to battle resumes.

third in the defeat of the disruptive party, usually meaning the penetration of his or her disguise (alihan). The third case is evidently the most interesting, but it gives rise to an anti-climax, since there is little or no explanation of why the character took on a disguise and caused so much disruption in the first place. So even at the end of a performance, there is really no dramatic resolution, only a stop, no satisfaction of spectators' interest but simply a forswearing of any further claims to their attention. That there is no such thing as character development also contributes to this impression of an almost fortuitous cessation of action at dawn.

A performance of wayang, as I have said, does not posit a theme, develop it, bring it to a climax, and then resolve it: as A. L. Becker has noted (1979), Aristotelian conventions are irrelevant to wayang. Like a series of gong periods in a gendhing, or a number of gendhing played in a series, a performance presents a repeating progression of sections that are distinguished by shifting degrees of focus. Spectators are not expected to pay rapt attention. Instead, they are drawn into the story at some times, while at others they pay little or no attention. For the most part, the regular structure of the performance provides a static framework, fragmenting the lakon into a collection of what are thematically only loosely joined parts. The result emphasizes the incidentals of music, jokes, gestures, and dialogue, which may have little intrinsic connection to the particular lakon. It is to these surfaces that spectators attend, without committing themselves, or being expected to commit themselves, to anything more.

Yet the art form also suggests the possibility of a spectator's pleasant forgetfulness. This disfocus, I must stress, is only one aspect of the enjoyment to be had in a performance of wayang. The popular taste for battles, jokes, and lightweight gendhing emphasizes the opposite tendency: to insist on simple contrasts and accessible language. So does the moral absolutism of commentary on wayang, as will be taken up in the next chapter. Nevertheless, a certain *chiaroscuro* is intrinsic to the experience of wayang, and I believe it is an important aspect both of its allure and of the resistance it evokes. In fact, clarity, focus, and the presentation of obvious oppositions, though extolled in exegetical remarks about wayang, do not necessarily win praise in performance. The pleasure in a loss of orientation and focus pertains to wayang just as it does to gamelan.

For example, the contrast between bad and good dhalang can be phrased in terms, respectively, of an unappealing clarity and a certain significant obscurity. An older dhalang told me that when a mediocre dhalang performs, the puppets appear clear and bright. When a good dhalang performs, in contrast, the puppets are *singup*, "dark, shadowy, mysterious," and so *angker*, "mystically charged." My informant described the language of different dhalang in the same way. If a dhalang uses everyday language in his narration (*janturan*), the sense is clear and the effect dull. By using Kawi (classical) vocabulary, a dhalang makes his performance more mysterious and powerful.

Many informants stressed this point, that a dhalang must use Kawi fluently. It was difficult for me to elicit explanations of what people meant when they said that without a fair proportion of Kawi words a performance would be unaffecting (*ora mranani*). Kawi vocabulary almost invariably substitutes archaic vocabulary for colloquial words of identical meaning. Only rarely does Kawi modify or add nuance to signification. Instead, it simply makes comprehension more difficult. I believe the pleasure of Kawi lies in large measure there: it inserts a kind of pause, a split-second delay between sound and sense, which is found pleasurable.[16] The pleasure taken in this kind of momentary free-fall of sound is perhaps comparable to the pleasure taken in a crowd scene.[17] People throng to night fairs in Jogja and other cities, to mill about quite aimlessly, snacking and looking at things for sale, but without feeling much need to talk or to find anything special to see or do. The same busy but diffuse environment is a part of the allure of a crowded and sprawling ritual celebration-cum-performance. The pleasure in either case lies in the absence of any compelling focus, in a kind of mild disconnectedness. I believe the pleasure in Kawi's suggestive obscurity lies in a similar absence of any immediately compelling sense.

The issue of sleep highlights the pleasurably disorienting aspect of wayang most succinctly. I have mentioned that sleep arouses ambivalent reactions in Java. Dhalang like to say that they teach spectators to *éling*, and some say that in enabling spectators to stay awake all

---

[16] The only analogue I can think of in English, and it is somewhat farfetched, is Spenser's deliberately archaized vocabulary in *The Faerie Queene*. Friends who know and love the work assure me it can be appreciated fully only if read aloud, and I am inclined to believe that a similar play on sound and a slightly delayed sense accounts for that fact.

[17] Bateson and Mead 1942 describes this pleasure in Bali.

night, a dhalang helps them to achieve an ascetic exercise. Others reject this claim on the grounds that you go to a wayang for pleasure, and no pleasurable activity can be counted an ascetic exercise. It remains true, in any case, that an eight-hour, nightlong performance induces somnolence almost inevitably. The pleasure of yielding to it and snoozing while the dhalang's voice drones on in description, say, of a palace, his elegant words superimposed on the shimmering sound of the gamelan, is irresistible. Yet while the young boys who stream inside and sprawl about on the floor after the invited guests have gone home sleep happily through much of the rest of the performance, their older brothers, fathers, and grandfathers, if they stay, struggle to stay awake. There appears to be in this concerted, if usually vain, attempt to remain conscious an effort to prove one's strength. Or at least, it is an effort to protect oneself. Sleep is, after all, a vulnerable state, and it is particularly risky to sleep in a public place.

The equivocation about wayang lies in its ostensible function of exciting people to éling, a function that dhalang are forever extolling, and its simultaneous suggestion of a loss of control over one's thoughts, feelings, and even consciousness. Even a person who does not fall asleep and remains alert, watching with focused attention throughout the performance, is believed to run certain risks. I have alluded to the risk of emotional involvement that the many forms of resistance point to. Certain popular beliefs about the dangers that lurk at a performance indicate suspicions of the art form as well. One frequently voiced fear is that while people are out enjoying a wayang their houses are being robbed. I think the fear is exaggerated; few houses are ever left empty in Java. The fear of robbery is really, I think, an image of distraction, a distraction induced by the dhalang's skill at creating an illusion. The more completely they fall under the sway of the dhalang's performance, the less conscious spectators become of the fact that they observe only an illusion. And in becoming so persuaded by the dhalang, Javanese sense their own sovereignty compromised: it is another version of submission. The fear is that one will be too deeply moved by the lakon and thus disturbed and troubled, or too trusting in the dhalang's perhaps inadequate or inauspicious aura (daya). Yet that submission, like the abdi-dalem's mindless contentment at court, exerts great appeal. As a result, whether intent upon the story and so inattentive to their surroundings, or sleepy and so unable to attend to anything, spectators indulge in a risky pleasure, entrusting themselves completely to the dhalang and his performance.

The distracting pleasure that gamelan and wayang proffer corresponds to an emotion Zoetmulder speaks of as central to the aesthetic of Old Javanese epic poetry (*kakawin*). Designated by the words "*langö, lengeng, lengleng* and their derivatives," that emotion

> is a kind of swooning sensation, in which the subject is completely absorbed by and becomes lost in its object, the appeal of which is so overwhelming that everything else sinks into nothingness and oblivion. All intellectual activity ceases; the perception of the object itself becomes vague, and in an experience of oneness that blurs the distinction between subject and object, consciousness of the self vanishes, too. (Zoetmulder 1974:172)

It is perhaps not surprising that this understanding of aesthetic pleasure has persisted over centuries in Java. What is striking about contemporary Javanese reactions to performance, however, is that such considerable defenses are raised against it. Yet this defensiveness may also have ancient antecedents. It is commonplace in Javanese conversation to liken a person too caught up in mundane affairs, and so ignorant of kebatinan, to a spectator of wayang who forgets that what he sees are only shadows on a screen. The same image, with the same disparaging intent, occurs in the twelfth-century *kakawin*, *Arjuna wiwaha*. Zoetmulder translates the passage, spoken by Indra disguised as a brahmin:

> "For it is as with the spectators of a puppet-performance (*ringgit*). They (are carried away), cry, and are sad (because of what befalls their beloved hero or heroine) in the ignorance of their understanding. And this even though they know that it is merely carved leather that moves and speaks. That is the image of one whose desires are bound to the objects of the senses, and who refuses to understand that all appearances are only an illusion and a display of sorcery without any reality." (Zoetmulder 1974:210)

Used here to describe a person with insufficient insight into the workings of the divine in the world, the simile can nevertheless be taken more literally. It indicates suspicion of wayang's illusion, and by extension, of the dhalang's power in creating that illusion. Of course, at the level of the cosmos, if there is a dhalang behind the phenomena of the world, he is the proper focus of one's attention. But then the human dhalang behind the illusion of wayang is a distracting, intermediate presence, generator of further illusions in this illusory world. In Java today, his power is neutralized, or at least whitewashed, as long as his performance is seen to consist in moral platitudes. But that domestication of the art form is a defensive, and I believe rather lame, justification. Whether attentive to the performance or not, a spectator enjoys a pleasurable but suspect distraction.

This conception of wayang as distraction helps acount for a curious but widely-held belief among Javanese that wayang was first developed by the Muslim proselytizers (*wali*) who spread Islam in Java. Although accounts vary in specifics, the story runs that the then-Hindu or Buddhist or animist Javanese were drawn to newly-built mosques by the sound of gamelan being played inside. Once gathered outside a mosque, people were granted entry to the mosque on the condition that they repeat a few syllables. These were the Muslim confession of faith, and the naive populace, by repeating them, was unwittingly converted to Islam. Wayang performances were then held in order to teach the precepts of the new religion. Although it is often granted that *wayang bèbèr* (illustrated scroll narratives whose painted figures resemble wayang) existed before the advent of Islam, the origin of shadow puppets themselves is attributed in this account to the Muslims. Some people add that the puppets are very highly stylized in deference to Muslim strictures against representing the human body. In some versions, wayang's origin is not explained in this way, but its elaboration and perfection are nevertheless attributed to the Muslim *wali*.

These accounts usually place no negative judgment upon such a manner of converting Java to Islam. If anything, people seem to admire the wiliness of the proselytizers, who knew how to play upon the Javanese taste for gamelan and performances to attain their ends. Yet the point remains that in these stories, gamelan and wayang become, in the hands of the sponsors of their performance, means to attract people, and then to subvert a crucial aspect of their identities, namely, their customs and beliefs.

DHALANG, DHUKUN, AND THIEVES

The ambivalence that wayang arouses is rendered not just in the manner in which performances are received and the tradition discussed. Ambivalent feelings also cluster about the dhalang himself, and I wish to take up the subject of the dhalang once more in order to show that these conflicting reactions stem from an impression of his insidious ability to induce distraction. That is, distrust of the art form is transferred to the artist, and that distrust is highlighted in popular associations—some conscious, some less explicit—that link dhalang to dhukun and thieves.

Dhukun, as possessors and transmitters of traditional wisdom, are thought both to resemble dhalang (inasmuch as both dhukun and dhalang are teachers) and to assist them. It is said of dhalang that they of course all go to dhukun to obtain certain kinds of mystical knowledge (ngèlmu). Specifically, they seek *rapal panyirepan* (from *sirep*, "to fall quiet," "to cease"), formulas that cause an audience to sit in silence, and "attractive power" (*daya penarik*), which will prevent spectators from going off to snack or going home for the night. The ability to keep spectators quiet is seen as a kind of influence exerted by one's potency. As mentioned in Chapter 1, one dhalang held Ki Nartosabdho "personally" responsible for the fact that a boy yelled out during his performance: that Nartosabdho was not able to keep the boy quiet indicated a decline in his potency. *Rapal panyirepan* should stave off such unflattering reflections on a dhalang's authority. This is one more example of the importance of controlling others' behavior to demonstrate one's own potency.

Such rapal are assimilable to other kinds of magic that are intended to guarantee a dhalang's popularity, because the public's silence and its favor are both seen as functions of the dhalang's influence. Dhalang are also said to go to dhukun to get magic that will ensure that they are engaged to perform often. Actually, it is interesting to note what is and what is not susceptible to magical manipulation about a dhalang's career. Talent (*bakat*) seems to be constitutional: either you have it or you don't. Neither being born into a long line of dhalang nor any kind of asceticism can assure a person of possessing or obtaining talent. Ascetic exercises and ngèlmu provided by a dhukun can, however, make a dhalang "accepted" (*katrima*): popular, famous, and rich. The ability to perform well, that is, has to do with *bakat*, also to some degree with training and practice. This has little to do with whether or not one is a hit with the masses (*diarepi masyarakat*), however, which depends on ascetic exercises, ngèlmu and the state of one's batin, plus, finally, the potency of the dhukun one applies to for assistance.

Dhalang routinely say about all their colleagues that they seek the intercession of dhukun to attain success, and every dhalang denies such practice just as routinely in his own case. If he does admit to having consulted a dhukun, a dhalang minimizes the fact. He only went once or twice, to only one dhukun, or perhaps the dhukun came to him and provided him with unsolicited instruction. The denials, I believe, reflect a feeling that a dhalang should not need to go to a dhukun. A dhalang is supposed to possess ngèlmu. So he should never have needed to obtain it from someone else. (It is always more flattering to his status to have gotten his ngèlmu from non-human sources, as Ki Nartosabdho, among many others, claims to have done.) Pak Cerma said he never went to dhukun because then "people would say I was successful only because I had found a powerful dhukun." Many Javanese attribute the phenomenal success of Java's current top two dhalang to just such a cause: each must have a potent dhukun and maybe a wealth-seeking spirit (inthuk). In making this (libelous) assertion, people repeat the pattern of seeing in obvious power only a manifestation of some hidden source. And in denying any truck with dhukun, dhalang obey the Javanese rule of avoiding or disclaiming all connection with people whose status rivals their own, since dhalang and dhukun are seen as comparable experts in ka-kuwatan batin.

Javanese associate dhukun with thieves, as well as with dhalang. A thief discovered in a village is beaten to death in short order. Village officials are now responsible for taking a thief to the nearest jail, and some villagers express the opinion that it is better to beat a thief only to the verge of death, so that he will die in jail rather then in the village. Then there follow no annoying government inquiries. A man who steals in his own hamlet, for that matter, may enjoy some clemency, though the social disgrace is then great. But beyond one's own hamlet, in the undifferentiated realm of *wong* (literally, "people," by extension, "non-kin and strangers"), moral strictures carry no weight, and thieving is only a mortally risky gamble. The moral neutrality of stealing is epitomized in the category of "great" or "noble thieves" (*maling agung* or *maling utama*, from *maling*, "thief"; *agung*, "great"; *utama*, "noble"). These thieves steal from rich people who live in faraway villages or cities, best of all in that jungle of wealth and amorality, Jakarta. They then come home to the village and distribute the take among their kin and neighbors. The verb for "distribute" here is *ngeteri*, which is most often used in reference to the practice of sending food to the homes of substantial contributors to a ritual celebration. The word therefore suggests pretty young réwang coming in the door carrying trays of goodies on their shoulders. In the case of thieves, presumably, money, clothes, and radios substitute for spiced coconut and sticky-rice snacks.

A thief, to be successful, needs great ngèlmu. This endows him with knowledge essential to the success of his venture: knowledge of which house to rob, and when; how to make the owners sleep soundly and be unaware of any danger, if they are at home; how to break into the house soundlessly, without arousing the attention of the neighbors and without suffering any interference from the village dhanyang; and, should he be detected, how to disappear or elude his pursuers by taking shelter in or under precisely the right species of tree or bush. All this requires knowledge of numerological magic (pétungan) and formulas (rapal), plus great kakuwatan batin.

I have never spoken with an admitted thief in Java, but it would not surprise me if such a person also disclaimed ever having gone to dhukun. Criminals have their professional pride, after all. What is interesting is that many people assume that dhukun are simply thieves become too old, or for some other reason unable to steal. A dhukun, in this view, is a retired thief. Certainly, thieves and dhukun are thought to be in cahoots. Although a dhukun cannot put a price on his instructions, he can expect that, should his pupil make a big heist, he will receive some token of gratitude. It is but a small step to see dhukun and thieves as allies, although this impression does not seem to sully the popular image of dhukun. That thieves should number among a dhukun's pupils, even that the dhukun himself was previously a thief, seems to garner him no particular censure.

If dhalang and dkukun are linked in the popular mind, and if thieves and dhukun are seen as transformations of one another, a special relationship is also said to exist between thieves and dhalang. The relationship is defined in part negatively, in that a dhalang is believed able to overpower a thief. If a thief enters a village intending to commit a robbery but finds a performance of wayang going on, he will become so interested in it he will forget all about thieving. He may even be struck by the truth of the moral lessons a dhalang includes in a performance and thereby persuaded to give up thieving altogether. In any case, dhalang assured me, he will fear the dhalang's aura, which holds the entire hamlet in his thrall for the duration of the performance. Should a thief go ahead and steal, however, he is sure to be discovered. He will be unable to leave the village without arousing someone's suspicions, and whatever ngèlmu he possesses will prove useless in this area of the dhalang's temporary but inescapable authority.

Dhalang make these claims quite insistently, probably to counteract the opposite but also widespread opinion that great ritual celebrations that include performances present thieves with unparalleled opportunities to break into houses without getting caught. If a whole family is off at a ritual celebration, it has made itself vulnerable to theft. And the coming and going of so many strangers in the village means that a thief will arouse little suspicion. He succeeds, therefore, by taking advantage of his victims' distraction.

One often becomes aware, in speaking with Javanese, that they speak of spirits and thieves almost interchangeably. Conceived of as intruders pressing against one's doors, both categories evoke the same reactions: the need to be watchful, attentive, conscious, on guard. The areas where both spirits and thieves are considered numerous— "to the north" people said in the village where I lived, that is, toward the mountains—are the same. Both spirits and thieves are active at night, and they are defended against by both practical and mystical methods. Dhalang are believed to have a special capacity to fend off thieves and spirits alike.

The relations of dhalang with thieves are not purely negative. Dhalang like to boast of the special consideration that thieves show them. When dhalang go off to perform in areas known to harbor great numbers of thieves (e.g., "to the north"), it is said that men there are especially deferential to them. They show special zeal in helping to set up the performing area and making sure that everything suits the dhalang's wishes. These people are presumed thieves. The respect they show dhalang is attributed to their interest in ngèlmu. But since the ngèlmu that dhalang are said to provide in performance has nothing to do with the needs of thieves, I find that justification for thieves' great deference thin. I think the conception of a particular bond between dhalang and thieves represents instead an unarticulated but real perception of affinities in what they do.

Dhalang and thieves mediate between different realms. A thief crosses the boundaries between inside and outside the village and the house. He uses ngèlmu to overcome his victims' awareness, to enlist the aid or at least toleration of local spirits, and to become invisible. A dhalang also enters a village and displaces established patterns of authority in the village and the house—even the king may not interrupt him. In displacing the sponsors, the dhalang repeats a thief's stealthy ingress, usurping authority, at least apparently, as the thief usurps property. Most importantly, he plays on his audience's consciousness and attention, to the profit, it is said, of thieves. That people attending a performance are thought particularly vulnerable to theft stems not just from their not being at home, but also from their not being in full control of their own thoughts and feelings. This affinity between dhalang and thieves is especially clear in the fact that the formula with which a dhalang obtains silence from his spectators, and the one with which a thief makes his victims sleep, are both called *rapal panyirepan*.

My contention is that the many appreciations of a performance's effectiveness—its effects upon the sponsors' prestige and future fortunes, upon spirits, and upon spectators' emotions, moral attitudes, and attention—matter more than what wayang "means." If the meaning of a performance is understood as the formulation of an isolable message, then, as I have said, to seek the meaning of a performance of wayang seems to me misguided. I would prefer to speak of its resonance, evocativeness, or richness of associations, that is, of the ways in which it plays upon issues that preoccupy Javanese. Wayang does this through the medium of the performance, as much if not more than by the content of any particular lakon. This Javanese play, therefore, is "deep," to borrow Geertz's term for the Balinese cockfight (C. Geertz 1973a), not in the profundity or originality of its statements, but rather in how richly it evokes Javanese conceptions of the interplay of power and selves.

More specifically, attention and focus transpose onto the level of aesthetics' fundamental concerns about interaction: status, control, effectiveness, and subordination. The play on diffuse and clear focus in performance reiterates the contrast between dissembled and overtly demonstrated power, as the performance alternately draws spectators together in an attentive crowd and releases them in a mass of sounds and bodies. To win a spectator's attention is analogous to winning a subject's tribute or a foreigner's obeisance, particularly if spectator, subject, and foreigner all act "freely," under the sole compulsion of the center's attractive power. So the political ambiguity about relative status and authority that underlies relations between sponsors and guests has its counterpart in the ambiguity about relations between illusion and spectator. To what extent should spectators let themselves become subject to that illusion? To what extent does such subjection imply a loss of control? Relations between spectator and dhalang combine both domains, aesthetic and political, because the dhalang's authority—aesthetic in the medium of its exertion, political inasmuch as one person's power over another is always political—is demonstrated through the effectiveness of his performance.

But why puppets rather than people, and why shadows? Wayang kulit is only one of many Javanese performing arts, but it is indisputably the "high" art form in Javanese culture. Many people in Central Java prefer to see wayang wong (classical dance performances of lakon derived from or similar to those in the wayang kulit repertoire), or increasingly, *kethoprak* (folk drama). Women, especially, take greater interest in these broader, more "romantic" arts. Almost everyone, however, considers wayang kulit the truly important art form. Its superior prestige stems in part from the great age of the wayang tradition. It stems as well, I believe, from the particular characteristics of the medium itself. People always single out the stories when they contrast wayang kulit and *kethoprak*. *Kethoprak* stories do not *urut*, they do not fit together tightly, as wayang lakon do. More important than the stories, however, are differences in the nature of the two media. Women, it is said, need to see live actors on the stage. They cannot appreciate the beauty of shadows, and they like to indulge their romantic fantasies in the "realistic" love scenes. They also enjoy weeping through *kethoprak*'s shamelessly melodramatic twists of fortune. Men profess to find these aspects of kethoprak foolish, and most older men admit no taste whatever for kethoprak, except perhaps insofar as it relates historical tales and therefore *urut*. Women, in contrast, are thought little interested in seeing wayang, and many men say it is disgraceful for them to do so. Men justify this attitude on the grounds that women should not go traipsing about at all hours of the night. But kethoprak lasts most of the night, too, and a woman suffers no censure for watching it. More to the point, I think, is that wayang concerns potency, and that is not considered women's domain. Women do not possess, exercise, or really understand potency to any appreciable degree. They are said, by Javanese men and women, to be flighty, incapable of concentration, and self-control.[18] How could they then appreciate the significance of an art form that plays upon these nuances of consciousness and power? Better that they stick with the sex, slapstick, and accessible language of kethoprak. As everyone knows, they chat all through the important scenes in a performance anyway, and pay attention only when the hero and heroine or the clowns are on stage together.

I believe wayang's prestige depends on its capacity to suggest political and aesthetic correspondences much more richly than any other art form, including wayang wong. It can do so because of its unique arrangements. It is the only art form in which a single figure exercises thorough control over all aspects of the performance. True, there is a dhalang in wayang wong. He plays the *keprak*, sings suluk, and recites some narrative, but he does not run the show, since actors both speak their own lines and dance. Only the dhalang in wayang kulit determines the entire course of a performance down to the smallest detail, and so only in wayang kulit is the relationship between artist and spectator so clearly highlighted and so rich in associations. (Those lakon thought dangerous if performed with shadow puppets are thought lukewarm, neutral, unaffecting [*tawar*] if performed by dancers.) The use of puppets in wayang kulit makes possible the concentration of authority in a clear center or source. At the same time, as I have tried to argue, much about the dhalang's performance, such as the splintering of his voice, the hiding of his person, etc., dissimulates that fact. The tension affords a constant play on the dhalang's authority and its dissemblance.

Yet the question remains why an art form should be elaborated in this medium of shadows at all. Many theories have been proposed to explain the origins and persistence of shadow plays. Dutch scholars were partial to the view that wayang began as a representation of the souls of the dead, but there seems no way to prove this. I did not find Javanese much interested in the question. Although a few people, as I have mentioned, suggested that the Muslim aversion to representation caused people to stylize the puppets so thoroughly, they did not

[18] For a discussion of Javanese gender stereotypes, see Keeler Forthcoming a.

offer reasons for the use of shadow puppets rather than, say, rod puppets, which exist in West Java and are fairly popular in certain areas of Central Java.

My own hypothesis, for which I can claim only indirect support from my informants, is that one can see in the almost immaterial form of shadows the realm of kebatinan. The world of wayang is governed by the principles of spiritual power much more pervasively and demonstrably than is that of humans. It is a world thought not so much removed in time as distinct in nature from ours. In this respect, it resembles the world of spirits (*alam panglémunan*), which exists coextensively with our environment or sphere (*alam*), but which is invisible to all but the most spiritually adept. Shadows cast upon a screen seem an apt representation of such a world. The insubstantiality of shadows, their lack of color, their varying degrees of clarity and size, and the dissimulation of any agent responsible for their movement and speech, all effect a realization of what is mysterious and imperceptible, but in a manifest, if still largely immaterial, form. Shadows, that is, illustrate with particular force the paradox of characters, voices, and power both present and absent in the world. They are slightly material traces of an invisible source. So they represent with peculiar aptness the Javanese conception of spiritual power: its subtle nature, and its equivocal but pervasive effects.

9 · ON JAVANESE INTERPRETATION

People's relations with signs in Java, the degree to which they are master of or subject to them, at once indicate and determine their potency. This assumption about the relationship between self and signs has important consequences for Javanese epistemology. Exegesis of wayang exemplifies these consequences, and I will take it as a starting point for a more general discussion of Javanese interpretation. My point is that, like speech, the signs that are an art form, a tract of ngèlmu, or a dream, all pose a challenge to a person's autonomy, a challenge to which modes of interpretation are the defensive reaction. In interpreting such signs, a person seeks to control them, mastering and using—rather than falling subject to—their significance.

EXEGESIS AND THE STATUS OF WAYANG STORIES

Indigenous commentary on wayang fits into the politics of meaning in Java because its reductiveness constitutes another defense against a performance's impact: it indicates resistance to the performance in yet another register. At many points in the epic cycle, error, oversight, and passion cause characters to become caught in ethically subtle and problematic situations. Even the central dispute over the kingdom of Ngastina is by no means morally clear-cut, since each of the two camps can make justifiable claims to the throne. Yet contemporary Javanese commentary sees the Kurawa as unequivocally evil, given over to their envy, lust for power and coarseness, and the Pandhawa as good, models of fairness, potency, and patience. Their struggle is therefore the eternal one between good and evil. In stances in which certain "good" characters clearly diverge from the straight and narrow do little to shake this simplistic reduction of all events to clear-cut opposites. When, for example, in the *Bratayuda*, the wily and powerful Kresna tricks Arjuna into interceding, unfairly, in the struggle between Setyaki and Burisrawa, Kresna's stratagem is excused casually as a subterfuge justified by his ultimate end, the triumph of the good Pandhawa.

When people speak, as dhalang speak at particularly great length, of the exemplary function of wayang, they justify the claim with reference to precisely these clear moral contrasts. The most commonly espoused view of wayang's effect upon its audience describes it as an inducement to righteous behavior. First of all, the dhalang makes certain characters voice properly elevating remarks about the virtues of filial piety, the need to speak with proper refinement, the importance of doing ascetic rigors, etc. In addition to these clearly didactic statements, a performance is also believed to transmit beneficial moral influence through its examples of good and evil actions and the fruits they reap. To most commentators, this obvious moral instruction is the real essence of wayang's worth, the cause of its ceaseless appeal, and the indisputable justification for the whole tradition. Nuances in emotions and moral issues are sacrificed in such a reading of wayang, and exegesis reduces the meanings of lakon to a few moral sententiae.[1]

Javanese discussion of what wayang means usually focuses on one or two lakon, *Dewa Ruci* above all,[2] occasionally *Kresna duta*. These seem to me to fit certain theosophical prejudices of both Javanese and Western analysts (or apologists), but the conventional commentary does not constitute an exegetical approach applicable to other lakon. Actually, rather than deal with stories at all, most commentary concerns the pathokan. It is conventional and quite universally accepted wisdom among educated wayang enthusiasts that a performance of wayang represents the life of a single person. So the first section of a performance represents his birth and childhood, followed by adolescence, triumph over the passions, the pursuit of ngèlmu, and finally death.[3] Justifications for the scheme are often quite elaborate and

[1] James Boon, with his customary wit, punctures the pieties of moralistic interpretations of wayang (Boon 1984). He suggests that wayang's multiple voices preclude its conveying a normative message.

[2] A. L. Becker notes that the *Dewa Ruci* lakon appeals to Westerners because it follows the constraints of causal linear sequences that make up part of the Western dramatic traditions (A. L. Becker 1979:219). I think it is the same simplicity of line that lends it so well to Javanese exegesis.

[3] For a statement of this interpretation that has been translated into English, see Mangkunegara VII 1957. For a representative example of indigenous exegesis of wayang in Indonesian, see Seno-Sastroamidjojo 1964.

even ingenious. A point invariably made is that the hero's battle against the fanged monster, Buta Cakil, midway through the performance represents a man's struggle against his passions. Having subdued and killed these, he is ready to prepare himself for the acquisition of ngèlmu. (Several informants spoke in high dudgeon of "young dhalang" who conclude the battle with the monster's escape, not his death. This proves their failure to understand the "real meaning" of the scene, the contest with one's impulses. Even aside from the validity of the interpretation, which I find questionable, I never saw a performance in which the monster didn't die, and my informants' excitation always seemed to me misplaced. The conversational landscape in Java is, however, strewn with the bodies of such strawmen.) The dance performed at the end of a performance by a wooden puppet, called a *wayang golèk*, is glossed as a signal to the spectators that they must now "look for" (*golèk*) the real essence of the performance, viz., its moral instruction.

If the exegesis of lakon is stunningly reductive, this reading of a performance's structure is sheer addition, lacking any necessary connection to what happens in a particular performance. The result—and I believe it is the aim—in either case is to put a stop to associations to the performance. Every performance becomes perfectly equivalent to every other. To take the progress of all performances as Everyman's passage through life accomplishes this closure with particular efficacy, since it limits the meaning of the whole to the experience of only one person, and it posits the universal validity of that experience, at least as an ideal. Exegetes are thus saved from the implications of any particular lakon, and from any relevance of wayang to the rest of life except as expressed in the most domesticated of homilies. They are saved, in a word, from exegesis.

The willed poverty of wayang exegesis strikes me as a defense against the intricacies of analysis, judgment, and feeling that a more nuanced consideration of the corpus of stories would entail. Attitudes toward the historical status of wayang stories, in contrast, indicate not this reductive definitiveness, but rather its opposite, a generalized agnosticism. The results are much the same.

There is a curious vagueness about the status of the *Mahabharata* stories, which are the basis of most wayang lakon. People speak of lakon alternatively as *sejarah* or *crita*. The first term corresponds generally to English "history," the second to "story." The distinction in

Javanese is by no means hard and fast, but several informants spoke of sejarah as "what happened," and crita as "what people say." Whether or not wayang stories recount the history of Java is actually moot for Javanese. Many Javanese associate features of the landscape with stories and characters in wayang. The cave at which the monkey brothers, Sugriwa and Subali, suddenly became enemies is located by some north of the village of Wates; the village of Dwarawati near Jatinom is identified by some with Kresna's kingdom of that name; and several different sites are claimed as the mountain on which Arjuna meditated before slaying Niwatakawaca. However, many people are skeptical of these identifications, particularly people who have heard, as many Javanese have heard, that the stories come originally from India. What is remarkable is how little difference the issue of the stories' historical veracity seems to make. Connections between the present and known world, the art form, and the past, matter little to Javanese appreciation of wayang.

One reason many people speak vaguely about the historicity of stories stems from a habitual reluctance to pass judgment on the truthfulness of any statement. One man in Karanganom said that sejarah and crita are the same, since they both consist only in "things people say" (omongané wong). His tone implied that there was no use trying to decide what was true and what wasn't about them. Javanese often repeat another person's remarks, or traditional wisdom, and then add, "That's just what they say. I don't know myself." The comment disclaims the speaker's commitment to and responsibility for what he has said. It is one more manifestation of the reluctance to take responsibility (tanggung jawab). One Jogja dhalang answered my questions about the status of wayang stories by saying, "All lakon are crita: you can believe what you like. I don't take responsibility for them."

Such difficulty in pronouncing anything, including "history," true stems from the fact that to do so people must surpass the limits of their own perception. Javanese are not necessarily skeptical, but they see no reason to commit themselves to statements to which they feel no personal link. One doesn't say another person's stories aren't true; one simply doesn't say, just as one avoids lending money or getting involved in any situation in which trust must be extended. Incidentally, I believe Javanese can express belief in Gusti Allah so easily in part because there is so little one need believe about him. He is an anthropomorphic but otherwise largely blank entity.

More critical to Javanese than the historical veracity of wayang stories is their integrity: the way in which each important story links to others in the entire corpus. When I asked informants the difference between sejarah and crita, many spoke of the former as genealogy (sarasilah), and the latter as elaboration or embellishment (kembangan). Kembangan vary, but genealogies must remain unaltered. The distinction underlies that between principal and secondary lakon (lakon pokok and lakon carangan), but principal lakon already represent elaborations upon the basic genealogies. The point is that principal lakon must be internally consistent, their several strands contributing to the progression of the whole epic cycle. They must follow in order (urut). It is this inviolability, and the impression of an inevitable progression, I believe, that give the classical lakon pokok their power. Each enters into a cycle that moves like an unstoppable chain of associations until the end of the Bratayuda.

The power of this chain is great. That principal lakon are all of a piece was demonstrated to me whenever a dhalang began to tell me one of them. Once he got started, he couldn't stop. There is no point of resolution in these stories: each event leads to another, and that to another, until the end of the whole cycle is reached. It is as though there inhered in the mythical cycle a drive to be played out until exhausted. (I became reluctant to ask about any single Bratayuda lakon because I knew it would mean listening to everything that happens in the war after that point.) It is perhaps reductive reasoning on my part, but the unvarying structure of the performance (the pathokan) seems to me one way of breaking the chain, of imposing a beginning and, more importantly, an end within this long and implacable series.

Newer lakon, in contrast, are isolated units. The preference for new lakon that in no way advance the epic cycle represents a means of escape from the entangling stories of the whole corpus. Ignoring the issue of the historicity of the tradition further removes it from a person's geographical and historical environment. And if the power and prestige of principal lakon depend on their irreversible drive toward a conclusion, wayang exegesis seems to consist in draining just such energy from the tradition, in favor of its own speedy conclusion. The reduction of all lakon to a stereotypical account of individual development makes exegesis not an investigation but an imposition, of an invariant and so largely insignificant "meaning."

The need to diminish the significance of the stories in all these ways was impressed upon me in speaking with a dhalang from the Bagelen area. His father, he explained, knew that the stories came originally from India. But he used to say that they depicted traits of character (*watak*). "It mustn't *suluk*, but rather *sulek*," the dhalang quoted his father as saying (*Ora kena suluk, nanging kudu sulek*). He defined *suluk* (which normally refers to the long vocal lines with which a dhalang punctuates his performance) by means of an instance of *kérata basa*, folk etymologies of which Javanese are fond. He cited it as follows: " '*Suluk*: if you follow it, it keeps billowing upwards [*Suluk: yèn disusul, saya muluk*],' " and then explained, "It can make you confused, disoriented, upset [*bingung*]. You get involved checking to see if it happened in a particular place, you have to look for books or someone who witnessed it. But," and here he provided another kérata basa as a gloss, " '*sulek*: if you follow it, it gathers itself up [*sulek: yèn disusul, saya mulek*].' " He explained, "*Mulek* means to whirl round and finally come to a single point.[4] In this case, it means that one must seek out the important part of the story: if you take the story as representing different aspects of a person, then it is easy to interpret [*methèk*]."

These remarks point to the risks perceived in exegesis if exegesis calls for open-minded inquiry and/or judgments about truth value. The danger is that one will be drawn into a difficult and disorienting search for "proof," corroboration or conviction. The spatial imagery, common in Javanese remarks about emotional experience, implies a disconcerting loss of place: the analyst will follow something that is not confined in space or subject to gravity. Note that *muluk*, the billowing that is here disvalued, is precisely the word that Pak Cerma used to describe the pleasurable sensation of listening to gamelan, as quoted in the preceding chapter. The same displacement of thought or feeling can be found pleasurable and/or risky. But in the case of exegesis, it is neither exciting nor gratifying: it will only cause confusion.

The threat posed by a concern with objective facts, with the veracity of material outside people's own experience, lies in this possibility that they will be pulled toward a compelling, attractive, or elu-

---

[4] Poerwadarminta gives two definitions of *mulek*: "to gather without dispersing (smoke, odor); to whirl round (water)."

sive other. If on the contrary an object of inquiry concentrates itself in a single point, then the search for meaning becomes easy. It is easy to *methèk* ("to predict what will happen"; "to guess"; "to answer a riddle"), because instead of leading away it whirls itself into an ever more confined space. In the case of wayang exegesis, that point is a universal individual, and all difficulties are solved.

The word *suluk* was used in a similar way, but applied specifically to my own researches, by a man who ran a food stall along the highway near Karanganom. He spoke first of *katurangga*, a variety of ngèlmu in which a horse's qualities, characteristics, and weaknesses are discerned by the color and grain of its coat. He went on to mention other sorts of ngèlmu, including one that reveals the predictive capacity of doves on the basis of the color of their feathering, and other aspects of their appearance, and another that reveals people's personalities on the basis of their physical features. "If you really went after all that sort of ngèlmu, though," he told me, "you might end up changing your citizenship. Then *suluk*." *Suluk*, he explained, means "there's no end to it, it rises and rises and has the quality of something which appears very distant [and induces sadness]." The suggestion— actually, he used the particle *lho*, which implies warning—was that I would lose track of my own task, which was the pursuit of ilmiah, that rational, logical knowledge that is the defining concern of Westerners. I might instead become entangled in the pursuit of ngèlmu. While seeking ngèlmu is a worthy undertaking, it is also a dangerous one, since a novice may overstep his own capacity and go mad. As a Westerner and so of course one inexperienced in ngèlmu, I would stand in particularly great danger. Yet the allure of it might entice me to give up an essential element of my identity, my nationality.

A very different feeling, one of well-being, inheres in the impression of certainty. One day an old dhalang gave me a copy of a book of ngèlmu that he had copied by hand. It contained brief stories about the origins of certain wayang figures, some numerological formulas (pétungan), and sage counsel about proper behavior. He assured me that I would find it very useful, in that it would answer all my questions. He described his youth as an unhappy time when he had himself sought answers to many questions, until he had happened upon this particular text. Upon reading it, however, he was "no longer amazed" (*Sampun mboten gumun malih*). Released from astonishment, he was then content, and he felt sure I would enjoy the same benefit from reading the text.

NGÈLMU AND KÉRATA BASA

Though wayang stories and ngèlmu threaten the unwary with a dispersal of self, external objects and knowledge are not necessarily pernicious. Just as powerful heirlooms (pusaka) exert an equivocal power, so any type of ngèlmu is an aid to those who know it provided their potency is adequate to it—provided, that is, that they can exercise firm control over it. Two kinds of wisdom much appreciated by Javanese, the displays of ngèlmu a dhalang often includes in a performance and the device of kérata basa alluded to several times already, illustrate what such control consists of: the subjugation of phenomena by means of connections made apart from obvious sense.

A dhalang can show off his ngèlmu in performance in a variety of ways. The punakawan Pétruk's homiletic discourses on propriety and honesty are termed ngèlmu, as are much more esoteric accounts about the immaterial world. Many displays of ngèlmu repeat the correspondences between the cardinal points, gods, colors, traits, etc., that are a mainstay of the genre. Another favorite form is a *bantah*, which means literally "debate" but which is actually an exposition of any doctrine through a kind of catechism. Ki Anom Suroto gave the most impressive exposition of ngèlmu I have seen in his rendering of the classical bantah *Parta déwa*. In it, Pandhita Durna tries to discredit a mysterious newcomer to Ngamarta, a certain Parta déwa, who has been given the throne by the sons of the Pandhawa following the disappearance of their fathers. Durna challenges Parta déwa in a series of questions as to what is associated with the number of fingers on his hands. In a countdown from ten to one, Parta déwa names the following series: ten *pengarasan* (meaning unclear); nine *watak* ("character traits"); eight rules of priestly conduct; seven gods; six types of water; five kinds of *bayu* ("wind", "energy"); four kinds of *windu* ("eight-year cycles"); three types of light; two elements in any set of opposites; and one question, which he puts in turn to his challenger. This question leads to the exposition of five plus four plus eight more categories, and this non-classical section concludes with the manipulation of the figures to arrive at the magic date of 17/8/45.

This is something of a white rabbit pulled out of Indonesian displays of mystical rhetoric: it is the date of Indonesia's independence.[5]

The significance of this demonstration lies not in the content of the words, many of which were unintelligible to the spectators, and are so even to dhalang. It lies rather in the display that the scene affords of the dhalang's mastery. The dhalang names a vast array of phenomena that lack any connection among themselves. Order is not discovered within them, but is instead imposed upon them, through the device of the countdown. In this respect, the *bantah* resembles the entire performance, in which a story is ordered through the imposition upon it of a series of set scenes (pathokan). The countdown, furthermore, can organize the material so effectively only because the dhalang reels off all the categories so fluently. The routine relies for its power not on the subtlety of any analysis it makes of the world, but rather on the assertion of the dhalang's indomitable mastery.

Kérata basa constitute a system of linguistic glossing, the workings of which are less sheerly arbitrary than the imposition of order upon the diverse quantities named in the *bantah Parta déwa*. But especially when intended seriously, kérata basa also illustrate the tendency to assert meaning by imposing associations on and among words quite arbitrarily. Some examples of kérata basa have already been provided. The device depends on dividing a word into syllables, then fitting together other words containing those syllables in a phrase that illustrates or is otherwise connected to the meaning of the original word. For example, the word *dongèng* ("story", "legend") is separated into *do* and *ngèng*, and glossed *Dipaido, kénging* ("You may disbelieve it if you like"). Another name for the practice, *jarwa dhosok* (*jarwa*, "to clarify," "to render literary Javanese into popular speech"; *dhosok*, "to push, force"), shows that the device does not lay claim to scholarly authority, and the effect sought is often humorous or witty, as in the risqué example of the kérata basa for "penis" given in the preceding chapter. Nevertheless, this etymologizing plays a much more important role in Javanese culture than popular etymologies in English.[6]

There are dozens of standardized examples of kérata basa familiar

[5] For the text and an annotated translation of this segment of Ki Anom Soeroto's performance of *Parta déwa*, see Keeler Forthcoming b.

[6] A. L. Becker has discussed the place of kérata basa in wayang (A. L. Becker 1979).

to many Javanese. Furthermore, they make up a remarkable proportion of Javanese exegesis, and much mystical ngèlmu consists of kérata basa. Any older man with aspirations to the status of a respected elder (wong tuwa) or teacher of mystical wisdom (guru) will have many such etymologies ready for almost any topic that comes up. These may not have the epigrammatic turns of phrase typical of the more generally known examples, but they are pronounced with a more significant air. To give just one example: an older man I met at a dhalang's home said of the musical instrument, the bonang: " 'Bu: lé ngimamaké kaya ngapa [Mother: she takes on burdens like no one else], because she is the leader of the family; and nang: wong lanang, wewenang [male: he has authority].' So it is the bonang which is the leader and plays the opening of a gendhing, just as it was Sunan Bonang [one of the nine wali, propagators of Islam in Java] who gathered all the wali together." The example is slightly atypical in that its associations are unusually numerous and rich, but it is useful in indicating both the diversity of links possible and the tolerance for links missing. Bu and nang are derived from the word bonang itself, and each monosyllable is linked to a parent through the usual device of adding syllables at will. Each parent is then identified in the role of leader, which is fitted to the role of the bonang as the instrument that opens a gendhing. (Actually, the bonang opens only some gendhing under certain circumstances.) The same quality of leadership is taken to justify the name, Sunan Bonang, of one of the nine wali, although no claim is made for the priority of either instrument or person. What has happened is that the explicator has succeeded in connecting the word bonang to certain approved domains of meaning: parents and religion. The assimilation does not really tell one more about any of the three—musical instrument, parent, or Muslim proselytizer. It simply associates them linguistically and justifies those linguistic connections by a rather loose understanding of leadership. I believe it is this assertion—which passes for an uncovering—of subtly motivated connections, connections whose motivation is linguistic, numerological, and formulaic, and still somewhat arbitrary, which makes kérata basa in ngèlmu so compelling.

Ngèlmu and kérata basa are not really intended to expand a person's understanding. They do not represent an analysis of the world. Instead, they assert control by the imposition of a grid upon data. They concern truth only inasmuch as they appeal to what is already assumed true: that father and mother run a household, say, or that Indonesia attained independence on August 17, 1945. Sense is kept subordinate to the demands of the interpreter, who insists upon links outside sense, or at most bound within a circumscribed and always pre-established sense.

It is not incidental that the links ngèlmu and kérata basa disclose in phenomena concern numbers and sounds much more than sense. Aural associations among the names for things stand somewhere between self and phenomena, between an impervious individual and an imposing object. That is, they assert an independent support for the links an interpreter may make between phenomena. But they do so outside obvious sense, by a more mysterious correspondence. Phonic repetition constitutes a kind of alternate web of links among things, outside all material or other cognitive connections. At the same time, sounds are more malleable than things, being far fewer in number. So an interpreter can work with the word *bonang* more freely than with the image—of a number of brass pots suspended over ropes—it evokes, particularly if he is free to treat the word as a number of sounds he can separate and join at will.

DREAMS AND PORTENTS

I have suggested that the exegesis of wayang, understandings about ngèlmu, and rhetorical displays involving kérata basa bespeak a cautious attitude toward knowledge. In the case of ngèlmu, control over the material becomes especially important, since if its accumulation is not carefully gradated, it threatens the well-being and even sanity of the learner. Interpreters or investigators in all the fields mentioned above, however, try to maintain firm control over the data under study. They restrict in advance the range of experience the data might evoke, and/or the degree of emotional involvement or intellectual credence they place in it. Interpretation may well constitute a pursuit of sense and a consideration of what is true and what is questionable. Yet the sense and range of references that signs are permitted to make remains circumscribed. Outside the realm of appropriate interpretations, people avoid committing themselves to either belief or skepticism.

Sense is not always predetermined in Javanese interpretation, and people do not always avoid passing judgment on the veracity of what they perceive. In the interpretation of dreams, determining the truth value of signs becomes crucial. Nevertheless, the interpretation of dreams represents another form of defense against phenomena. Dreams are examined closely not to attain insight, as a post-Freudian Westerner claims to do, but rather to attain foresight, and with that foresight the ability to defend oneself from—or at least prepare oneself for—future events. At the same time, the greater pertinence of truth value credited to dreams brings another emphasis: on the importance of signs' insulation from any obvious source or agent.

Dreams are divided into four types, distinguished according to their significance. In general, the greater the degree of reference to prior events and familiar context, the less truth is believed to inhere in a dream. Dreams that are strange or difficult to unravel are thought more significant than those of obvious content. A dream's import is further graded according to when a person dreams it, whether in the early, middle, or late portion of the night. Only dreams obtained during the last three hours of sleep before dawn are thought likely to contain true signs. (Numerological formulas [pétungan] provide formulas with which to ascertain both the probability of a dream's fulfillment in life and when that fulfillment is likely to take place.) It is also essential to determine whether a dream's source is the dreamer's own experiences and wishes, a bothersome spirit (dhemit), or an ancestral spirit, or God. Only the last two agents can provide truthful dreams. The dreams considered most important of all lack images of any kind. They consist only of some statement, presumed to be God's own words.

Interpreting particular dream content consists of checking it against invariant symbolic meanings. Most people spoke of dream symbolism as "backwards" (kosok balèn): pleasant dreams presage misfortune, whereas unpleasant elements foretell happiness. If people dream of being praised and applauded, for example, they should expect to see themselves publicly shamed. If on the other hand they dream of wild tigers or of feces, they can look forward to obtaining money or advancement. This rule is not invariable, however. To dream of losing a tooth signals someone's death, the location of the tooth indicating whether it is a relative on the dreamer's maternal or paternal side, or the dreamer himself or herself, who will die.

People's reactions to a dream, or to the interpretation they or a wong tuwa can make of it, should be guarded. If a dream suggests good fortune, they should simply put it out of their minds. To antic-

ipate happy events would diminish their likelihood and/or cause the
dreamer disppointment and disarray. Indications of imminent misfortune, however, should prompt a person to exercise caution. One
morning when Pak Cerma had planned to travel to Klaten, he decided against it because a disturbing dream during the night had made
him believe any movement outside the village ill-advised. Dreaming
of a tooth falling out may prompt a person to do ascetic exercise in
order to avert its significance. In any case, though, the accuracy of an
interpretation can only be determined with hindsight. "Oh yes,"
dreamers think to themselves at some future time, "this must be what
that dream was about."

As I have said of obscure language in wayang, reserved reference in
dreams—meaning that is held in reserve—is often thought more
powerful than signification in immediately intelligible sense. Clear
connection to the dreamer's experience, or worse, to one's particular
desires, vitiates a dream's significance. Immediate intelligibility or
immediate reference indicates a dream's origin in experience, proving that it has no progressive referential function. Such a dream is
dismissed as "the flower of sleep" (kembanging turu). Elements of a
dream that are obscure, however, suggest greater significance. Furthermore, obscure signs imply the dream's origin in an external
source. The dreamer then acts as a conduit through which messages
flow, and interpretation becomes a manner of appropriating those
signs.

Specifically, interpreting a dream enables a person to achieve, or
at least to try to achieve, some mastery over events, whether through
ascetic action or perhaps just a spiritual readying. The dreamer of significant dreams has become empty of personal desire and memory,
just as a wong tuwa must in order to make himself a conduit to potency and powerful speech. Actually, the more obvious analogue to
the dreamer is the préwangan, whose consciousness and voice have
been usurped by an external agent, thereby enabling him or her to
provide truthful messages. In the case of dreams, truthful messages
are predictive ones, and if the message presages disaster, the dreamer
hopes it is only provisional and so still subject to manipulation.

The Javanese interpretation of dreams brings out two points: that
their predictive significance depends on their insulation from the
dreamer, and that they are of interest to the degree that they enable
a person to control events by anticipating them. This second point,
that one tries in Java to take active control of signification, was illus-

trated in reactions on the part of members of Pak Cerma's family to another kind of sign. One evening Pak Cerma's son Sigit sat talking quietly and rather anxiously with an older neighbor. The older man kept repeating counsel often given by older people to younger ones: that Sigit must be careful, on guard (*sing ati-ati*), must stick close to home and not take any unnecessary risks, and that he must be ready for whatver might befall him. What prompted the advice in this case was that at three o'clock that morning, a lizard (*cecak*) had fallen on Sigit while he sat up working on some government forms. This is a very ominous sign to Javanese. It betokens the imminent death of a relative. I was told that there are two ways to respond to this sign. One cannot prevent the death itself but one can, through ascetic exercise, try to avert its impact by making it refer to some very old, perhaps very distant relative. The other reponse came out in talking with other members of Pak Cerma's family. Sigit's brother Parto reported that a lizard had fallen on him recently, too. But he had managed to catch it and rip apart its jaw. Parto spoke quite jauntily: by doing this, he had made the disaster "befall the lizard" and so prevented its realization in later events.

The meaning of the sign, namely, disaster, remains in either case. One can only try to alter or direct its significance by interceding between sign and event. In the ascetic mode, one tries to diffuse the sign's importance by shifting its fulfillment away from oneself toward some less invested object. The move suggests catching meaning like a hand grenade, and quickly tossing it someplace else. By the more direct action of ripping the lizard's jaw, the sign is neutralized by its immediate fulfillment. The opposite of reserved reference, this case of forced referentiality dramatizes the ominous power of unrealized signification. Here, by putting a stop to the progress of reference, signification is controlled. Such at least is a person's hope. Eerily, it was a morning barely two weeks later when the youths' older brother Sarna passed a truck on his motorbike, crashed head on with a bus, and was killed. Everyone in the family then surmised that this event was what the falling *cecak* had foreshadowed.

INTERPRETATION AND THE DISSEMBLED SELF

The extent to which signs can be judged truthful in Java depends, as I have said, on their removal from any obvious, personal self, that is, on their insulation from personal desires and the distortion these imply. Insistence on the dissimulation of self in a wong tuwa's other-worldliness, the dhalang's dissembled presence, and a dream's opacity reflect the distrust of a personal agent in the generation of signs. The greater the demand for truth or efficacy, the more the presence of a mediating, interpreting self must be obscured. A wong tuwa must show himself to be without desire (pamrih). The dhalang must dissimulate his own voice and presence in performance. A dreamer must not recognize his or her own desires and experience in a dream's content. In the West, such a suppression of personal investments would be intended to enable a person to uncover objectively verifiable connections among data. In Java, however, it means fitting data to externally established systems, systems neither generated by the data's particular nature nor obviously dependent upon the analyst's point of view or wishes.

Ngèlmu, dreams, and falling lizards all illustrate these principles in specialized areas. Another specialized kind of interpretation is employed in the pursuit of a thief. When Pak Lurah Karanganom tried to obtain positive identification of the person who stole his jewelry, he went to several dhukun. Most would not make any comment on the identity of the thief, indicating only various methods by which Pak Lurah could assure the brooch's recovery. However, one dhukun did use a method that is sometimes applied in such circumstances. It consists of reciting certain formulas (rapal) and then asking a young, prepubescent child to look in a mirror and describe the person he or she sees in it. The description should enable the child's listeners to discern the culprit's identity. The person who reads the image must be a child because children are not caught up in the jealousy, intrigue, and politicking inherent in social and sexual maturity. Once again, self-interest is thought to rule out the possibility of foresight, whereas innocence assures the veracity of the child's words.

A much more frequent manifestation of the need to dissimulate an interpretive, mediating presence lies in the pervasive pattern in Javanese speech of using direct rather than indirect quotation. I cited in Chapter 1 a use to which this pattern is often put: when a person attributes remarks implying his or her own high status to another speaker. But the pattern's use is by no means restricted to such stratagems. Any recitation of a previous encounter turns into something like a reenactment, each speaker quoted (supposedly) verbatim. As such, it is another instance of the assumption of voices described in Chapter 5. Each quoted speaker's voice should be distinguishable, just as the voices of different characters must be distinguishable in a performance of wayang. The reason for such meticulous repetition of people's words, or its pretense, lies in the need to dissimulate the mediating role of the speaker. Of course, people are fully aware that such a retelling may include modification and distortion. Yet the rhetorical motive remains, I think, a claim to truthfulness based on the transparency of the present speaker to the incident recounted. The speaker as narrator ostensibly disappears.

In this thoroughly everyday pattern in Javanese interaction stands a summation of the contrasts between Western and Javanese attitudes toward interpretation. In the West, we think that language's first responsibility is to be representational, that it should conform to the shape of the world. At the same time, however, in using language, Westerners seek to make their particular interpretation expressive of their particular, unique selves. Interpretation asserts their presence in the world, in the meeting of phenomena and self. By rendering the world—the past, other people, the environment—in accurate and expressive language, in making a "powerful analysis," Westerners lay claim to superior perceptiveness.

Indirect quotation emphasizes that meeting. The higher a Westerner's status, the more worthy of attention his or her interpretations become, and the more likely he or she is to use indirect quotation. The complex grammatical changes wrought in indirect quotation in Western languages illustrate the importance of the distinction between direct and indirect discourse. They also tend to distinguish more and less educated speakers: those who can and those who cannot claim authority to make significant interpretations of phenomena. To speak in indirect discourse maintains the integrity of, and draws attention to, the speaking self.

Claims to analytic power and the use of indirect discourse may characterize intellectuals more than others in the West. But political leaders are also judged by their ability to articulate a view of the world, and they are expected to be able to express the often inchoate ideas and wants of their constituents. (If their analyses succeed best when they are simplistic and conventional, they should nevertheless appear to present "a bold alternative" to prevailing views. Even a return to the good old days must be presented as a radical departure from current policies, which are held responsible for the dismal present.) No matter what one's role, an individual's particular perspective should grant him or her an "original" opinion, and we value such originality highly. One should think for oneself, draw one's own conclusions, and thereby prove that one is "his own man." Like Javanese, we want to be able to influence the world, but we hope to do so by bringing our uniqueness to bear on the world's otherness. We then overcome subjectivity by capitalizing upon it. We believe that that triumph requires an initial interpretive skill, the ability to observe, understand, and only then attempt to modify the world. Experience, interpretation, and action are supposed to proceed always in that order. Interpretation that precedes experience is deemed prejudice. Mental illness is thought of as improper interpretation, best righted, in the opinion of some, through a reinterpretation.

The contrast I am drawing between Java and the West is, of course, more conventional than real. Westerners impose models upon experience arbitrarily (cf. neo-evolutionary anthropology), and Javanese constantly observe, analyze, and act upon their experience. Each of these aspects of interpretation is essential to cognition and action. But the two traditions, Javanese and Western, differ in emphasis.

In Java, only people who have successfully rid themselves of personal or idiosyncratic traits are thought capable of passing accurate judgment on events. A wong tuwa can discern meaning in the world because he no longer suffers the distortion of perception implicit in self-interest. His effectiveness in the world, and the impact he can have on events, are believed to depend on a similar loss of personal investment, and this matters rather more than his interpretive skill alone. If this view overlaps with Western notions about objectivity, it nevertheless differs importantly in that it suggests not an original or penetrating analyst, but rather a venerable and almost anonymous conduit of potency. A wong tuwa who looks at a young person taking his leave to go to town and says, "Better not go today. Wait until another day," has noticed something that alerts him to danger or obstacles in the young person's path. This is, certainly, an interpretive act. The wong tuwa is capable of it, however, because in his loss of pamrih and the resultant increase in the power of his batin he has become sensitive to the play of mystical forces in the world. But his batin is powerful because it is not constrained by his particular identity.

In Java, therefore, interpretation does not begin with an opening onto experience. It is not the abandonment of positions such as we claim to attempt on the forefronts of knowledge, a move that would seem to Javanese a reckless surrender of control. It is instead a meticulous processing of information in ways that keep it subject to the interpreter's grasp. This permits interpreters to resist experience—to show fortitude in the face of any setback, and to be "not amazed" in the face of any phenomena—and so able to maintain their own power, dignity, and identity in the world.

10. CONCLUSION

In contemporary anthropology, much is made of the ways in which meaning is constructed by a culture's members. The interpretive act by which sense is asserted, such as in the interpretation of art or dreams or language, is a moment in which such constructions of meaning become particularly clear. It seems therefore a particularly vital point at which to observe a culture's workings. The meeting of individuals and events that interpretation implies is a reapplication of principles, occasionally a revision, rarely, in Java at least, a radical reconsideration of them. But in interpreting phenomena of whatever sort, people act upon fundamental understandings of their proper interaction with the world.

I wish to suggest that interpretation is in itself a kind of interaction, one constrained by culturally given patterns and comparable therefore to other kinds of social behavior. It is for this reason that I have treated Javanese interpretation as susceptible to analysis in terms similar to those I have brought to bear on Javanese social life and Javanese shadow plays. Since, however, I have dared to construe the art form in ways at variance with traditional Javanese interpretations, I will conclude with a consideration of how interpreting a non-Western art form challenges some of our own hermeneutic assumptions. If we are going to analyze the ways others approach interpretation, we must also be ready to question the ways we do so. More specifically, in the present context we must ask whether the guidelines we formulate in interpreting texts still hold when we look at a non-Western art form. Are our interpretive principles applicable to texts that are not of our making?

Clifford Geertz, the most famous proponent of an interpretive approach in anthropology, has discussed current interpretive modes in the social sciences, laying particular emphasis on the frequently invoked models of social life as performance and social life as text (C. Geertz 1983). Adherents of the dramaturgical model see in collective life publicly enacted performances that (in the case of what Geertz calls the ritual theory approach) try to resolve conflict among social actors, and/or that (in what Geertz calls the symbolic action approach) convey specific meanings about the nature of the world. Geertz characterizes his own work on the "theatre state" in nineteenth-century Bali as a combination of the two, taking Balinese social life and expressive culture combined as a "dramatized statement of a distinct form of political theory" (1983:29), a statement that not only asserts the theory but also draws people into its enactment.

Adherents of the textual model, Geertz continues, treat text and action as comparable in that both have meanings that persist beyond the moment of speaking or doing: both become "inscribed." Summarizing Paul Ricoeur's understanding of inscription as the fixation of meaning, Geertz states:

> When we speak, our utterances fly by as events like any other behavior; unless what we say is inscribed in writing (or some other established recording process), it is as evanescent as what we do. If it is so inscribed, it of course passes . . . ; but at least its meaning—the *said*, not the *saying*—to a degree and for a while remains. This too is not different for action in general: its meaning can persist in a way its actuality cannot. (C. Geertz 1983:31; cf. Ricoeur 1981)

Geertz suggests that in taking on the notion of text, we can make of our role as observers of social life something akin to that of translator, exegete, or inconographer, and he cites Becker's work on wayang as an example worthy of emulation.

Geertz's succinct summary of these interpretive approaches helps to bring out the particular challenges and opportunities afforded by the study of a performing art. The value of such a study for cultural analysis stems from the fact that an art form provides us indigenously generated representations of people's lives while still constituting a part of those lives. Both observed and lived, and so both a representation of social life and an instance of it, a performance provides a commentary upon interaction and yet also exemplifies it. At the same time, analyzing a performing art should persuade us to examine any untoward assumptions the use of some metaphors might foster. It can do so because a performing art overturns the distinctions between "social life," "performance," and "text," upon which such metaphors depend.

To analyze a performing art as a form of interaction, and so a form or manifestation of social life, counters the more common practice of seeing social life as a kind of performance. When social life is likened to a performance, the latter tends to become a generic term, one actually possessed of relatively little explanatory power. Specifically, if we play on the notions of role, appearance, and scenario to analyze everyday life, we are liable to presume Western understandings of a self as self-conscious actor, choosing among scripts and affecting roles. When an actual performance is analyzed in the context of social life, its explanatory power can prove much greater. Unable to say that a performance is "like a performance," we must ask what a performance in a particular place actually looks like. This should encourage us to consider how "selves" are represented, therefore, and what is thought important or interesting about them and their actions. It should, furthermore, encourage us to think about the medium in which the performance takes place. Since that medium implies a form of interaction—between performance and spectator—but an obviously constructed one, it suggests focal issues in interaction more generally. By putting aside the dramaturgical model in favor of drama itself, we give up universalizing statements about self and role and take up the challenge to analyze specific conceptions of self and interaction.

If the dramaturgical model turns perforce tautological when applied to actual performances, the textual model proves particularly interesting and problematic when applied to a performing art. Ricoeur, as Geertz has noted, sees texts as fixing the "said of speaking," thereby enabling the meanings of discourse to develop through time. Ricoeur compares this to the way that action, although fleeting, develops meanings in the form of its consequences. A performance, however, is both text *and* action. As a result, Ricoeur's distinction makes it possible to look for different kinds of meanings in performance, seen on the one hand as text and on the other as action. At the same time, however, a performance points up some of the difficulties in using a textual model that makes action comparable to texts.

If a dramatic presentation is based on a script to which actors give voice, then the audience indeed receives a text, though in the form of speaking. This means that the process of interpretation has already been initiated by the actors and director. Yet if drama in performance is a partially interpreted text, it is also a form of action, or really, of actions. There is the action taking place within the world of the play, and there is the action of staging the play in the world outside it. Asking about the consequences of these two kinds of actions, in an effort to establish their significance, means on the one hand attending to the effects that action in the play has upon its characters, and on the other, attending to the effects that staging the play has upon its players, sponsors, and audience. We should, moreover, consider the relations between the two. Debate about the effects of violence in movies and television on the actions of spectators in the rest of life illustrates how problematic that issue can become.

Yet when a performance proposes an interpretation of a text, by supplying appropriate gestures and tone, it emphasizes the status of speech and action as events, rather than in the forms by which they may be fixed. This suggests that interpreting such a performance should proceed not from a meditation upon the text as fixed upon a page, but rather from the experience and/or memory of the performance, seen as an ephemeral event.

The problem with Ricoeur's account of action in general is that he exaggerates its fixity, in order to support his comparison of action with texts. We cannot recover an event with nearly the degree of confidence with which we recover writing. As a result, we must modify the way we conceive of the meanings that inhere in events, and ask whether our reliance upon a textual model is suitable to something—whether a performance or any kind of action—that is experienced very differently from reading, and is much less subject to retrieval.

Of course, the notion of text is often expanded far beyond Ricoeur's relatively restricted usage of it, as for example in Becker's wide-ranging use of the term (1979), or, for that matter, Geertz's (1973a). Yet as long as the concept of writing is taken as constitutive of texts, and by analogy, as long as we take the fixing or objectifying of action as constitutive of its meaning, we run the risk of separating meaning from event, and casting off the latter as an unwanted husk. Unlike a text, action is experienced only within specific contexts. In analyzing it, as a result, we must not lose sight of what J. B. Thompson, paraphrasing Ricoeur, calls the "doing" of action, in too-hot pursuit of "the significance of what is done" (J. B. Thompson 1981:15).

A performance of wayang poses these problems particularly clearly. It is quite resistant to being made into a text. It is shaped by convention, but it is not scripted. Indeed, with the ambiguous exception of sung verse, the traditional arts in Java almost never take the form of written texts. Javanese seem unwilling to accept the impoverishment of language necessary to fix it upon the page, stripped as it then becomes of so much of its tone and contextual meanings. That wayang lakon are preserved in only three- or four-line summaries bespeaks the inadequacy of writing to convey anything in wayang beyond "what happens." What matters in performance is what is proper to performance: the tone, manner, and style of movement and speech. So even more acutely than scripted drama, a performance of wayang emphasizes its own nature as an ephemeral event.

How then can we talk about what a performance of wayang means? How could we, following Ricoeur, look for a text, and how could we look for the consequences of a performance as "meaningful action"? In response to the first query, if meaning inheres in what remains inscribed in a text, then we should look to what is fixed about the tradition as a whole—the pathokan and the recurrent conventions of plot, taken as a kind of textual basis for every performance. A. L. Becker does just this, establishing some fixity of meaning in the ephemera of performance.

In addressing the second query, if we take the meaning of action to lie in its consequences, and if we take a performance of wayang as a kind of action undertaken by its players and sponsors, then we can look for its meaning in the effects it has after it takes place. Javanese themselves believe that a performance becomes "inscribed in the world." They believe that its consequences surpass the intentions of its agents, since a performance is thought capable of exerting mystical influence over its sponsors, spectators, and surroundings long after it takes place. They also believe that its importance surpasses its immediate context, as it redounds on the status of the sponsors and the reputation of the dhalang and his troupe. Furthermore, since a performance as part of a ritual celebration draws many people into its workings, as providers of labor and/or as guests or spectators, it can have important ramifications in their social lives. For example, the extent of a neighbor's financial support and labor will affect his or her relations with the sponsoring family for years to come. In all these ways, a performance of wayang fits Ricoeur's description of "meaningful action considered as a text," since its meanings persist long after its occurrence.

Nevertheless, to insist upon the textual nature of a performance, or upon its consequences in the world, in order to determine its meaning, would be to restrict the nature of its significance. I have tried to demonstrate that the meaningfulness of a performance of wayang resides above all in the nature of the relations it establishes in the course of the performance itself. It is because meaning need not develop out of or after the event, because a performance of wa- yang need not be mulled over in exegetical rumination to yield up its significance, that it provides such a rich source of insight into Jav- anese culture. What is said and done in a performance matter to Jav- anese, who make much of its moral instruction. More importantly, however, the "saying" and the "doing" of the performance implicate essential concerns in Javanese culture about the nature and effects of all interaction. It is because the relationship between dhalang and spectator resonates so deeply with other relationships in Javanese life that it exercises such fascination for Javanese, and we must as a result not put that relationship aside as the incidental means for conveying a more enduring message. We must take it, as Javanese themselves take it, altogether seriously. Just as hermeneuticists have gained in- sight into the nature of texts by pondering the act of reading itself, so we can gain insight into the nature of wayang kulit by pondering the act of watching it, and by pondering the difference between that act and the act of reading.

Watching a performance of wayang, I have tried to show, evokes Javanese understandings about the constitution of the self and about appropriate modes of interaction. Essential to these ideas is the issue of power, as manifested in a concern with potency, status, and per- sonal sovereignty, and as implemented in several different kinds of relationships: in face-to-face encounter, in the family, in village pol- itics, and in activities linked to healing, to ritual needs, to aesthetic pleasures, and to interpretive efforts. The transposition of such core concerns into so many different registers does not yield perfectly con- gruent patterns. Still, many of the same tensions, following as they do from certain contradictory impulses, reappear.

What wayang does not do is resolve such contradictions that ap- pear in ideology and in life, and in that respect it does not instruct. An emphasis upon meaning such as the exegete of texts might wish in a study of performances is misleading insofar as it holds up the promise of either a radical questioning or a proposed resolution to problems in the world of its spectators. Wayang certainly helps to

propagate a particular view of the world. But it can do so above all
because to participate in the event of a shadow play means to repeat
patterns of interaction common to other domains of life. In this way
it constitutes—to return to Ricoeur's terms for a moment—additional instances of "saying" and "doing," rather than any isolation of
the "said" or the "meaningful" in the rest of life.

I insist upon this not to demean wayang kulit, but rather to point
to where its richness lies. Only when we release wayang from an obligation to convey explicit messages to its spectators can we recognize
the range of associations implicit in attending any performance, or
any part of one. Only when we treat the performance as an event, as
an experience of great evocative power rather than as some elaborate
heuristic device, do we escape the intellectualist prejudices and expectations we bring to the study of texts, or for that matter, to many
studies of ritual seen as cognitively instructive or transformative experiences. (For a critique of the latter, see Schieffelin 1985.) Some
Javanese see wayang as a vehicle for molding people's ideas. Those
political interests, however, that have sought to use wayang to pro-
pound a particular message, whether currently or in the past, have
exaggerated the effectiveness of the turns of plot and dialogue to alter
people's attitudes and behavior, and they have neglected the greater
significance of the medium itself.

This is not to say that the wayang tradition is ossified or impervious
to change. No doubt it has changed just as the world in which its performances take place has changed. I am myself inclined, for example,
to see the recent popularity of highly conventionalized stories about
wahyu as emblematic of the current era. Wahyu account for sudden
shifts in power in the world, very much a concern in a society where
such shifts have been many and dramatic since World War II. Highly
stereotypical plots, at the same time, assure all present that everything—the course of the performance, the tenor of the audience's response, and implicitly the world at large—is under control. Yet even
if older dhalang, as I have mentioned, disparage the current proliferation of wahyu stories, it is unclear how differently stories that were
popular in earlier eras were actually performed. It is also unclear how
the aristocracy's greater patronage of the tradition in the past may
have affected its contents. Unfortunately, it is very difficult to establish with any certainty what performances were like a century ago, or
fifty years ago, or even thirty. Had we clearer records of a range of
earlier performances, we could speak more confidently of the links

between the content of performances and their particular historical and political contexts. Yet I believe the format of the performance has changed relatively little, and the continuity of the medium is more important than changes in particular lakon: it is the medium even more than the contents that resonates so deeply with other domains of Javanese life.

Those domains are many. In the Javanese family, the father's role is glorified and constrained in such a way as to make his power at the same time unquestioned and largely unexercised. Villagers who press their headman into particular molds seek to determine the nature and extent of his power over them in much the same way. The dissembled center—king, ritual sponsor, or dhalang—reiterates the paradoxically effective but absent figures of authority that the father and headman are pressed to become. Each of these figures should support and protect people, but in no way impinge on their personal autonomy. The spectators who impose a conventional meaning upon a performance of wayang define their relationship with the art form and with the dhalang in a similarly idealizing yet defensive way. Certainly, family members, villagers, and spectators all seek to gain certain benefits from the very power that they distrust. The authority of the father, the influence and perhaps patronage of the lurah, the influence (berkah) and esoteric wisdom (ngèlmu) communicated by a dhalang in performance, are all judged at least potentially beneficial. The pleasure afforded by a performance of wayang as entertainment is also great. At the same time, however, submission to a powerful political authority, classically to the king, and surrender of self-conscious control, such as to the dhalang, constitute seductive and mistrusted alternatives to the personal sovereignty, clarity, and guardedness Javanese norms prescribe. Whether in political or aesthetic subjection to headman or dhalang, dissimulation of a superior's control mitigates the impression of a loss of personal control or autonomy. The dissimulated self also gains a particular authority: a diffuse but idealized and highly respected position as agent both operating within and surpassing the world. The peculiar fascination of the dhalang in Javanese culture stems from this fact: that he is at once a dissembled authority, one whose power is great, non-coercive, and unworldly, and a dissembled interpreter, one who mediates between an unreal but persuasive and distracting world, and our own.

GLOSSARY

The following glossary gives only *ngoko* terms, followed by brief definitions.

abangan	syncretist Muslim
abdi-dalem	servant at a royal court
aji-aji	a magical formula, usually granting invulnerability
alihan	a change of form
alus	smooth; refined; elegant
antawacana	the differentiation of voices in wayang
basa	any mix of the speech levels *krama* and *madya* in speech; polite manners; to use refined speech and manners
batin	the imperceptible, subtle, spiritual, or mysterious; a person's reserve of potency, enabling him or her to be sensitive to the imperceptible forces at play in the world
bayan	a lesser village official, below the rank of *lurah* and *carik* (village notary)
berkah	beneficent mystical influence
céngkok	embellishment; decoration; variation
crita	story; what people say
daya	energy (positive or negative); aura; mystical influence
dhalang	puppeteer
dhanyang	a territorial spirit
dhukun	a magic specialist to whom people turn for cures, advice, and other mystical assistance
éling	to remember; to be conscious; to be mindful or careful
gamelan	the Javanese percussion orchestra
gendhing	a musical composition played on the *gamelan*
guru	a teacher, often referring to a teacher of mystical wisdom
ilmiah	science, knowledge based on mundane perceptions
inthuk	an evil spirit able to supply people with stolen money in return for the souls of the recipients and/or their kin
isin	ashamed; embarrassed; affronted
jagongan	an evening gathering of males held in observance of a ritual occasion
jathilan	a dance form in which male dancers use props resembling horses

jodho	to fit; to be suitable to one another; to be mystically compatible
kakuwatan	strength
kakuwatan batin	mystical strength; spiritual potency
kalah	to be defeated
kalah kuwat	to be less strong; to be overwhelmed; to lose out
kalurahan	the smallest administrative unit in Java, usually translated village, consisting of several hamlets
kasar	rough, crude
kaul	a vow
Kawi	Javanese vocabulary used in the performing and literary arts
kebatinan	anything to do with spiritual power and mystical energy
kérata basa	rhyming folk etymologies
krama	a term applied to all forms of high Javanese
krama andhap	self-humbling vocabulary
krama inggil	honorific vocabulary
lair	visible; apparent to the senses; mundane
lakon	the plot of a performance
lakon carangan	a *lakon* that does not adhere closely to the major events in the Indian epics on which the classical *lakon* are based
lakon pokok	a *lakon* that constitutes an essential part of an epic cycle
laku	an ascetic exercise (literally, a step)
lali	to forget; to be thoughtless
ludrug	folk drama with transvestites playing all female roles
lungguh	village lands the use of which goes to village officials in lieu of a salary
lurah	the village headman
madya	middle Javanese, consisting of vocabulary items from other speech levels plus a few specifically *madya* items
malih	to take on another form (see *alihan*)
mandi	to be effective or powerful (e.g., medicine or venom)
modin	village religious official; any person able to officiate at a *slametan*
nduwé gawé	to hold a ritual celebration on a large scale (literally, to have work)
ngalah	to give way voluntarily from a position of superior strength or wisdom
ngalamun	to let one's thoughts wander aimlessly
ngebleng	a type of ascetic exercise in which a person fasts and goes without sleep for three days in an enclosed space
ngèlmu	mystical wisdom based on immaterial or subtle forces

ngoko	low Javanese
nunggal weton	to be born on the same conjunction of five- and seven-day cycles as another person
pamrih	self-interest; desire; envy
pathet	a musical mode
pathokan	requirements; the requisite structure of a performance of *wayang*
pétungan	numerological calculations, used to determine the compatibility of prospective spouses, propitious days and times for important activities, etc.
prabawa	a person's impressive presence or influence, attributed to great spiritual power
préwangan	a medium
punakawan	servant-clowns that appear in the performing arts
pusaka	an heirloom, often believed to have great *daya*
rapal	a magical formula
réwang	neighbor or relative who assists in a person's ritual need
ruwatan	a preventative ritual, to stave off mystically caused misfortune
sabetan	a puppeteer's ability to manipulate puppets
sah	paid off; fulfilled; formally acknowledged
sajèn	offerings to spirits
sanggit	a puppeteer's dramatic capacity
santri	a devout Mulsim (whether orthodox or modernist)
sejarah	history
slametan	a ritual meal, held in observance of any individual or group occasion
suluk	long vocal lines sung by the *dhalang* during the course of a performance
tanggung jawab	to take responsibility; to be responsible
tarupan	setting up for a ritual occasion
tembang	Javanese sung verse
wadhah	a vessel or container
wahyu	mystical boon (usually in the form of a glowing ball of light that descends from the sky)
wajib	obligatory; small sum of money given to the *modin* at the time of a *slametan*
watak	characteristic; personality trait
wayang kulit	shadow puppet
wayang wong	dance drama (literally, people puppets; a human shadow play)
wedi	fear; fear and respect for one's superiors

weton	the conjunction of five- and seven-day cycles on which a person is born
wong liya	non-kin (literally, other people)
wong tuwa	a parent; an elder; any person thought to have great wisdom or spiritual power

BIBLIOGRAPHY

Anderson, Benedict
   1965   *Mythology and the Tolerance of the Javanese.* Cornell Indonesia Project Monograph no. 37. Ithaca, N.Y.: Cornell Modern Indonesia Project.
   1966   "The Languages of Indonesian Politics." *Indonesia* 1:89-116.
   1972a *Java in a Time of Revolution.* Ithaca, N.Y.: Cornell University Press.
   1972b "The Idea of Power in Javanese Culture." In *Culture and Politics in Indonesia,* edited by Claire Holt, Benedict Anderson, and James Siegel, 1-69. Ithaca, N.Y.: Cornell University Press.
Austin, J. L.
   1962   *How to Do Things With Words.* Cambridge, Mass.: Harvard University Press.
Bateson, Gregory, and Margaret Mead
   1942   *Balinese Character: A Photographic Analysis.* New York: New York Academy of Sciences.
Becker, A. L.
   1979   "Text-Building, Epistemology, and Aesthetics in Javanese Shadow Theatre." In *The Imagination of Reality: Essays in Southeast Asian Coherence Systems,* edited by A. L. Becker and A. A. Yengoyan, 211-43. Norwood, N.J.: Ablex Publishing Corporation.
Becker, Judith
   1979   "Time and Tune in Java." In *The Imagination of Reality: Essays in Southeast Asian Coherence Systems,* edited by A. L. Becker and A. A. Yengoyan, 197-210. Norwood, N.J.: Ablex Publishing Corporation.
Belo, Jane
   1970   "A Study of Customs Pertaining to Twins in Bali." In *Traditional Balinese Culture,* 3-56. New York: Columbia University Press.
Boon, James
   1977   *The Anthropological Romance of Bali 1597-1972: Dynamic Perspectives in Marriage and Caste, Politics and Religion.* Cambridge: Cambridge University Press.
   1984   "Folly, Bali, and Anthropology." In *Text, Play, and Story: The Construction and Reconstruction of Self and Society,* edited by Edward Bruner, 156-77. 1983 Proceedings of the American Eth-

nological Society. Washington, D.C.: American Ethnological Society.

Brandon, James

1970   *On Thrones of Gold.* Cambridge, Mass.: Harvard University Press.

Clara van Groenendaal, Victoria

1982   *Er zit een dhalang achter de wayang: De rol van de Vorstenlandse dalang in de Indonesisch-Javaanse samenleving.* Amsterdam: De Goudsbloem.

Errington, James Joseph

1981   "Changing Speech Levels Among a Traditional Javanese Elite Group." Ph.D. thesis, University of Chicago.

1984   "Self and Self-Conduct Among the Javanese *Priyayi* Elite." *American Ethnologist* 11, no. 2:275-90.

1985   *Language and Social Change in Java: Linguistic Reflexes of Modernization in a Traditional Royal Polity.* Athens, Ohio: Ohio University Center for Southeast Asian Studies.

Errington, Shelly

1983   "Embodied Sumange' in Luwu." In *Journal of Asian Studies* 43, no. 3:545-70.

Forthcoming *Meaning and Power in a Southeast Asian Realm.*

Geertz, Clifford

1960   *The Religion of Java.* Glencoe, Ill.: Free Press.

1962   *Peddlers and Princes: Social Change and Economic Modernization in Two Indonesian Towns.* Chicago: University of Chicago Press.

1963   *Agricultural Involution: The Process of Ecological Change in Indonesia.* Berkeley: University of California Press.

1965   *The Social History of an Indonesian Town.* Cambridge, Mass.: MIT Press.

1968   *Islam Observed: Religious Development in Morocco and Indonesia.* New Haven: Yale University Press.

1973a   "Deep Play: Notes on the Balinese Cockfight." In *The Interpretation of Cultures,* 459-90. New York: Basic Books.

1973b   "Person, Time and Conduct in Bali." In *The Interpretation of Cultures,* 412-53. New York: Basic Books.

1980   *Negara: The Theatre State in Nineteenth Century Bali.* Princeton, N.J.: Princeton University Press.

1983   "Blurred Genres: The Refiguration of Social Thought." In *Local Knowledge,* 19-35. New York: Basic Books.

1984   "Cultural and Social Change: The Indonesian Case." *Man* n.s. 19:511-32.

Geertz, Hildred

1961   *The Javanese Family.* Glencoe, Ill.: Free Press.

Goffman, Erving
    1967   *Interaction Ritual*. Garden City, N.J.: Doubleday Inc.
Hefner, Robert
    1983   "The Problem of Preference: Economic and Ritual Change in Highlands Java." *Man* n.s. 18:669-89.
Heins, Ernst
    1970   "Cueing the Gamelan Orchestra in a Performance of Wayang Kulit." *Indonesia* 9:101-27.
Hood, Mantle
    1954   *The Nuclear Theme as a Determinant of Patet in Javanese Music*. Groningen: J. B. Wolters.
Hüsken, Frans
    1979   "Landlords, Sharecroppers and Agricultural Labourers: Changing Labour Relations in Rural Java." *Journal of Contemporary Asia* 9:140-51.
    1983   "Kinship, Economics and Politics in a Central Javanese Village." Paper presented to the Seminar on Cognatic Forms of Social Organization in Southeast Asia, Amsterdam, January 1983.
Jay, Robert
    1969   *Javanese Villagers*. Cambridge, Mass.: MIT Press.
Kats, J.
    1923   *Het Javaansche Tooneel*. Vol. 1, *Wayang Poerwa*. Weltevreden: Volkslectuur.
Keeler, Ward
    1975   "Musical Encounter in Java and Bali." *Indonesia* 19:85-125.
    1983   "Javanese Generations: Gender Roles and Intergenerational Ties in Javanese Myth and Ritual." Paper presented at the SSRC Conference on Gender Roles in Insular Southeast Asia, Princeton, December 1983.
    1984   *Javanese: A Cultural Approach*. Athens, Ohio: Ohio University Center for International Studies.
    1985   "Villagers and the Exemplary Center in Java." *Indonesia* 39:111-40.
Forthcoming a   "Speaking of Gender in Java." To appear in a collection of essays on the construction of gender in Southeast Asia, edited by Jane Atkinson and Shelly Errington.
Forthcoming b   "Mystic Debate and *Mission Impossible*." To appear in a collection of essays on literature and translation in Southeast Asia, edited by A. L. Becker.
Koentjaraningrat R.
    1967   "Tjelapar. A Village in South Central Java." In *Villages in Indone-*

sia, edited by R. Koentjaraningrat, 244-80. Ithaca, N.Y.: Cornell University Press.

Lévi-Strauss, Claude

1962   *La Pensée Sauvage*. Paris: Plon.

1964   *Le Cru et le Cuit*. Paris: Plon.

Long, Roger

1982   *Javanese Shadow Theatre: Movement and Characterization in Ngayogyakarta Wayang Kulit*. Ann Arbor: UMI Research Press.

Mangkunegara VII, K.G.P.A.A.

1957   *On the Wayang Kulit (Purwa) and Its Symbolic and Mystical Elements*. Translated by Claire Holt. Southeast Asia Program Data Paper no. 27. Ithaca, N.Y.: Cornell University Southeast Asia Program.

Moertono, Soemarsaid

1968   *State and Statecraft in Old Java*. Cornell Indonesia Project Monograph no. 43. Ithaca, N.Y.: Cornell Modern Indonesia Project.

Mulder, Niels

1983   "Abangan Javanese Religious Thought and Practice." *BKI* 139, no. 2/3:260-67.

Parnickel, B. B.

1980   "Towards an Interpretation of the Metempsychosis Motif in Wayang Purwa Lakons." *BKI* 136, no. 4:427-81.

Parsons, Anne

1969   "Is the Oedipal Crisis Universal?" In *Belief, Magic and Anomie: Essays in Psychological Anthropology*, 3-66. Glencoe, Ill.: Free Press.

Peacock, James.

1968   *The Rites of Modernization: Symbolic and Social Aspects of Indonesian Proletarian Drama*. Chicago: University of Chicago Press.

Pigeaud, Th.

1938   *Javaansche Volksvertoningen*. Batavia: Volkslectuur.

Poerwadarminta, W.J.S.

1939   *Baoesastra Djawa*. Groningen: J. B. Wolters.

Ras, J. J.

1978   "De Clownfiguren in de Wajang." *BKI* 134, no. 4:451-65.

Rassers, W. H.

1959   *Panji, the Culture Hero*. The Hague: Martinus Nijhoff.

Ricoeur, Paul

1981   "The Model of the Text: Meaningful Action Considered as Text." In *Hermeneutics and the Human Sciences*, edited and translated by John B. Thompson, 197-246. Cambridge: Cambridge University Press.

Schieffelin, Edward L.
1985 "Performance and the Cultural Construction of Reality." *American Ethnologist* 12, no. 4:707-24.
Schulte Nordholt, N. G.
1982 "De Positie van de Lurah: Een kritische beschouwing naar aanleiding van enkele lurah-verkiezingen in Midden-Java." *BKI* 138, no. 1:98-126.
Seno-Sastroamidjojo
1964 *Renungan Tentang Wajang Kulit*. Jakarta: Kinta.
Siegel, James
1969 *The Rope of God*. Berkeley: University of California Press.
1979 *Shadow and Sound: The Historical Thought of a Sumatran People*. Chicago: University of Chicago Press.
Soepomo Poedjosoedarmo
1968 "Javanese Speech Levels." *Indonesia* 6:54-81.
1969 "Wordlist of Javanese Non-Ngoko Vocabulary." *Indonesia* 7:165-90.
Solomonik, I. N.
1980 "Wayang Purwa Puppets: The Language of the Silhouette." *BKI* 136, no. 4:482-97.
Sumarsam
1984 "Inner Melody in Javanese Gamelan." In *Karawitan: Source Readings in Javanese Gamelan and Vocal Music*, vol. 1, edited by J. Becker and A. Feinstein, 245-304. Ann Arbor: University of Michigan.
Sutton, R. Anderson
1984 "Change and Ambiguity: Gamelan Style and Regional Identity in Yogyakarta." In *Aesthetic Tradition and Cultural Transition in Java and Bali*, edited by S. Morgan and L. J. Sears, 221-45. Madison, Wis.: University of Wisconsin Center for Southeast Asian Studies.
Thompson, John B.
1981 "Editor's Introduction." In Paul Ricoeur, *Hermeneutics and the Human Sciences*, 1-26. Cambridge: Cambridge University Press.
Turner, Victor
1967 *The Forest of Symbols*. Ithaca, N.Y.: Cornell University Press.
1969 *The Ritual Process*. Chicago: Aldine Publishing Co.
Uhlenbeck, E. M.
1978 *Studies in Javanese Morphology*. Translation Series no. 19. Koninklijk Instituut voor Taal-, Land- en Volken-Kunden. The Hague: Martinus Nijhoff.

Ulbricht, H.
　1970　Wayang Purwa: Shadows of the Past. Kuala Lumpur: Oxford University Press.
Valeri, Valerio
　1985　Kingship and Sacrifice: Ritual and Society in Ancient Hawaii. Translated by Paula Wissing. Chicago: University of Chicago Press.
Van Ness, Edward, and Shita Prawirohardjo
　1981　Javanese Wayang Kulit. New York: Oxford University Press.
White, Benjamin
　1983a　" 'Agricultural Involution' and its Critics: Twenty Years After." Bulletin of Concerned Asian Scholars 15,2:18-31.
　1983b　Notes on Processes of Agrarian Differentiation in Post-Colonial Java. Manuscript in possession of author.
Wilner, Ann Ruth
　1970　"The Neotraditional Accommodation to Political Independence: The Case of Indonesia." In Cases in Comparative Politics: Asia, edited by Lucian Pye, 242-306. Boston: Little, Brown and Co.
Zoetmulder, P. J.
　1974　Kalangwan: A Survey of Old Javanese Literature. The Hague: Martinus Nijhoff.

INDEX

abdi-dalem, 31, 155–56, 166–67, 169–70, 202–203, 209, 223–24, 232
aesthetics: of *gamelan*, 226–29; of *wayang*, 229–33
agricultural labor, 68, 74, 90–91, 105, 107, 134
alihan, malih, 10, 207–209, 210, 211, 230
ancestors. *See* spirits, ancestral
antawacana, 189, 196–98, 199
aristocracy, 26, 28, 32, 41, 65, 67, 95, 107, 115, 116, 155–56, 168, 171, 172, 176, 184, 267
asceticism, 25, 40, 41–48, 49, 54, 83, 86, 97, 98, 100, 112, 119, 121, 123, 126, 129, 132, 136, 137, 160, 161, 172, 183, 200, 204, 208, 210, 219–20, 222, 232, 235, 244, 255, 256
audience, 5, 6, 7, 8, 9, 10, 11, 12, 15, 17, 141, 152, 174, 176, 178, 180, 182, 183, 184, 185, 188, 189, 212, 213–19, 225, 229–34, 235–40, 243, 263, 264, 265, 266, 267, 268

basa, 29, 30, 31, 65, 70, 71, 80, 110–11, 136, 170, 178. *See also krama*; language; *madya*
batin. See lair
berkah, 45, 84, 98, 104, 111, 137, 202, 268
birthday. *See weton*
Bratayuda, 193, 195, 214–15, 217–18, 243, 247

children and child-rearing, 31, 33, 51, 56–84, 113, 118, 122, 135, 136, 197, 257
clients. *See* patrons and clients
conflict, interpersonal, 37, 72, 75–78, 80, 82, 87, 110, 151–53, 212–13, 220, 223; in *wayang*, 191, 212–13
consciousness, 72, 118, 120, 123, 205, 213, 217, 219–24, 226, 228, 232,

233, 238, 239, 241, 255. *See also* memory
curing, 42, 51, 87, 93, 107, 114, 115–19, 208; and vows, 125–27, 135

dhalang, 3–14, 18, 27, 32, 33, 43–44, 84, 85, 127, 128, 135, 140, 141, 142, 156, 160, 161, 162, 165–79, 211, 215, 216, 218, 219, 220, 229, 232, 233–40, 241, 243, 246, 247, 249, 251, 252, 257, 265, 266, 268; evaluation of, 5, 10, 40, 175, 183–85, 188–200, 217, 230–31; and kin, 32, 183, 184; selection of, 172–75; social status, 15, 70, 165–73; training, 7, 183–84; and sponsors, 172–79, 180
dhanyang, 84, 97–98, 104, 109–112, 165–66, 170, 177, 211, 217; and vows, 126–28, 131, 134; and *wayang*, 165–66, 217–18
dhukun, 112, 114–19, 124, 127, 140, 161, 171, 221, 234–37, 257
dramaturgy. *See sanggit*
dreams, 42, 83, 107, 130, 243, 254–56, 257

education, 31, 68, 69, 70, 72–73, 98, 126, 149, 183–84, 186
elder, respected. *See wong tuwa*
emotions, 32, 56–68, 70–79, 133, 151, 159–60, 161, 163, 176, 209, 222, 224, 227, 244, 248, 253, 255; in marriage, 52, 53, 54; and spirit possession, 117–18; and vows, 125–27, 129–30, 132; and *wayang*, 217, 218, 239. *See also isin; kagèt; wedi*
encounter, face-to-face, 14, 25–38, 40, 45–46, 48–50, 57, 65–68, 73, 75–80, 84, 106, 114–15, 133, 139, 142, 150, 153, 163, 164, 204, 212–13, 220, 266
etymology, folk. *See kérata basa*
exchange, 4, 84, 106, 113, 124, 128, 162, 237; and asceticism, 46, 47; and

exchange (cont.)
    ritual celebrations, 142, 143, 146–47,
    153, 154, 157, 158, 159, 202; with
    spirits, 116–18, 121–22; among spon-
    sors and dhalang, 177, 178; and vows,
    129, 131
exegesis, 16, 21, 42, 205, 213, 243–60,
    262; of wayang, 217, 230, 243–50

family relations, 25, 28, 36–37, 51–84,
    85, 105, 137, 202, 220, 222, 252,
    268
father, 9, 18, 32, 51, 56, 60–63, 65, 68,
    70–84, 86–87, 92–93, 99, 104, 112,
    136–37, 160, 186, 192, 268; and son,
    51, 68, 71–84, 99, 115, 122, 130,
    134, 160, 184, 212, 222; in wayang,
    211–12, 244
fear. See wedi

gamelan, 3, 4, 6, 12, 13, 15, 170, 173,
    180–83, 191, 198, 225–27, 229, 233,
    234, 248. See also musicians
gender, 6, 7, 8, 36, 88, 95–96, 98, 104,
    113, 114, 181, 209, 210; and family,
    51–84; and mediums, 122; and per-
    forming arts, 240–41; and ritual cele-
    brations, 143–47, 150, 157–58; and
    wealth, 53–56, 72–73, 88, 95
genealogy, 26, 183, 209, 220–21, 247
God, 42, 44, 45, 46, 48, 82, 100, 113,
    117, 121, 123, 126, 128, 129, 131,
    134, 159, 177, 219, 220, 221, 246,
    254; and potency, 41, 46, 82
guru, 81–83, 107, 112, 137, 156, 252

headman, village. See lurah

isin, 32, 41, 54, 63, 66–67, 76, 79, 94,
    152, 160, 176
Islam, 23, 40, 99, 102, 110, 114, 166,
    234, 241, 252. See also santri

Javanese language. See language

kagèt, 58, 63, 226
Kawi, 183, 192, 231
kebatinan, 21, 38–40, 109, 114, 124,
    148, 151, 169, 174, 218, 222, 231,
    233, 235–39, 242, 259. See also ascet-
    icism; ngèlmu; potency
kérata basa, 223, 248, 250, 251–53

kethoprak, 152, 240
king, 48, 85, 86, 111–12, 127, 140,
    151, 152, 168, 171–72, 178–79, 192,
    202, 211, 212, 213, 218, 224, 268;
    and dhalang, 169–72, 178, 239
kinship, 5, 26, 27, 32, 33, 36–37, 42,
    51n, 67, 78, 92, 93, 105, 113, 115,
    126, 134, 159, 194, 204, 218, 221,
    222n, 223–24, 254; and asceticism,
    160, 204; among dhalang, 7, 32, 183;
    and ritual celebrations, 142–45, 155.
    See also family relations
krama, 24, 28, 29, 34, 136, 152, 178.
    See also basa; language
Kurawa, 206, 207, 211, 214, 216, 243

lair: and batin, 39, 47, 78, 119, 151,
    173, 174
lakon, 8, 13, 15, 16, 176, 183, 188, 190,
    191, 192–95, 198, 203–205, 206,
    207, 211, 212, 213–18, 229, 230,
    232, 240, 241, 247, 265, 267, 268;
    and exegesis, 217, 230, 243–50; prin-
    cipal, 194, 214, 247; secondary, 194,
    195, 214–15, 247
language: learning, 64–66, 136; and lin-
    guistic etiquette, 40, 46, 53, 65, 70,
    71, 80, 84, 110–11, 113, 119, 136–
    37, 138, 139, 160, 161, 162, 170,
    210, 244; literary, 183, 187, 235;
    magical, see rapal; in wayang, 192,
    193, 197, 198, 209, 230, 231, 241,
    251. See also basa; Kawi; kérata basa;
    krama; madya; ngoko; speech; vows
lurah, 27, 33, 84, 86–108, 112, 137,
    138, 144, 145, 149, 152, 155, 162,
    166, 172, 268
luwaran kaul, 125, 126–28, 129–31. See
    also vows

madya, 28, 29, 34, 35
magic. See dhukun; kebatinan; ngèlmu;
    rapal; wong tuwa
Mangkunegara VII, 244n
marriage, 43, 52–56, 69–70, 93, 94, 95,
    100, 147
medium. See préwangan
memory, 116, 129, 139, 146, 147, 202,
    203, 209, 210, 219–24, 226, 230,
    231, 255. See also consciousness
mother, 51, 56–65, 69, 72–80, 186
music. See gamelan

musicians, 5, 6, 7, 8, 10, 11, 12, 14, 32, 141, 165, 170, 173, 175, 176, 180–83, 226, 227, 228, 229, 252
mysticism. *See kebatinan; ngèlmu*; potency

Nartosabdho, Ki, 173, 189, 190, 193, 195, 197, 199, 200, 235, 236
neighbors, relations among, 6, 113, 115–16, 142, 143–45, 148–50, 153–55, 156, 236, 237
ngebleng, 42, 45, 48, 220
ngèlmu, 81–84, 99–100, 102, 121, 122, 123, 171, 235, 243, 244, 245, 249, 250–53, 257, 268; *ngèlmu padhalangan*, 183, 188, 200
ngoko, 24, 28, 29, 30, 35, 65, 104, 161
numerology. *See pétungan*

orchestra. *See gamelan*; musicians

pamrih, 48–49, 112, 124, 207, 211, 255, 256–57, 259
Pandhawa, 9, 194, 204, 206, 207, 208, 214, 216, 218, 243, 244, 250
pathokan, 190–94, 230, 244, 245, 247, 251, 265
patrons and clients, 86, 90–91, 101, 105, 106, 114, 134–35, 155–56, 166, 167, 224
performance, structure of. *See pathokan*
pétungan, 5, 110, 160, 237, 249, 254
politics, 15, 25, 40, 51, 73n, 85–108, 171, 172, 200, 224, 228, 240, 241, 258, 267, 268
possession, spirit: involuntary, 116–19, 221–22; and mediums, 120–24; and trances, 100–102
potency, 19, 20, 32, 46–49, 51, 55, 56, 111, 112, 113, 135–37, 140, 141, 171, 172, 176, 192, 200, 204, 215, 222, 237, 241, 242, 250, 259; and asceticism, 41–48; and curing, 116–19; and *dhalang*, 169, 176, 199, 235–36; and encounter, 38–41; in the family, 70, 72, 77, 78, 79, 81, 82, 84; and gender, 41, 54, 77–79, 84, 241; and *lurah*, 85–108; and mediums, 120–23; and *ngèlmu*, 81–82; and ritual celebrations, 151, 152, 154, 155, 156, 157, 160n, 164; and speech, 48–49, 118–

19, 136–40; and vows, 129; and *wayang*, 205–213, 243
power, 25, 48–49, 51, 86–88, 92, 94, 102, 107, 108, 111, 112, 154, 157, 163, 165, 170, 171, 172, 175, 178, 182, 200, 203, 204, 210, 212, 219, 221, 224, 239, 240, 241, 242, 243, 250, 260, 266; and gender, 78; and potency, 19, 39, 48, 78, 103, 105, 123; and speech, 118–19; and wealth, 54–55, 78
préwangan, 112, 119–24, 255
punakawan, 12, 15, 110, 191, 192, 193, 197, 198–99, 206, 208–212, 229, 250
puppeteer. *See dhalang*
puppets. *See wayang golèk; wayang kulit*

rapal, 81, 82, 83, 100, 137, 139, 221, 237, 239, 257, 258
respect. *See wedi*
réwang, 6, 141–42, 142–45, 148–50, 153, 174, 237, 265
ritual: ritual celebrations, 5, 51, 87, 100, 110, 127, 138, 141–64, 165, 167, 168, 172, 174–79, 180, 201, 202, 231, 237, 238, 265. *See also réwang; slametan*; sponsors of ritual celebrations
ruwatan, 173, 177–78, 193, 204, 211

sabetan, 174, 188–89, 229
sanggit, 189, 190–96, 197, 198, 214
santri, 23, 99, 102, 166
self, 17, 19, 37–38, 45, 46, 47–49, 51, 84, 88, 107, 119, 124, 132, 136, 140, 162, 200, 204, 221, 239, 241, 242, 249, 253, 255–60, 263, 266, 268
servant-clowns. *See punakawan*
servant of the court. *See abdi-dalem*
sexuality, 39, 41, 45, 47, 52–53, 54, 59, 80, 99, 110n, 147, 223, 257
shame. *See isin*
slametan, 70n, 125, 127, 128, 129, 131, 147, 149, 157–59, 177
sleep, 12, 13–14, 41, 42, 45, 97, 110n, 182, 222–23, 227, 229, 231–32, 237
speech, 19–20, 48, 70n, 72, 77, 78, 79, 112–13, 117, 118, 124, 133, 135–40, 141, 160, 161, 162, 208, 234, 242; and potency, 136–40, 163; and quotation, 34, 257–58; and voice, 117–18,

speech (*cont.*)
119, 121–24, 132, 157–64, 165, 177, 178, 198, 201, 255, 258; and vows, 126, 130–32

spirits, 42, 45, 46, 75, 82, 86, 87, 100, 102, 104, 107, 109–112, 113, 139–40, 151, 159, 170, 174, 177, 221–22, 236, 237, 242, 254; ancestral, 83–84, 111, 126, 159, 161, 162, 163, 174n, 254; and *dhukun*, 116–19; and *pré-wangan*, 120–24; territorial, *see dhan-yang*; and vows, 126–29

sponsors of ritual celebrations, 5, 6, 7, 8, 9, 11, 13, 14, 17, 20, 142–60, 163–64, 177, 178, 199, 234; and *dhal-ang*, 6, 8, 11, 141, 165–69, 173–74, 175–79, 180, 185, 190, 199, 201, 215, 239, 265, 268; and guests, 141–54, 157–60, 162–64, 165, 169, 173–74, 240; and representatives, 11, 141, 142–60, 163–64, 177, 178, 199, 234

status, social, 19, 25–38, 42, 45, 57, 67, 68–70, 78–79, 80, 105, 107, 111, 112, 115–16, 134, 140, 142, 167, 200, 204, 220–21, 224, 239, 258; of *dhalang*, 15, 74–75, 165–72; and gender, 41, 53–56, 77–78; and linguistic etiquette, 28–38, 46; and potency, 38–41, 46, 70, 77–79; and relative status, 25–38, 136, 142; and ritual celebrations, 141–58; among *wayang* characters, 4, 205–213; and wealth, 26, 27, 35–36, 115

stories, *wayang*. *See lakon*

suluk, 4, 9, 10, 183, 190, 241

thieves, 236–39, 257

village headman. *See lurah*

vows, 112, 124–36, 161, 177

wayang golèk, 13, 245

wayang kulit (*wayang*), 19, 20, 40, 127, 136, 140, 141, 147, 152, 166, 172–79, 180–85, 186n, 188–201, 202–219, 224–25, 229–34, 243–48, 250–51, 264–68; description of a performance, 3–14; financial arrangements, 5–6, 13, 128n, 167, 173; manipulation of puppets, *see sabetan*. *See also dhalang; lakon; sanggit*

wayang wong, 15, 166n, 240, 241

wealth, 42, 72–73, 86, 94, 95, 98, 106, 134–35, 142, 160n, 202, 254; and family, 53, 54, 55, 56, 78; and potency, 39, 86, 116, 124; and power, 54, 78; and ritual celebrations, 142, 146, 148, 150, 155, 156, 167; to "seek wealth," 112–14, 131, 236; and social status, 26, 27, 35–36, 115. *See also* exchange

wedi, 55, 63–64, 66, 67n, 70, 71, 72, 78, 81, 111, 117, 136

weton, 80, 82, 84, 170

wong tuwa, 43, 76, 106, 112, 114, 127, 130, 137, 208, 221, 252, 254, 255, 257, 259; and curing, 116–19; and *lu-rah*, 89, 102–104; and mediums, 121–24

writing, 19, 128, 130, 147, 186n, 187, 188, 190, 200, 262, 264, 265

LIBRARY OF CONGRESS
CATALOGING-IN-PUBLICATION DATA

Keeler, Ward.
Javanese shadow plays.

Bibliography: p.
Includes index.
1. Wayang.   2. Shadow pantomimes and plays—Indonesia—Java.
3. Ethnology—Indonesia—Java.   4. Java (Indonesia)—Social
life and customs. I. Title.

PN1979.S5K44 1987   791.5   86-16851
ISBN 0-691-09425-X (alk. paper)   ISBN 0-691-02836-2 (pbk.)